ACCENTS ON SHAKESPEARE

General Editor: TERENCE HAWKES

Making Shakespeare

Making Shakespeare offers a lively introduction to the major issues of stage and printing history, whilst also raising questions about what a 'Shakespeare play' actually is.

Tiffany Stern reveals how London, the theatre, the actors and the way in which the plays were written and printed all affect the 'Shakespeare' that we now read. Concentrating on the instability and fluidity of Shakespeare's texts, her book discusses what happened to a manuscript between its first composition, its performance on stage and its printing, and identifies traces of the production system in the plays that we read. She argues that the versions of Shakespeare that have come down to us have inevitably been formed by the contexts from which they emerged, being shaped by, for example, the way actors received and responded to their lines, the props and music used in the theatre, or the continual revision of plays by the playhouses and printers.

Allowing a fuller understanding of the texts we read and perform, *Making Shakespeare* is the perfect introduction to issues of stage and page. A refreshingly clear, accessible read, this book will allow even those with no expert knowledge to begin to contextualise Shakespeare's plays for themselves, in ways both old and new.

Tiffany Stern is Senior Lecturer at Oxford Brookes University. Her previous publications include *Rehearsal from Shakespeare to Sheridan* (2000) and, with Simon Palfrey, *Shakespeare in Parts* (2005). She has edited *King Leir*, is editing Sheridan's *Rivals*, and is particularly interested in the way theatrical performance impacts on the writing and revision of plays.

ACCENTS ON SHAKESPEARE
General Editor: TERENCE HAWKES

It is more than twenty years since the New Accents series helped to establish 'theory' as a fundamental and continuing feature of the study of literature at the undergraduate level. Since then, the need for short, powerful 'cutting edge' accounts of and comments on new developments has increased sharply. In the case of Shakespeare, books with this sort of focus have not been readily available. **Accents on Shakespeare** aims to supply them.

Accents on Shakespeare volumes will either 'apply' theory, or broaden and adapt it in order to connect with concrete teaching concerns. In the process, they will also reflect and engage with the major developments in Shakespeare studies of the last ten years.

The series will lead as well as follow. In pursuit of this goal it will be a two-tiered series. In addition to affordable, 'adoptable' titles aimed at modular undergraduate courses, it will include a number of research-based books. Spirited and committed, these second-tier volumes advocate radical change rather than stolidly reinforcing the status quo.

IN THE SAME SERIES

Shakespeare and Appropriation
Edited by Christy Desmet and Robert Sawyer

Shakespeare Without Women
Dympna Callaghan

Philosophical Shakespeares
Edited by John J. Joughin

Shakespeare and Modernity: Early Modern to Millennium
Edited by Hugh Grady

Marxist Shakespeares
Edited by Jean E. Howard and Scott Cutler Shershow

Shakespeare in Psychoanalysis
Philip Armstrong

Shakespeare and Modern Theatre: The Performance of Modernity
Edited by Michael Bristol and Kathleen McLuskie

Shakespeare and Feminist Performance: Ideology on Stage
Sarah Werner

Shame in Shakespeare
Ewan Fernie

The Sound of Shakespeare
Wes Folkerth

Shakespeare in the Present
Terence Hawkes

Making Shakespeare

From stage to page

TIFFANY STERN

Routledge
Taylor & Francis Group

LONDON AND NEW YORK

First published 2004
by Routledge
2 Park Square, Milton Park,
Abingdon, Oxon OX14 4RN

Simultaneously published in
the USA and Canada
by Routledge
270 Madison Avenue,
New York, NY 10016

Routledge is an imprint of the
Taylor & Francis Group

© 2004 Tiffany Stern

Typeset in Baskerville by
Florence Production Ltd,
Stoodleigh, Devon

British Library Cataloguing in
Publication Data

A catalogue record for this book is
available from the British Library

Library of Congress Cataloging
in Publication Data

Stern, Tiffany.
Making Shakespeare : the pressures
of stage to page / Tiffany Stern.
    p. cm. – (Accents on Shakespeare)
Includes bibliographical references and
index.
1. Shakespeare, William, 1564–1616
– Criticism, Textual.   2. Shakespeare,
William, 1564–1616 – Stage history.
3. Transmission of texts – England –
History.   4. Drama – Editing –
History.   I. Title.   II. Series.

PR3071.S67 2004
822.3'3–dc22   2003017129

ISBN 0–415–31965–X (pb)
ISBN 0–415–31964–1 (hb)

To my brother Jonty

Contents

Illustrations

General editor's preface

In our time, the field of literary studies has rarely been a settled, tranquil place. Indeed, for over two decades, the clash of opposed theories, prejudices and points of view has made it more of a battlefield. Echoing across its most beleaguered terrain, the student's weary complaint 'Why can't I just pick up Shakespeare's plays and read them?' seems to demand a sympathetic response.

Nevertheless, we know that modern spectacles will always impose their own particular characteristics on the vision of those who unthinkingly don them. This must mean, at the very least, that an apparently simple confrontation with, or pious contemplation of, the text of a four-hundred-year-old play can scarcely supply the grounding for an adequate response to its complex demands. For this reason, a transfer of emphasis from 'text' towards 'context' has increasingly been the concern of critics and scholars since the Second World War: a tendency that has perhaps reached its climax in more recent movements such as 'New Historicism' or 'Cultural Materialism'.

A consideration of the conditions – social, political, or economic – within which the play came to exist, from which it derives and to which it speaks will certainly make legitimate demands on the attention of any well-prepared student nowadays. Of course, the serious pursuit of those interests will also inevitably start to undermine ancient and inherited prejudices, such as the supposed distinction between 'foreground' and 'background' in literary studies. And even the slightest awareness of the pressures of gender or of race, or the most cursory glance at the role played by that strange creature 'Shakespeare' in our cultural politics, will reinforce a similar turn towards questions that sometimes appear scandalously 'non-literary'. It seems clear that very different and unsettling notions of the ways in which literature might be addressed can hardly be avoided. The worrying truth is that nobody can just pick up Shakespeare's plays and read them. Perhaps – even more worrying – they never could.

The aim of *Accents on Shakespeare* is to encourage students and teachers to explore the implications of this situation by means of an engagement with the major developments in Shakespeare studies over recent years. It will offer a continuing and challenging reflection on those ideas through a series of multi- and single-author books which will also supply the basis for adapting or augmenting them in the light of changing concerns.

Accents on Shakespeare also intends to lead as well as follow. In pursuit of this goal, the series will operate on more than one level. In addition to titles aimed at modular undergraduate courses, it will include a number of books embodying polemical, strongly argued cases aimed at expanding the horizons of a specific aspect of the subject and at challenging the preconceptions on which it is based. These volumes will not be learned 'monographs' in any traditional sense. They will, it is hoped, offer a platform for the work of the liveliest younger scholars and teachers at their most outspoken and provocative. Committed and contentious, they will be reporting from the forefront of current critical activity and will have something new to say. The fact that each book in the series promises a Shakespeare inflected in terms of a specific urgency should ensure that, in the present as in the recent past, the accent will be on change.

Terence Hawkes

Acknowledgements

Making Shakespeare started life as a series of lectures given to the English Faculty at Oxford. I am indebted to the students who attended those lectures – particularly Pascale Aebischer, Paige Newmark and Pierre Hecker – whose probing questions have become part of what this book is about. To Merton College, Oxford, I am deeply grateful for the Junior Research Fellowship that enabled me to embark on this project; Clare Hall, Cambridge, kindly provided the Visiting Fellowship that enabled me to complete it. Most of all I thank my current institution, Oxford Brookes University, which generously granted me leave to write up.

I have benefited enormously from the assistance of Gareth Mann and Tracey Sowerby, who took time out from their own work to read mine; their intelligence and historical acumen rescued me from countless errors. Ralph Hanna, an astute and sagacious friend – as well as an excellent drinking companion – gave thoroughly helpful criticism and asked the questions that needed to be asked. I cannot do enough justice to Gordon McMullan, David Scott Kastan and Andrew Gurr who read chapters sent to them at short notice; their help, criticism, and attentive reading has improved the book in countless ways; its errors are, of course, my own. Last, but by no means least, Terence Hawkes has been a tremendously supportive and encouraging general editor, and a wise, diligent and thoughtful reader.

The staffs of the Cambridge University Library, the British Library, the Huntington Library and the Folger Shakespeare Library have all been extremely helpful; the assistance I have received from the staff at the Bodleian, who have put up uncomplainingly with my daily demands, has been invaluable. The following libraries and people allowed me to reproduce images from their collections: Guildhall Library, Corporation of London (2.1); Library of the Rijksuniversiteit, Utrecht (2.2); the Syndics of Cambridge University Library (2.3; 5.1); the Bodleian Library, University of Oxford (4.1); the Huntington Library, San Marino, California (4.2; 5.2); the British Library (5.3); the Marquess of Bath, Longleat House, Warminster, Wiltshire (5.4); David Bolton (7.1).

The work and friendship of colleagues across the globe has informed this book in numerous ways. Peter Holland has, from the first, been an inspiration; Alan Dessen does not know how important his email, sent to me in Poland, really was – he deserves very special thanks for his encouragement and great help then and now. The Shakespeare Association of America, the International Shakespeare Association, a Huntington Library conference on Redefining Theatre History, and the Bodleian Library have provided the most wonderful intellectual environments in which to test out some of the ideas put forward here. My thanks for comments, conversation and companionship from John Astington, Mark Bland, Al Braunmuller, Doug Brooks, David Carnegie, Jean Chothia, Tony Dawson, Gabriel Egan, Jay Halio, Jonathan Hope, Bill Ingram, William Long, Scott McMillin, Laurie Maguire, Randall Martin, Stephen Orgel, Simon Palfrey, Eric Rasmussen, Michael Warren. I am also grateful to an insightful letter sent me from an anonymous member of the SAA; portions of this book are responses to points it made.

People whose company was important during the time when *Making Shakespeare* was being completed include Kate Bennett, James Cannon, Ivona Dragun, Sam (John-in-London) Eidinow, Elspeth Findlay, Kerensa Heffron, Wojtek Jajdelski, Justyna Lesniewska, Richard McCabe, Bryan Magee, Arkady Ostrovsky, Vlatko Vedral, Marcin Walecki, all my colleagues at Oxford Brookes – but in particular Michelle O'Callaghan, Steve Matthews and Anna Richards, and all my colleagues at the Jagiellonian University, Kraków – in particular Marta Gibinska and Zygmunt Mazur. I am indebted to Joy Moore for numerous kindnesses here and in Canada. Rebecca Hewitt's friendship has cheered and enriched the last few years; the love of Artur Ekert, who put up with me – and put me up – while in Cambridge has shaped them. I owe a huge debt of gratitude to my uncle Patrick Tucker who first stimulated my interest in Shakespeare and the theatre and to my parents Geoffrey and Elisabeth Stern who nurtured and encouraged that interest – and me. My brother Jonty (Jonathon) Stern's warmth, kindness and thoughtfulness deserve more than I can say or give. To him this book is affectionately dedicated.

Textual note

As this book focuses on texts, it is important to present Shakespeare passages in the form in which they were first printed. For that reason, quotations are given as they appear in quarto (Q) or folio (F). Quarto texts were consulted using *Shakespeare's Plays in Quarto: A Facsimile Edition of Copies Primarily from the Henry E. Huntington Library* ed. Michael J. B. Allen and Kenneth Muir (Berkeley and Los Angeles: University of California Press, 1981); they are referred to by page signature. Folio texts were consulted using the Norton Facsimile of *Mr. William Shakespeares Comedies, Histories, & Tragedies* (*The First Folio*), prepared by Charlton Hinman (New York: Norton, 1968); they are referred to using the through-line-numbers (TLN) of that edition. A modern act-scene-line reference is also supplied, taken from the *The Riverside Shakespeare* ed. G. Blakemore Evans *et al.*, second edn (Boston and New York: Houghton Mifflin, 1997). Speech-prefixes have, to avoid confusion, been regularised except in instances when they are themselves the subject of examination. Similarly, 'i' and 'j' and 'u' and 'v' have been regularised in quotations, except, again, when the use of either is under discussion.

1
Prologue

It is a truism to say that a play printed on the page is not the same as a play in performance. What is less often considered is that one version of a play in performance is different from others. Shakespeare's plays were written and rewritten throughout their production, taking markedly different forms on their first day, on subsequent days, for court and for revivals. Censorship, changes in playhouse personnel, audience reactions all took their toll, and their shadows can be seen through the texts that have come down to us, as this book will illustrate. But plays were also shaped by other circumstances: they were written primarily for London performance in certain buildings whose size and construction also informs the content of the texts. Subsequently printed in a variety of forms and marketed to different readers, plays were then moulded to and by the books in which they were published. *Making Shakespeare* is about the playtexts we have, and the way they relate to events in the theatre and printing houses of the past. It explores the distance between the texts that have survived, what the author wrote, what the reviser rewrote, what was initially performed, what was subsequently performed and what was first printed. The contents of Shakespeare's plays may have been in their nature 'fluid', as is often said; but this is also a book about the 'fluidity' of the material conditions of production.

Recent scholarship, which has stressed the importance of the multiple contexts that brought about Shakespeare's work, attempts to 'situate' plays inside the culture that helped generate them. This book concentrates on the contexts that directly impacted on the nature of the playtext in the playhouse and the printing house, examining the full process of production undergone by a text to bring it from what Shakespeare wrote to what was published in quarto and folio. *Making Shakespeare* is thus a 'stage-to-page' book with a difference. It shows everything that goes into making a play – but it also shows how the versions of plays we have are only written testaments to moments in the life of an unstable text. It introduces the major issues of stage history and printing history, whilst raising questions about what a 'Shakespeare play' actually is.

Concerned as it is with situation and circumstance, *Making Shakespeare* considers plays not one by one, but context by context. No prior knowledge is assumed; instead, the chapters describe how London, the theatre, the actors, the way plays were written and printed, affect the 'Shakespeare' that we now read. The book straddles performance and bibliographical issues; it shows what happened to a manuscript between its first composition, its performance on stage and its printing, and how leftovers of the production system have worked their way into the plays that we read. It argues that the way actors received and responded to their lines, the props and music anticipated and used in the theatre, and the continual revision and remodelling of plays by the playhouses and printing houses have formed the versions of Shakespeare that have come down to us. Included in the book is a discussion of the knotty question of revision (who did it? when did it happen? and what can be learned from notions of a revising author?) and a look at 'new' bibliographical issues, such as the way books were typeset and what effect this has on the text. Each chapter explores a different practical context for shape-shifting Shakespeare; each is illustrated verbally and, sometimes, with pictures. The book aims not to give a dictatorial series of 'readings'; rather, it builds up a familiarity with particular passages and references, while providing the background material and tools to allow readers to contextualise Shakespeare's plays – in old and new ways – for themselves.

The opening chapter, 'Text, Playhouse and London', is concerned with buildings – both the buildings of early modern London and, more locally, the buildings in which Shakespeare's plays were enacted. The structure of the early modern theatres and the layout of early modern London itself became a feature of Shakespeare's writing, and this chapter illustrates how these and other contingent factors have formed Shakespeare's plays and are manifested in them. The history of the establishment of the Theatre, the Globe and Blackfriars is discussed in terms of the plays written for those buildings; London life, playhouses, bear-baiting pits, theatrical audiences, theatrical flags and theatrical candles are shown to have impacts on the writing as well as the performance of Shakespeare.

The next chapter, 'Additions, Emendations and Revisions', explains what happens to Shakespeare's plays over time and how that is manifested in quarto and folio. It looks at plays revised during the process of writing, and plays revised after performance in the light of censorship, or criticism – or simply in order to maintain their currency. It shows, too, how signs of revision can be found, even in plays that exist only in one form. The playhouse of the time demanded a flexible and fluid text; just how unfixed that text was, and how receptive to change, is examined in this chapter.

What does it mean to share a number of productions amongst the same small group of people? The fourth chapter, 'Rehearsal, Performance and Plays' puts Shakespeare's works in the context of the people who acted in them. It looks at members of the playing company – clowns, tragedians, 'boys' and a series of other typecast actors – and it examines the way the writing reflects these people or types. It also asks how theatrical companies dealt with the quantity of texts that had to be learned and relearned. The process of putting together a performance is discussed, with a look at actors' preparation from the moment when separate scripts ('parts') are received, through individual 'study', to brief collective rehearsal. How are the players and the way they perform reflected in the plays themselves?

Chapter 5, 'Props, Music and Stage Directions', investigates the practical stage. It compares verbal props and physical props, showing how actual props functioned symbolically rather than realistically. Colour, music, stage-hangings and words joined together to make statements to the audience – but how were those statements perceived? And how were the plays designed to accommodate the artefacts of the early modern theatre?

Shakespeare was an actor writing for actors: he wrote anticipating the way his texts would be disseminated and learned.

Chapter 6, 'Prologues, Songs and Actors' Parts', explores the life of different fragments of the play, arguing that the theatre was, in many ways, more interested in 'parts' of the work than in the whole. By paring Shakespeare's plays back down into the separate pieces of paper that made them up, this chapter shows how the printed versions relate to theatrical manuscripts, and examines the implications of this relationship.

Looking at the corrections, improvements and errors that arise from the way texts were readied for performance and for the printing house, Chapter 7, 'From Stage to Printing House', shows how, even by the time of publication, the plays of Shakespeare were distinctly different from what their 'author' had written.

The stage-to-page trajectory of this book, an approach currently without its own defining 'ism', is a particular example of a more general trend in recent modern criticism. As part of its aim to 'restore Shakespeare's artistry to the earliest conditions of its realization and intelligibility', that criticism initially aligned itself with two particularly strong movements from the 1980s.[1] It took its interest in the importance of context from new historicism, and its interest in textual indeterminacy and instability from the postmodern project to 'decentre' the text and query the nature of 'authorship'. The next step was to start considering the various factors involved in the construction of a Shakespeare text, and to question the authority residing in the plays themselves. Studies mostly concentrating on *King Lear* – the test-case for revision – had already begun to point out that Shakespeare's plays were regularly altered and adapted by a number of different agents. Principal amongst the 1980s work was Peter Blayney's *The Texts of 'King Lear' and Their Origins: Nicholas Okes and the First Quarto*, which explained the printing house background to the two variant texts of *Lear*. That was swiftly followed by a fascinating collection of essays arguing that the quarto and folio versions of *Lear* constituted two slightly different plays: *The Division of the Kingdoms: Shakespeare's Two Versions of 'King Lear'* edited by Gary Taylor and Michael Warren. The later exciting and notorious *Complete Works of Shakespeare*, edited by Stanley Wells and Gary Taylor, responded to issues arising out of the new interest in textual instability by printing *Lear* separately in two versions and – more controversially – renaming Falstaff 'Oldcastle' in *1 Henry IV*, Imogen 'Innogen' in *Cymbeline*, and retitling *Henry VIII* 'All Is True' in an attempt to present 'Shakespeare' not as written by the author but as performed in the theatre.[2] Arising from this was a renewed interest in collaboration: had we been too certain not just in the stability of texts, but in the stability of authorship itself?[3] Questions were asked not only about how 'fixed' any printed text was, but what constituted a text at all.[4]

'Context' and 'indeterminacy' were themselves inflected by various other concerns radically different in their nature. One was theatre history, a subject that has been of continual interest to Shakespeareans and that, unlike most other approaches to Shakespeare, has never been outdated or replaced – though it has also been slow to accept new interpretative methodologies. It came to greater prominence than ever during the 1990s with the growth of general concern in the material conditions that shaped the playhouse, traceable to a combination of practical events and technological advances. The discovery of the Rose theatre site, the building of the new Globe in London and the new Blackfriars in Virginia have returned attention to early modern playhouses as buildings: just how did the original places of performance impact on the texts performed in them?[5] At the same time, new historical material was and is being made available in huge quantities allowing criticism with an empirical base to flourish. *REED (Records of Early English Drama)* has since 1979 been publishing manuscript county records illustrating habits of performance outside London; internet sites are beginning to make rare books – and so bookbased scholarship – accessible to universities situated miles away from rare-book libraries.[6]

As a movement, however, the stage-to-page field, combining theatre history and book history, reaching towards a 'Shakespeare' defined by multiple contexts rather than authorial intention, has only lately been theoretically situated. A series of notable recent books have begun the process. Principal among them are two collections of essays: *A New History of Early English Drama*, ed. John D. Cox and David Scott Kastan (New York: Columbia University Press, 1997); and *A Companion to Shakespeare*, ed. David Scott Kastan (Oxford: Blackwell, 1999). Both attempt to recover specific historical contexts and actions in playhouse and printing house that produce meaning(s) in the light of questions about textual and authorial instability.[7]

Making Shakespeare is part of a critical movement that, in the same spirit, concentrates not on 'Shakespeare' the individual author but on the collaborative, multilayered, material, historical world that fashioned the Shakespeare canon. The book provides both a summary of stage and textual history and an alternative way of understanding the dissemination of theatrical manuscripts. It inherits a tradition that perhaps once saw the study of 'literature' and the study of 'history' as separable if not separate activities. By redefining ideas of textual and authorial instability in a rooted, historical context, it aims to create a newly vibrant meeting point between the two.

Text, Playhouse and London

Potential spectators going from London to the Globe theatre on the Bankside could cross the Thames in two ways. There were ferry-boats plying the river, the watermen shouting out their route: 'Westward Ho!' from which the Dekker and Webster play got its name, or 'Eastward Ho!' from which the Chapman, Jonson and Marston play took its title. These could be hailed to cross the river, and functioned much like taxis now. Whenever theatres were forcibly closed, watermen feared for their jobs and made vigorous complaints: 'wee yor saide poore watermen have had muche helpe and reliefe for us oure poore wives and Children by meanes of the resorte of suche people as come unto the . . . playe howse'.[1] For the audience, the raucous cries of the ferrymen were part of the preliminary entertainment on the way to the theatre; the play-titles show how the ferryman's language also became part of theatrical discourse. The alternative way over the Thames was via London Bridge, a street over the water, filled with shops and houses, merchants and moneylenders. A toll was charged to enter London Bridge on horseback, however, and it was also necessary to pay a waterman to row over the river – so that in general only people with spare cash and the intention of spending it would cross the Thames to experience the pleasures of the Bankside. At the Southbank exit from London Bridge, visible both to those on the bridge and to those on the river itself, was a gatehouse. Impaled above the gatehouse were the heads of traitors (see Plate 2.1): a grim reminder for Londoners entering into the bad suburbs (the 'liberties') – where 'the licentious, dangerous, unclean, or polluted' were located – that transgression would have the direst results.[2]

Plate 2.1 Claus Jan Visscher, *Long View of London* (1616). Reproduced by permission of Guildhall Library, Corporation of London.

The heads over the gatehouse prompted a number of fairly predictable jokes. When Catesby in *Richard III* bandies words with Hastings, he says: 'The Princes both make high account of you', adding in an aside, 'For they account his Head upon the Bridge' (TLN 1869–70, 3.2.69–70).[3] But the heads also form part of a network of less straightforward references. They were black in appearance, having been parboiled and, often, coated in tar to prevent erosion. Of the Bishop of Rochester, executed on 22 June 1535, it is recorded that his miraculous head, after 'parboiling in hot water . . . grew daily fresher and fresher'.[4] In the theatres, just down the road, 'black' characters were created when the actor either masked his face with a black vizard or 'pitched' it by artificially colouring it with a burnt cork; the same processes were used to make 'devils', also black.[5] A blackened actor, irrespective of character, had an immediate resemblance not just to a stage devil but also to the condemned traitors the audience would probably have seen on its way to the theatre. To many of Shakespeare's audience watching *Othello* for the first time, the hero has a doomed aspect: he is a traitor even before he has opened his mouth.

Places and environments have always been infused with meaning, and early modern London was filled with buildings and details that were strongly part of the routine both of Shakespeare and of his London-based audience. Even the ways by which Londoners approached the playhouses might, as shown, have an affect on what they understood from the plays they saw there; the very bustle of London, its noises and imagery, were part of the plays put on. Consideration of just a couple of important London landmarks that characterised the approach to the Globe and the Blackfriars theatre usefully shows how place was part of thought, and highlights the question raised by this chapter: how did the playhouses – as places – impact on the works performed in them?

If the bridge approach to the Globe may have promoted, sanctioned or simply become an element of early modern racism, so the Ludgate approach to the Blackfriars playhouse was part of the way early modern Londoners thought about – or knew about – the history of their city. For Ludgate, one of the entrances into the walled city of London, was famously decorated with 'with images of *Lud* and other Kinges'. Spectators attending Blackfriars, where Shakespeare's company performed from 1609, would have been familiar with Ludgate's famous decorations, as the gate was directly up the road from the theatre. They would have known, too, that the gate was not just a triumphant record of English kingship and its (semi-spurious) links to ancient Rome; it was also a prison. As the antiquarian John Stow recorded, Ludgate was, in 1586, fully refurbished:

> the same gate being sore decayed was clean taken down, the prisoners in the meane time remayning in the large Southeast quadrant to the same Gate adjoyning, and the same yeare, the whole gate was newly and beautifully builded with the images of *Lud*, & others, as afore, on the East side, and the picture of her Majestie, Queene *Elizabeth* on the West side.[6]

On Ludgate, then, Queen Elizabeth completed a line of kingship extending from the mythical king Lud; in being carefully placed to one side of Ludgate the Queen created her own historical context. But the gate also had another memorable image, so memorable as to define it in some way. This was, as the poet Henry Vaughan attests, a picture of the ancient king Cymbeline. When lust is high, writes Vaughan, 'itchy blood' hunts for a mate 'From the Tower-wharf to Cymbeline and Lud'.[7] 'Cymbeline and Lud' was an alternative way of saying 'Ludgate'.

Any writer of plays for the Blackfriars playhouse would have known the pictorial image of Cymbeline on Ludgate – as would his audience. Familiar, too, would have been Cymbeline's context as one of a line of early monarchs, concluded by Elizabeth and fronting both an entry and a gaol. It is telling, then, that Shakespeare's play *Cymbeline* runs through the history of some of the prominent early London kings who embellished the gate: Mulmutius who 'made our lawes / Who was the first of Britaine, which did put / His browes within a golden Crowne, and call'd / Himselfe a King' (TLN 1436–9, 3.1.58–61); Cassibellaunus who 'Made *Luds-Towne* with rejoycing-Fires bright, / And Britaines strut with Courage' (TLN 1411–12, 3.1.32–3). It is also telling that prisons and prison images run through *Cymbeline*; that Imogen is the Queen's prisoner (TLN 86, 1.1.72); that the Welsh cave of Arviragus and Guidarius is likened to 'A Cell of Ignorance: . . . A Prison' (TLN 1589–90, 3.3.33–4). At a pivotal point in the play Posthumus is thrown in jail because he has been mistaken for a Roman soldier. The play, of course, is not in any sense about Ludgate, though the repeated references to King Lud and to gates in general in it are significant: Guidarius and Arverigus stoop to go through the 'gate' of their cave (whereas 'The Gates of Monarchs / Are Arch'd so high, that Giants may jet through / And keepe their impious Turbonds on', TLN 1558–60, 3.3.4–6); Cloten threatens the king's true sons with 'Ile . . . on the Gates of *Luds-Towne* set your heads' (TLN 2378, 4.2.99–100). More, the play is, on a minor level, a function of having been performed near Ludgate; it seems to anticipate mental associations that will join monarchs of the past to a monarch of the recent present, and perhaps suggest that, at least historically, 'Britain' has been – like Hamlet's Denmark – a prison as well as a place of triumph.

Shakespeare's plays were, of course, performed in the provinces as well as in London, and the London-based associations work only on a London-based audience: that, presumably, is another reason why the plays do not overuse London analogies. Nevertheless, Shakespeare's surroundings, Shakespeare's London, clearly affected what the playwright wrote, as well as what the audience saw and the associations they might draw from it. Similarly, the theatres of early modern London are not simply referred to in Shakespeare's works; they are part of their fabric. Shakespeare's plays were written to be performed in certain types of building and those buildings – their dimensions, their construction, and their milieu – imposed a variety of understanding on the audiences who attended them. Moreover, as permanent theatre buildings were themselves a relatively new idea, Shakespeare, in the process of writing, was not only using but *creating* a new kind of dramatic text fitted for this new kind of environment.

The first ever permanent theatre in London was probably the Red Lion, about which very little is known other than that it was erected by John Brayne around 1567 and that it did not exist very long. The next purpose-built theatre in London, put up in 1576 was, by contrast, a great and immediate success. As a result, it was condemned by Puritan preachers: 'It is an evident token of a wicked time when plaiers wexe so riche that they can build suche houses.'[8] It too, was built by John Brayne, this time together with his brother-in-law, James Burbage, who had been a strolling player for the Earl of Leicester's Men. It was erected on a rented field in Halliwell, one of the suburbs or 'liberties' of London, which were less subject to London jurisdictions than the City itself, and was called 'the Theatre', a name that seems to have been borrowed from classical texts. From classical texts, too, must have come the inspiration for the Theatre's round shape. In other respects, as well, the Theatre was entirely a local Tudor building: it was made from wood, and had sides of irregular length and a thatched roof. When Shakespeare became attached to the company performing at the Theatre is unclear. He is known to have been a member of the Chamberlain's Men, who performed at the Theatre from 1594 to 1596, and a shareholder in the company from 1599. The first plays Shakespeare wrote, then, were intended for performance in the Theatre: *Love's Labour's Lost, Richard II, Romeo and Juliet, A Midsummer Night's Dream, King John, The Merchant of Venice, 1, 2* and *3 Henry VI, 1* and *2 Henry IV* and *Much Ado About Nothing*.

The Theatre was a great success, not only because good young authors were writing for it but also because good young actors were performing in it. Most notable amongst the up-and-coming players was James Burbage's son, Richard Burbage. He would become not only one of London's most famous actors but also the player for whom many of Shakespeare's major roles were written. Disaster struck the popular playhouse in 1597, however. The Brayne family and the Burbage family had, for some time, been furiously quarrelling over finances. On one occasion James Burbage leant out of his window to shout 'whore' and 'murdering knave' at Brayne's wife and her friend Robert Miles; afterwards Richard Burbage beat Miles with a broom-staff and threatened Nicholas Bishop, appointed to collect money for Mrs Brayne, by 'scornfully and disdainfullye playing with this deponents nose'.[9] At the same time, the theatre itself was increasingly threatened by local ill-feeling. Not only was the subject matter of its plays thought questionable but the very place itself was said to breed unwholesomeness.

> I am persuaded that Satan hath not a more speedie way & fitter schoole to worke and teach his desire to bring men and women into his snare of concupiscense and filthie lustes of wicked whoredome, than those places and plaies, and Theatres are: And therefore it is necessarie that those places and Plaiers shoulde bee forbidden and dissolved and put downe by authoritie, as the Brothell houses and Stewes are.[10]

Then the last blow struck. Giles Alleyn, who had rented to James Burbage the field on which the Theatre had been built, declined to renew the lease on the land. He went so far as to refuse even to let the actors enter the field to collect their wooden theatre, as, technically, he owned the buildings erected on his site; in reclaiming his field, he thus also acquired the Theatre for his own use.

What must it have been like for the Chamberlain's Men to see the building they had constructed rendered inaccessible because it was trapped on a piece of land that belonged to someone else? Shakespeare in *The Merry Wives of Windsor* seems to relate memories of the physical loss to general emotional outrage. In that play Ford compares misdirected love (to someone he in fact should 'own' – his wife) to 'A fair house, built on another mans ground, so that I have lost my edifice, by mistaking the place, where I erected it' (TLN 975–7, 2.2.215–17).

Eventually the actors, probably including Shakespeare, certainly including the brothers Richard and Cuthbert Burbage, went into Alleyn's field by night on 28 December 1598. With the help of the master-builder Peter Streete, they dismantled the Theatre and, as the legal documents put it, carried 'all the wood and timber therof unto the Banckside in the parishe of St. Marye Overyes, and there erected a newe playehowse with the sayd timber and woode'.[11] St Mary Overies was to become an actors' church; it still stands, though it is now known as Southwark Cathedral. In its choir are gravestones for Shakespeare's brother Edmund, also an actor, and the playwrights John Fletcher and Philip Massinger. In one wall is the tomb of the medieval poet John Gower, whom Shakespeare fictionalised as the narrator in his play *Pericles*. St Mary Overies (called 'overies' because it was over the river) and its Bankside parish were, like London Bridge and Ludgate, part of the complex fabric out of which Shakespeare's plays were woven.

Being on the South Bank of the Thames, the parish of St Mary Overies was situated in what was then Surrey, not London. So the players had changed more than just the environment of their playhouse; they had changed its milieu. But why did the players cross the Thames for their new venture? There was the pull of the relaxed laws offered by being in a 'liberty' of course, but London was surrounded by 'liberties'. Perhaps the Rose theatre, already flourishing on the Bankside, was seen to offer a ready-made audience primed to like plays, and willing to be diverted to a new and more glamorous playhouse. In addition, the particularly weak government of Surrey – and of Southwark in particular – would have been of huge appeal. Southwark was an administrative mess: nominally it came under the auspices of the Justices of Surrey, but in effect it was governed by one of three manors which made up the borough. The area which included Bankside was the Clink Liberty, named after the prison, which was under the authority of the bishop of Winchester. Winchester not only sanctioned but also took rent from the many prostitutes who clustered around his land and were popularly known as Winchester 'geese'. In this new, glamorous, seedy and fairly lawless environment, the company for which Shakespeare wrote could feel less restrained in their choice of play topic than when they were north of the London wall.

Part of making a clean break with the past involved changing the playhouse's name. The new building would no longer be called the Theatre; it was retitled the Globe. The symbolism implies that people were expected to know the history of the playhouse and its previous name. 'The Theatre' became 'the Globe', the stage became the world. As Duke Senior put it in *As You Like It*, thought to be the first Shakespeare play performed at the new Globe:

> This wide and universall Theater
> Presents more wofull Pageants then the Sceane
> Wherein we play in.
> (TLN 1115–17, 2.7.137–9)

Drawing out the analogy, the Duke also calls attention to the fact that, more locally, the Globe really *is* the Theatre. He toys with the fact and with the fiction of his environment – he is indeed speaking from a theatre in which tragedies as well as comedies are performed – but Jaques replies in a way that highlights, again, both the conceit (the world is like a theatre) and the move from Theatre to Globe:

> All the world's a stage,
> And all the men and women, meerely Players;
> They have their *Exits* and their Entrances,
> And one man in his time playes many parts.
> (TLN 1118–21, 2.7.139–42)

The Globe was a living metaphor, and the performances written for it, unsurprisingly, are often 'metatheatrical' – they draw frequent attention to their own theatrical natures and their consequent unreality.

To bridge the time between being denied access to the Theatre in 1597, pulling it down in 1598–99 and constructing the Globe theatre out of its remains in 1599, the Chamberlain's Men performed at the other round theatre that had been constructed in the liberty of Halliwell: the Curtain. Shakespearean plays that may have first been performed at the Curtain are those of 1598–99 and seem to have included *Henry V*, so that the prologue's famous diffidence about the inadequacies of 'this unworthy Scaffold . . . this Cock-pit . . . this Woodden O' (TLN 11–14) are probably references to the Curtain, not the Globe as is so often thought.[12] If *Henry V* is indeed a Curtain play, written just as the Globe was being readied for performance, the prologue's 'apology' has an aggressive dimension. Rather than displaying a modest humility for the inability of the stage in general to depict realism, the prologue seems designed to undermine the Curtain theatre, the suggestion being that the Globe's better-appointed 'O' will be an improvement. The much later Globe/Blackfriars prologue to *Henry VIII* is, by contrast, pointedly unapologetic for its surroundings. Instead, it forcefully puts the onus on the audience not to resent the staging but to use their imaginations and 'for Goodnesse sake . . . Thinke ye see / The very Persons of our Noble Story, / As they were Living' (TLN 24–8). It is always important to have a sense of which plays were intended for which theatres; the very buildings can inflect the way the text may be understood.

Before long, almost all the public theatres were situated on the South Bank (the 'Bankside') of the Thames in the county of Surrey. They were the Rose, the Hope, the Swan (all round theatres), and they came to be part of the essence of the South Bank – just as the South Bank, its buildings and its mentality, became a feature of the plays put on in its environs.

None of the South Bank playhouses was subject to London rules. Liberating as the lack of regulations was, however, the fact that the theatres were over the river and away from London itself raised practical problems. Advertising across the water was difficult, yet it was necessary that Londoners should know when a performance was to be expected. A number of solutions were devised. At one stage, the players sent posses across the Thames with drums and trumpets, shouting out the name of that day's play; later, they covered London with advertisements ('bills'), filling the city with printed mementoes of the theatre it had so pointedly rejected. An alternative system of visual imagery also came into being, able to market to the literate and illiterate alike; the theatres' appeal was broad and extended over different classes. When a play was to be performed, the Surrey playhouses flew flags from their rooftops to herald the fact. In that way, the buildings themselves could advertise across the water. 'Each Play-house', as William Parkes explained, 'advanceth his flagge in the aire, whither quickly at the waving thereof, are summoned whole troopes of men, women and children.'[13] The flags bore signs linked to the name of the theatre: a Swan for the Swan, probably a symbol of the Thames (see the picture of the Swan playhouse, Plate 2.2, p. 23), a rose for the Rose, a symbol of the rose-gardens the theatre replaced. Juliet's observation in *Romeo and Juliet* that 'that which we call a Rose, / By any other word [Q1 name] would smell as sweete' (TLN 837–8, 2.2.43–4) may also be a cruel joke about the Rose playhouse, said to be distinctly malodorous.[14] There was a 'picture of Dame Fortune / Before the Fortune Play-house' until it burnt down; on rebuilding it was renamed the Phoenix, after the mythical bird that is resurrected from the ashes of its grave. A phoenix, presumably, became the theatre's symbol.[15] Visual signs with symbolic import were part of the world of the theatre.

The picture on the flag of the Globe was not described until the seventeenth century, though there are enough references to it in the literature of Shakespeare's time for us to guess what it must have been: a god carrying the Globe on his back – either Atlas who, according to the Greek myth, was condemned to hold the world on his shoulders for ever, or Hercules who bore the world briefly as one of his twelve labours. So an elegy for the Globe's lead actor, Richard Burbage, maintains that the Globe should shut down now that its best actor is dead:

> Hence forth your waving flagg, no more hang out
> Play now no more att all, when round aboute
> Wee looke and miss the Atlas of your spheare.[16]

That the Globe's sign was further embellished with the words *Totus Mundus Agit Histrionem* ('The whole world plays the player'), is a pleasing idea, though an unlikely one: the motto hung above the Drury Lane theatre in the early seventeenth century and the story that it came from the Globe dates from about then.[17] References to the Globe's pictorial sign, on the other hand, are not just present but used metatheatrically in several Shakespeare plays. Hamlet on a number of occasions makes references to Hercules, creating moments that are both inside the fiction of the play *Hamlet* and outside it. When the Prince hears that the boy players are so popular that they are taking audiences away from the adult 'tragedians of the city', he exclaims 'Do the Boyes carry it away?' 'I' [ay] replies Rosencrantz, 'that they do my Lord. *Hercules* & his load too.' Suddenly *Hamlet* has moved from the troubles of Elsinore to the troubles besetting the Globe theatre: boy players have become fashionable and the adult players are losing audiences to them (TLN 1408–9, 2.2.360–1).

The good reputation of the youthful actors in 1601 – seemingly the date of this passage – will have been particularly galling to the Burbages, for the boys were performing in the Blackfriars Playhouse, a theatre that the Burbages owned but could not use.[18] Ever impetuous, James Burbage had acquired parts of the old Blackfriars monastery in 1596 and had converted them into a rectangular indoor theatre before finding that residents in the area would not countenance professional performances there (indeed, they went so far as to get an injunction to stop the theatre being used by adult players).[19] Burbage presumably had not anticipated this trouble: Blackfriars was in a precinct of London that was technically a 'liberty' though within the City walls. As it was, unable to mount productions in Blackfriars himself, he had been obliged to lease his theatre to a boy choir. Infuriatingly, the children had been able to perform plays at Blackfriars as they were not considered professional players: they were said to be putting on productions as part of their education, even though they charged money for performances. When the adult professionals started losing their own audience to a theatre they had let the boys have, they must have been filled with the anger of the powerless. In the following passage, Hamlet wonders why the talented tragedians have had to leave the city and perform in the country as 'travelling players':

Hamlet   what Players are they?

Rosincrantz   Even those you were wont to take delight in the Tragedians of the City.

Hamlet   How chances it they travaile? their residence both in reputation and profit was better both wayes.

Rosincrantz   I thinke their Inhibition comes by the meanes of the late Innovation?

Hamlet Doe they hold the same estimation they did when I was
   in the City? Are they so follow'd?
Rosincrantz No indeed, they are not.
Hamlet How comes it? doe they grow rusty?
Rosincrantz Nay, their indeavour keepes in the wonted pace; But
   there is Sir an ayrie of Children, little Yases, that crye out
   on the top of question; and are most tyrannically clap't for't:
   these are now the fashion, and so be-ratled the common Stages
   (so they call them) that many wearing Rapiers, are affraide
   of Goose-quils, and dare scarse come thither.
                              (TLN 1371–91, 2.2.326–44)

'Little eyases' are young hawks – the boy players are birds of prey
consuming the scavenged remains of others' business.

   Hardly surprisingly, the boy players, situated within the walls
of London, often put on plays about life inside London; theatres
outside the walls, meanwhile, often performed what have come
to be known as 'history plays', plays based around the kings of
England. Playhouses outside London had, after all, London itself
as their backdrop: Surrey theatres looked across the river to the
Tower and St Paul's. The fiction of the English history plays will
thus have felt different from the fiction of other plays that might
also loosely be called historical, like 'Roman' plays: the 'history'
plays performed in those theatres were flanked by the flurry of
the London they were concerned with yet slightly removed from.
References like 'Here is the Indictment of the good Lord *Hastings*,
/ Which . . . may be to day read o're in *Paules*' (*Richard III*, TLN
2199–201, 3.6.1–3), or 'this is the way / To *Julius Caesars* ill-
erected Tower' (*Richard II*, TLN 2261–2, 5.1.1–2 – the Tower of
London was, at the time, thought to have been built by Julius
Caesar) were, for as long as they were performed in the London
liberties, 'situated'. London was, literally, the theatres' backdrop,
and it was part of the plays' context.
   Other dubious professions not approved of in London also
operated freely in Surrey. Bear-baiting took place in buildings
similar to the theatres – indeed, one theatre, the Hope, doubled as
a bear-baiting pit. These amphitheatres were the nearest rivals
to the playhouses, for both charged the same entrance fee, both put
on shows that lasted for about two hours, both started at the same
time and held roughly equivalent audiences. Often playhouses
and bear-baiting rings are discussed in the same breath, as when

Lambarde describes the prices of various entertainments: 'such as goe to Parisgardein, the Bell Savage, or Theatre, to beholde Beare baiting, Enterludes, or Fence play . . . first pay one pennie at the gate'.[20] Yet the sport and the drama were, in many ways, rivals – competing for roughly the same audience at the same time of day. Plays had to offer an entertainment at least as compelling as the visceral, bloody, brutal sport of killing or maiming bears, dogs and bulls. This rivalry may even be behind some of the visual cruelty of Shakespearean and other drama of the time. Plays are often surprisingly bloody – given that so much else is left to the poetry. There is the heavy, dark sticky blood that pervades *Macbeth* and cannot be washed off Lady Macbeth's hands, that fills the wounds of dead Henry VI until they 'Open their congeal'd mouthes, and bleed afresh' as Richard approaches (*Richard III*, TLN 232–3, 1.2.56). There is the sparkling and oddly erotically charged blood of *Julius Caesar*: the wound which Portia voluntarily makes in her thigh as a proof of her constancy to Brutus, and the gashes in the body of Caesar that 'ope their Ruby lips' (TLN 1488, 3.1.260) but cannot speak, so that Antony dearly wishes that he could 'put a Tongue / In every Wound of *Caesar*' (TLN 1765–6, 3.2.228–9).[21]

Bears in the bear-baiting pits were chained to a stake before being attacked by dogs: sometimes they had been blinded first; sometimes they were provoked to frenzy by having pepper blown into their noses. The idea was to release the dogs to worry at the chained bears who would then lash out, attacking and killing where they could. It is usual to find a Shakespearean tragic hero comparing himself to a baited bear and drawing up equivalencies. One early example is in the Theatre play of *2 Henry VI*, when the army of Richard, Duke of York, is compared to bears and Richard to the man in charge of the bears or 'bear-ward':

Clifford Are these thy Beares? Wee'l bate thy Bears to death,
  And manacle the Ber[w]ard in their Chaines,
  If thou dar'st bring them to the bayting place.
Richard Oft have I seene a hot ore-weening Curre,
  Run backe and bite, because he was with-held,
  Who being suffer'd with the Beares fell paw,
  Hath clapt his taile, betweene his legges and cride,
  And such a peece of service will you do,
  If you oppose your selves to match Lord Warwicke.
            (*2 Henry VI*, TLN 346–55, 5.1.148–56)

The comparison of stage-world and bear-pit can be found in unexpected places. It is little surprise to find Macbeth confronting his last fight with 'They have tied me to a stake, I cannot flye, / But Beare-like I must fight the course' (*Macbeth*, TLN 2396–7, 5.7.11–12), but perhaps more striking to find Olivia in the comedy *Twelfth Night* accusing the 'man' (actually a woman) she loves of having 'set mine Honor at the stake, / And baited it with all th'un-muzled thoughts / That tyrannous heart can think' (*Twelfth Night*, TLN 1331–3, 3.1.118–20). Perhaps because of the tension between bear-baiting ring and theatre, the only two actual creatures brought on stage in Shakespearean plays are a bear and a dog (*Winter's Tale*, *Two Gentlemen of Verona* and, perhaps, *Midsummer Night's Dream*), as though the Shakespearean playhouses attempted to counter the bear-baiting pit by, in a sophisticated way, being it.

Bear-baiting was also advertised with flags: early 'long views' of London sometimes show playhouses and bear-baiting houses with their flags up. So the South Bank waved its coloured flags indicating violence, sex and the theatre, all of which came to be associated, and the last of which might offer a ritualised, philosophical version of the former two. Bored Londoners could look across the Thames to the dangerous, seedy, exciting, liberated Surrey side; some would be tempted across to enjoy one pleasure or another, perhaps not minding too much which, as contemporary poems makes clear:

> Speake Gentleman, what shall we do to day?
> Drinke some brave health upon the Dutch carouse?
> Or shall we to the *Globe* and see a Play?
> Or visit *Shorditch*, for a bawdie house?[22]

In the mind of the Londoner, then, theatregoing was imbued with the glamour of sin that it picked up from its surroundings, and then dealt with in its plays.

Why might a spectator, given the choice, go to the theatre rather than engage in some of the many other Bankside pleasures? There are any number of reasons, of course, quite apart from the interest in being told a story, but one important pull of the theatre was its use of language. First, plays provided a source of jests and anecdotes; they supplied the quips and one-liners that could be used to spice up conversation later: 'So there be among them that will get jestes by heart, that have gathred a Common-place booke out of

Plaies, that will not let a merriment slip, but they will trusse it up
for their owne provision, to serve their expence at some other
time.'[23] Indeed, the very language of flirtation could be picked up
from the theatre; a lawyer's clerk is described as someone who dare
only 'attempt a mistresse' with 'Jests, or speeches stolne from
Playes'.[24] For those who could not read, the theatre was one of
the few places that would offer the carefully honed and crafted
language of love; already by 1598 Marston is horrified by 'Luscus'
who learns phrases of Shakespeare's *Romeo and Juliet* off by heart:

> Luscus what's playd to day? faith now I know
> I set thy lips abroach, from whence doth flow
> Naught but pure Juliat and Romio.

Luscus, as Marston goes on to explain:

> [Hath] made a common-place booke out of plaies,
> And speakes in print, at least what ere he sayes
> Is warranted by Curtaine plaudit[e]s,
> If ere you heard him courting Lesbias eyes;
> Say (Curteous Sir) speakes he not movingly
> From out some new pathetique Tragedie?
> He writes, he railes, he jests, he courts, what not,
> And all from out his huge long scraped stock
> Of well penn'd playes.[25]

But people of the time acquired more than just jokes and
speeches from the theatre. They enriched their vocabularies with
the new terms that the plays freely presented to them. 'English' was
in a state of development, swelling with foreign phrases brought
from overseas by merchants. It was being forcibly enlarged, too, by
humanists trying to make the tongue capable of producing the
'copiousness' they so admired in Latin.[26] Shakespeare was, like
Jonson, a minter of new words and bold in his acquisition of
others: new words were crowd-pullers (estimates as to how many
words Shakespeare really created vary; he is certainly the first
writer on record to use various compounds such as 'bloodstained'
and 'watchdog' as well as to turn nouns such as 'gossip' into verbs).
The playhouse introduced new terms into common parlance.
Richard Tarlton, the Theatre's most famous clown, notoriously
brought the word 'prepuse' (foreskin) 'into the Theater with great

applause'.[27] A Tarltonian catchphrase was 'without all the paraquestions'.[28] Shakespeare's clowns similarly have a fascination with the word: Costard in *Love's Labour's Lost* juggles with the term 'remuneration', while in the same play Don Adriano de Armado (described by King Ferdinand as 'One, who the musicke of his owne vaine tongue, / Doth ravish like inchanting harmonie', TLN 177–8, 1.1.166–7) calls his boy a 'tender Juvenal' because the phrase is 'a congruent apathaton, appertaining to thy young daies, which we may nominate tender' (TLN 324–6, 1.2.13–15). Osric in *Hamlet* interposes 'palpable' into a sentence; Polonius relishes the word 'mobled'. Arguing against the closure of all theatres in the 1640s, actors wrote that it was on the stage that 'the most exact and natural eloquence of our English language [is] expressed and daily amplified'.[29] When the theatres were indeed closed, it was feared that the language would suffer as a result:

> The *Stage* . . . having much conferd and contributed to the inrichment of [language], it being the *Mint* that daily coyns new *words*, which are presently received and admitted as *currant*, . . . the plucking downe of which will I feare, not only *retard* the perfectioning of our Language towards which it was advancing amain, but even quite hinder and *recoyle* it, and make it return to its former *Barbarisme*.[30]

If Shakespeare's vocabulary is rich, that is partly because 'words' were what his audience were paying for.

Fixed theatres, though a relatively new concept, were constructed using a symbolic architecture familiar to anyone of the early modern period. That architecture can be seen in the depiction in Plate 2.2 of the interior of the Swan theatre. The drawing itself, a copy made in Holland by the Dutchman Aernout van Buchel of a picture drawn by his friend Johannes de Witt when in London, is unlikely to be entirely accurate, but does usefully illustrate some of the essential elements about the way stages were housed within theatres.[31] It is the only contemporary picture of the inside of an English round theatre that has been found.

Though the theatre is itself circular, its stage is rectangular and protrudes or thrusts out into the middle of the auditorium. The stage is also elevated or, as Thomas Platter, visiting London from Germany in 1599, put it, 'they play on a raised platform, so that

Plate 2.2 Swan Theatre, by Johannes de Witt, as copied by Aernout van Buchel, *c.* 1596. Reproduced by permission of the Library of the Rijksuniversiteit, Utrecht.

everyone has a good view'.[32] A raised, thrust stage had the further advantage of providing plenty of room underneath to keep props and, if necessary, actors waiting for an entrance from below.

Over the top of the stage there is a thatched covering supported by pillars; such a covering, and the pillars themselves, are features of the plays written by Shakespeare. So, while structurally necessary, pillars also provide useful 'trees' on which Orlando in *As*

You Like It can hang his love poems, as well as hiding places behind which Claudius and Polonius can watch the Prince in *Hamlet* (with the additional advantage that the audience can see both the observer and the observed). They might also have been used as ways of separating the stage into two (perhaps representing Troy and Greece in *Troilus and Cressida*, or Egypt and Rome in *Antony and Cleopatra*). The covering supported by the pillars also served a practical purpose: it kept the rain or sun off the actors and their fine clothes. But the underside of this covering was, as contemporary references make clear, painted with images of stars, clouds and zodiacal signs. Most theatres, the Globe amongst them, seem to have had such an awning over their stages at least after about 1600. Unsurprisingly, this internal roof decorated with star images was called 'heaven', or 'the heavens', while the area below the stage was 'hell'. In an epitaph for the actor Richard Burbage, the playwright Ben Jonson wonders 'What need hee stand at the judgement throne / Who hath a heaven and a hell of his owne?'[33] Naturally this all relates to the stage/world analogy so carefully spelt out by the company that owned the Theatre/Globe. In the middle of this metaphorical sandwich, where the actors performed their play, was 'the world': if players had their own heaven and hell, they had their own living-space too.

So actors performed in a play-world that was different from the larger 'real' world that surrounded the stage, but that was intended to be a reflection of it. Similar heaven/hell distinctions were frequently made in other buildings of the time. Old churches, even now, often still have roofs painted with stars and angels: the heavens. Below, obviously, is the grave where the people are buried; it is also, traditionally, the location of purgatory and hell. Between heaven and hell in church and theatre alike lies the world of the living. Unlike the church's heaven, however, the heaven of the theatre did not extend out over the spectators: even references in plays that seem to be dealing with universal truths are, in a different sense, appealing more strongly to the fiction of the theatre. When Hamlet, occupant of 'this distracted Globe' (TLN 782, 1.5.97), gestures towards 'this brave o'rehanging firmament, this majestical roof' (TLN 1347–8, 2.2.299–301), he is, on one level, talking in universal terms, but also, in a fashion typical of him, undercutting what he says; when he goes on to observe that heaven is 'fretted with golden fire', he draws attention to the glory not of the actual sky but of the underside of the stage roof, a fretted structure described by the poet Thomas Middleton as 'naylde up with many a Starre'.[34]

The locations of heaven and hell within the theatre also have a practical effect on the way, for instance, members of the audience 'read' an actor's place of entrance and exit. To enter from or exit into heaven has supernatural connotations. In Shakespeare's *Cymbeline* Posthumus is on the point of despairing in prison when Jupiter descends from heaven on the back of an eagle. The hope Jupiter offers, and the riddling prophecy he gives, mark a turning point in the play, as does Juno's heavenly entrance to bless the marriage of Ferdinand and Miranda in *The Tempest*.

To enter from, or exit into, hell, on the other hand, clearly indicates evil, death – or both. A voice or a sound coming from hell is ominous, and plays stress the location of a sound if it comes from under the stage. In *Antony and Cleopatra*, the eerie whining of the hautboy (an earlier version of the oboe) from beneath the ground marks the beginning of Antony's final downfall.

Musicke of the Hoboyes is under the Stage.

2 Sold.	Peace, what noise?
1 Sold.	List list.
2 Sold.	Hearke.
1 Sold.	Musicke i'th'Ayre.
3 Sold.	Under the earth.
4 Sold.	It signes well, do's it not?
3 Sold.	No.
1 Sold.	Peace I say: What should this meane?
2 Sold.	'Tis the God *Hercules*, whom *Anthony* loved, Now leaves him.

(TLN 2482–92, 4.3.12–17)

There is a metatheatrical reference in this passage, too, to the sign of the Globe, Hercules, which was also Antony's sign: the theatre itself is giving up on its hero.

The trap-door in the centre of the stage was the entrance from hell. Indeed, the Rose playhouse's Elizabethan prop inventory, transcribed in the eighteenth century, seems to have included 'j Hell mought' (one hellmouth) with which to cover the trap; perhaps, like a German hellmouth described in 1594, it resembled 'the broad wide mouth of an huge Dragon'.[35] Even when not as obviously the lipped and toothed mouth of hell as this, the stage trap-door retained hellish or bad associations: it is the bloody hole in which Lavinia is raped in *Titus Andronicus*, the grave in *Hamlet*, the place from which the apparitions in *Macbeth* come and go.[36] So whenever the hole gaped open on the stage, the audience knew that something evil or with deathlike connotations was happening, or about to happen. The trap presumably came to represent a cumulative evil. Much in the theatre, props particularly, worked in this way, borrowing their natures partly from the collective character they had built up through use in many plays.

The trap, naturally, also doubled as the grave when characters needed to be buried on stage. So the ghost of Hamlet's father, who has clearly come up from the grave, has, by association, also come up from 'hell'. Almost certainly he enters the stage from the trap. Hamlet asks the ghost to tell 'why the Sepulcher / . . . Hath op'd his ponderous and Marble jawes, / To cast thee up againe?' (TLN 633–6, 1.4.48–51). The ghost exits to hell or at least clearly resides there, for his voice is heard emanating, as Hamlet is careful to point out, from 'the cellarage' under the stage. Hamlet calls the ghost 'old Mole' (TLN 859, 1.5.162) signifying that he burrows in the blackness under the ground. In terms of the metaphorical stage, therefore, the ghost in *Hamlet* is evil: the audience watching the play and hearing Hamlet wonder whether he is to meet 'a Spirit of health, or Goblin damn'd' (TLN 624, 1.4.40) may have felt that they knew the answer. The theatrical structure could impose a layer of simplicity on to the plays that modern readers, seeking for complex meanings in printed, footnoted editions, can miss.

The fact of the audience itself, its very presence, was also, selectively, part of the play. In the indoor and outdoor theatres of the time, spectators and actors clearly saw each other and borrowed reactions from one another. Watching plays today is thus a very different experience from watching plays in the early modern theatre. Audiences nowadays sit in the dark, unable to see the reactions of other spectators; a modern audience is a collection of solitary beings, not a crowd with crowd-responses. As trained and responsible spectators, moreover, we tend to sit quietly and keep ourselves to ourselves: we do not physically or vocally take part in the action, so that the separation of actor from audience is complete. But Shakespeare's original audience was as well-lit as the actors, as visible and, sometimes, as talkative. This was an audience constantly in need of taming. It might throw stones or even lathes. It often threw fruit, which was available for sale throughout performances. One poem asks the spectators of a play performed at the Red Bull playhouse to 'forbeare / Your wonted custome, banding Tyle, or Peare, / Against our curtaines, to allure us forth', and jest books relate amusing retorts made by actors under bombardment:

> in the Play Tarltons part was to travel, who kneeling down to aske his father blessing, [a] fellow threw an Apple at him, which hit him on the cheek. Tarlton taking up the Apple, made this jest.

> Gentleman, this fellow, with this face of Mapple,
> Instead of a pipin, hath throwne me an Apple,
> But as for an Apple, he hath cast a Crab,
> So instead of an honest woman, God hath sent him a drab.

> The people laughed heartily . . .[37]

Actors were expected to respond to events outside the texts, and seem to have had a body of known jokes with which to do so. These playhouse jests were features of one-off performances, and were not consistently attached to any particular play; they seldom ended up in print. Thus the play on paper often does not record the play performed. A hint of what some of the standard jokes might have been is provided in a muddled and probably 'memorial' text of *Hamlet* from 1603 (memorial texts themselves will be discussed in the next chapter). Speaking of clowns, Hamlet rails against the jesters so feeble as to have only one set of jokes to bring in to each play – jests so predictable that the audience can anticipate them all in advance:

> you have some . . . that keepes one sute
> Of jeasts, as a man is knowne by one sute of
> Apparell, and Gentlmen quotes his jeasts downe
> In their tables, before they come to the play, as thus:
> Cannot you stay till I eate my porridge? and, you owe me
> A quarters wages: and, my coate wants a cullison:
> And your beere is sowre . . .
>
> (Q1 F2a–b)

Confronted by such an active audience, plays kept their appeal as wide as possible: there were spectators who would 'damn' levity, and spectators who would 'damn' seriousness, indeed audiences seem to have clapped and hissed their way through performances, necessitating frequent alterations and revisions of plays – a point that will be returned to. John Davies writes a poem to playwrights whose trade he describes as being 'full of toile': 'It's easie to cry Hisse; but, tis not so / To silence it, and Claps of hands to raise.'[38]

The cheapest places at the Globe theatre were in the open air of the yard surrounding the stage. They were for standing audience only, and the people who gathered there were collectively known as 'penny stinkards', 'garlick breaths' and, punningly, 'understanders' – understanders, because they stood under the stage. Whenever a Shakespearean play insults the brutal nature of a lower-class crowd it seems to be turning its criticism towards this element of the audience, partly contemptuously, and partly to provoke a response. Antagonism was one of the ways a playhouse ensured involvement, and mutual insults were part of the theatre's stock-in-trade: 'What's the matter you dissentious rogues' says Caius Martius (later Coriolanus) at the start of *Coriolanus*, 'That rubbing the poore Itch of your Opinion, / Make your selves Scabs' (TLN 174–5, 1.1.165–6). He is taunting a crowd who are rebelling because they are starving as a result of corn shortages. As Britain had itself suffered corn shortages just the year before the play was performed (in an earlier famine in 1598, Shakespeare had himself been accused of hoarding malt at his Stratford home), the sentiment was incendiary.[39] Often Shakespeare utilises the spectators so that they become, unwittingly, part-actors in the plays they are observing. They can then supply the massed army that the *Henry V* prologue could not come up with. When Henry ends his 'Once more unto the Breach, / Deare friends' speech with a three-part expression designed to elicit applause, he urges the audience to cry out and swell the multitude: 'Cry, God for *Harry*, England, and S[aint]. *George*' (TLN 1117, 3.1.1–34). In *King John*, the monarch tries to persuade the people of Angiers that he is their rightful king:

> Doth not the Crowne of England, proove the King?
> And if not that, I bring you Witnesses
> Twice fifteene thousand hearts of Englands breed.
> (TLN 580–2, 2.1.273–5)

Here the spectators are again goaded by the speech to cheer, though, even if they do not, they have still been dragged into the fiction of the theatre, becoming by implication not only observers but part of what they are watching. This drama changes spectators into participants.

It was often said, at the time, that plays were written in layered form, each layer to appeal to a different class of spectator located broadly in different parts of the playhouse: bawdy jokes and rustic clowns for the stinkards standing in the pit, high poetry for the gentlefolk. Joseph Hall writes of the upper echelons (literally) of the audience, the 'gazing scaffolders' (the scaffold was the structure in which the sitting audience were placed) who particularly enjoy iambic verse, and of the 'dead stroke' or 'low' audience who are really interested only in clowning:

> if [the poet] can with terms Italianate,
> Big-sounding sentences, and words of state,
> Faire patch me up his pure *Iambick* verse,
> He ravishes the gazing Scaffolders: . . .
> Now, least such frightfull showes of Fortunes fall,
> And bloody Tyrants rage, should chance appal
> The dead stroke audience, mids the silent rout
> Comes leaping in a selfe-misformed lout,
> And laughes, and grins, and frames his Mimik face,
> And justles straight into the Princes place . . .[40]

All this would partly, but not wholly, change when another theatrical move was made by what were now called the King's Men. This was when, now under royal patronage, the company finally gained the right, in 1609, to perform in their Blackfriars theatre in London. They continued to play in the Globe theatre in the summer months – indeed, the Globe, having burnt down in 1613, was rebuilt even more finely – but from 1609 onwards Shakespeare's plays seem to have been written with the indoors Blackfriars theatre in mind. What works within a small artificially lit theatre can, after all, be adapted to work outdoors on a large naturally lit stage; the reverse is not necessarily the case.

The Blackfriars was in a rectilinear room, but it seems to have retained the properties of a round theatre. Its galleries were curved, so that from the auditorium it looked at least semicircular; it had a heaven and a hell, and a thrust stage surrounded by audience on all sides. One fanciful picture from the 1670s (Plate 2.3) depicts an indoor stage of the 1630s or 1640s (datable by the hats of the audience); the picture is not theatre-specific but can be taken as a rough guide to what indoor theatres in general were like.

Here is a playhouse lit by candles depending from chandeliers and surrounding the stage as footlights. A contemporary poem named the Blackfriars theatre 'the Torchy Fryers' and a wealth of artificial light was a Blackfriars feature.[41] Lighting immediately had huge effects not just on the look but also on the structure of plays. In the indoor Blackfriars theatre, provision had to be made for the regular trimming and replacing of candles: fire inside a timber-framed London would put the whole city at risk. Any play put on at the Blackfriars, therefore, had to have regular breaks on a roughly half-hourly basis during which candles could be tended. In what seems to be a direct response to this, any Shakespeare play written to be performed at the Blackfriars – that is to say, written after 1609 or, like *Measure for Measure*, revised for performance in the Blackfriars – is divided into five acts: five acts mean four act-breaks for candle-trimming. On the other hand, plays written before 1609, to be performed at the Globe only, simply have scene-breaks, and would have been enacted straight through without pause. But, of course, the five-act structure is classical (the plays of Seneca and Terence were divided this way). Sometimes it is thought that Shakespeare in his later years suddenly developed an interest in form. Actually, it seems more likely that Shakespeare changed his manner of writing to conform to a new playhouse, though the result would have been the same – writing to a five-act structure affects the way a play develops its story.

The auditorium of the Blackfriars was much smaller than that of the Globe. The Blackfriars' indoor stage was, similarly, narrower and shallower than the Globe's outdoor one: candles were expensive, and the larger the acting-area, the more lighting would have been required. As, in addition, the audience at Blackfriars could pay to sit on the stage itself, the kinds of texts that could be performed in the new playhouse were automatically limited.[42] Fighting armies with long halberds could not be countenanced, for the weapons might well damage spectators huddled around or on the stage. So plays with major battles were not written for the Blackfriars theatre. Moreover, spectators, who were charged more for performances at Blackfriars than at the Globe, tended to be from the richer classes, which itself put constraints on the

Plate 2.3 Illustration from the title page to Francis Kirkman's *The Wits, or, Sport upon Sport* (1673). Reproduced by permission of University of Cambridge Library.

plays produced. Court fashion became of enormous importance; sumptuous dances, known as masques, which were then very much in vogue in court circles, become regular features of later Shakespearean works. There is a dream-masque in *Henry VIII* very peripheral to the action, and a masque also in *The Tempest*. Music in general was a private-theatre staple, and it took a very different form from the basic, brash music that belonged to public theatres such as the Globe. Outdoor theatres needed instruments that were loud and martial if they were to be heard, like drums and trumpets or cannon. All Shakespeare's major tragedies, and most of his so-called 'history plays' with their battles and marches, were written for the Globe. Such music would, however, have been deafening in the enclosed space of the Blackfriars with its subtle acoustic. Instead, flutes, lutes and 'broken consorts' were chosen, with, in addition, the accompaniment of the odd boy singer to bolster the theatre's already established reputation for high-quality choral music. Music would be played in the four act breaks: 'the encurtain'd musique sounds', wrote Brathwait, 'to give Enter-breath to the *Actors*, and more grace to their *Action*'.[43] Music would also stop the audience from getting restless during act breaks. The plays written after the Shakespeare company acquired the Blackfriars theatre include those often called Shakespeare's 'late plays' or his 'romances': *Pericles, Cymbeline, The Tempest, The Winter's Tale*. Each of these has a dark side, but each is wistful, romantic, yearning, hence the term 'romance'. These are static plays – presumably because the Blackfriars stage was smaller than the stage of the Globe – so they tend towards the aesthetic of fixed things, painting, sculpture, stately dance, tableaux, the conscious art of the theatre. Written to be played by candlelight, broken into separable units and tied over with sweet music, they have a dreamy quality that can be traced directly to the practical necessities offered by the new theatre.

Sometimes, particularly over the Christmas season, plays were performed at court. That may be hinted at in some texts too. The single version of *Macbeth* that survives shows signs that it may be a version of the play specially prepared for one-off performance. The play includes a scene in which Macbeth visits the witches to ask whether Banquo's sons will indeed inherit the crown. In answer, he is shown a procession of '*eight Kings, and Banquo last, with a glasse in his hand*' (TLN 1658, 4.1.112–13). In the looking-glass Macbeth sees a line of kings that seems to 'stretch out to'th'cracke of Doome' (TLN 1664, 4.1.117). But the fact that Banquo heads a succession of kings has already been made by the procession, provoking a question as to why the mirror is needed. The answer may be that this version of *Macbeth* is to be played before King James, a direct lineal descendant from Banquo. Other aspects of the play – its many witch scenes (James had written a tract on witches, *Demonology*, in 1597) – suggest that *Macbeth* may have been reworked for royal performance. Then, in the glass as Banquo passes by, the King sees himself reflected at the end of the line of kings, just as he hears the prediction that his blood-line will rule for ever.

So Shakespeare's London, its buildings, its court, its playhouses, becomes a feature of Shakespeare's texts and of the mentality of Shakespeare's audience. The plays of Shakespeare are thus a product of Shakespeare's environment both specifically and more generally; to have a sense of the early modern London stage is not just to understand the plays *in situ* – in the place for which they were written – but also to understand the way place imposed itself on the writing as well as the performance of Shakespeare.

3
Additions, Emendations
and Revisions

One way a playwright could cancel what he had just written in manuscript was to cross it out, scribbling over the rejected words or phrases. Heminges and Condell, the two actors who gathered together Shakespeare's plays and published them in the 1623 folio, declare that Shakespeare seldom erased any fragment of text in this fashion: 'His mind and hand went together: And what he thought he uttered with that easiness, that wee have scarse received from him a blot in his papers' (A3a). Shakespeare, his friends claim, was so effortlessly creative that he hardly ever stumbled, even over a phrase.

It has been convincingly argued that Heminges and Condell were giving Shakespeare little more than formulaic praise.[1] Commendation of a similar kind is lavished on the works of the now nearly forgotten playwright Thomas Randolph, whose very childhood chatter was publishable – he had 'lisp'd Wit worthy th'Presse'. His natural ease in writing is compared with the scrawlings of lesser playwrights whose pages look like crossed account books; who

> . . . blot
> A quire of Paper to contrive a Plot,

And ere they name it, cross it, till it look
Raced with wounds like an old mercers Book.[2]

Indeed, Ben Jonson, who countered the praise that Shakespeare never blotted out a line with the bitter retort 'would he had blotted a thousand', pointed out that easy composition sometimes means writing before thinking: Shakespeare 'flow'd with that facility, that sometime it was necessary he should be stop'd . . . His wit was in his owne power; would the rule of it had beene so too.'[3] Jonson's resentment will have been fuelled by the fact that his own careful and long-pondered plays were frequently criticised for a laboured lack of spontaneity:

. . . thy Witt
As long upon a Comoedie did sit
As Elephants bring forth; and . . . thy blotts
And mendings tooke more time then Fortune plots.[4]

This chapter explores the way Shakespeare wrote, rewrote and revised his plays. Did Shakespeare in fact blot his copybook? What other kinds of changes might a composing author make and where can they be found? In showing that plays were regularly and frequently altered by a number of people, the chapter raises some larger questions – how 'fixed' is any playtext – and what, exactly, is 'the author' and 'the play'?

The one piece of continuous handwriting that is thought to be Shakespeare's is actually full of crossed words, rewriting and over-writing. It forms a section of a manuscript play, *The Booke* [i.e. playscript] *of Sir Thomas Moore*, which is written, in all, by six people, none of whose names are provided. Their individual 'hands' are commonly designated as belonging to playwrights A, B, C, D, E and S. 'Hand S' in *Thomas Moore* is thought to be that of Anthony Munday, author of numerous plays including *The Downfall of Robert, Earl of Huntingdon* (1601), and *John a Kent and John a Cumber* (*c.* 1594). He was famous for his ability to come up with good plots, but his play *Thomas Moore* was rejected by the public censor, the Master of the Revels, for being seditious. That rejected play was then returned and, at some later point, was revised by five people, most of whom made their emendations on to the rejected manuscript, some of whom wrote revisions on to separate pieces of paper that were then pasted into the playtext.

Why five people worked on the text is unclear; how they divided their labours between them is also unknown. Even the date at which the five performed their work is hard to determine. It is, moreover, suspected that the play was never performed and that what survives is a revised but subsequently re-rejected manuscript. The five revisers are thought to be: 'Hand A' (Henry Chettle), 'Hand B' (Thomas Heywood?), 'Hand C' (a professional scribe or prompter), 'Hand E' (Thomas Dekker). 'Hand D' is usually identified as Shakespeare's because of the appearance as well as the quality of its writing.[5]

Playwright D does not contribute much to *Thomas Moore*. He writes one crowd scene into the manuscript playtext, and provides one soliloquy which is written by Hand C on to a separate piece of paper and later pasted into the playbook; inconsistencies between these passages and the rest of the text show that D has written in isolation, without access to the full copy of the play for which his inserts are intended. D thus shows how little knowledge a collaborator needed to write his text, and this makes him important in the history of co-authorship, whoever he is. Here is a transcription of part of D's crowd scene as it appears on the manuscript page. It is heavily abbreviated, and, for ease of reference, the abbreviations have been spelled out in italics. C has later revised over the text and has changed some of D's speech-prefixes: C's alterations are reproduced in bold. In this section, the English crowd are crying out against admitting foreigners into the country, flooding England with their babies and their alien food. At this point in history, 'foreign food' seems to be defined particularly as root vegetables: the writer (from here on, for the sake of convenience, 'Shakespeare') may want to emphasise that true Englishmen eat meat rather than vegetables. At the same time he points out that food which is disturbingly foreign to one period is native to another:

Linc   they bring in straing rootes, which is merely to the vndoing of poore prentizes, for what*es* ~~a watrie~~ a sorry pa*r*snyp to a good hart

~~*oth*~~ **william**   trash trash,: they breed sore eyes and tis enough to infect the Cytty w*ith* the palsey

Lin   nay yt has infected yt w*ith* the palsey, for theise basterd*es* of dung as you knowe they growe in Dung haue infected vs, and yt is our infeccion will make the cytty shake which pa*r*tly Coms through the eating of parsnips

~~Clown.~~ **Clown. betts**   trewe and pumpions together

> . . .
> Enter the L maier Surrey
> Shrewsbury

~~Sher~~ **Maior**   hold in the king*es* name hold
Surrey   frend*es* masters Countrymen . . .[6]

[Modernised transcript:
Lincoln   They bring in strange roots, which is merely to the
  undoing of poor [ap]prentices, for what's ~~a watery~~ a sorry
  parsnip to a good heart?
~~Oth~~ *William*   Trash! Trash! They breed sore eyes, and 'tis enough
  to infect the city with the palsy.
Lincoln   Nay, it *has* infected it with the palsy, for these bastards
  of dung (as you know, they grow in dung) have infected us,
  and it is our infection will make the city shake – which partly
  comes through the eating of parsnips.
~~Clown.~~ **Clown. Betts**   True, and pumpions [pumpkins] together

> . . .
> *Enter the Lord Mayor, Surrey,*
> *Shrewsbury*

~~Sher~~ **Mayor**   Hold! In the king's name, hold!
Surrey   Friends, masters, countrymen . . .]

  Authorial revisions in *Thomas Moore* are made by the very proce-
dure Heminges and Condell had so specifically denied: by crossing
out erroneous words and phrases and rewriting them. Revisions
are made throughout the dialogue; changes to the designation of
character on the left were made later by C when trying to sort
out who speaks what (the layout of the manuscript suggests that
Shakespeare wrote the dialogue first, and added the names of the
speakers afterwards). This kind of revision, made hastily in
the process of writing a draft text, is called *currente calamo* (literally
'with a running pen'). When Lincoln's speech is changed from
'what's a watery parsnip to a good heart?' to 'What's a sorry
parsnip to a good heart?' Shakespeare is shown making a false
start and correcting it, *currente calamo*. The revision alters the direction of the sentence. Where 'watery' would have made 'parsnip'
the subject of criticism, 'sorry' – hardly an outrageous slur on the
vegetable – throws criticism back on to its speaker, now made,
himself, to seem rather ridiculous. It allows (or inspires), too, the

joke in the next line: 'sorry' parsnips are indeed so because they breed 'sore eyes'. Shakespeare, like most writers, revised during the process of writing itself.

The *Thomas Moore* fragment also shows another feature that relates to notions of the revising author – the use or reuse (depending on dating) of a verbal formula employed elsewhere. Surrey's opening speech to the crowd, 'friends, masters, countrymen' is highly reminiscent of Antony's 'Friends, Romans, Countrymen' (TLN 1618, 3.2.73) in *Julius Caesar*, just as Hamlet's 'words, words, words' in *Hamlet* (TLN 1230, 2.2.192) is matched by Troilus' 'Words, words, meere words, no matter from the heart' in *Troilus and Cressida* (TLN 3322–3, 5.3.108). Even in the heat of creation – or perhaps because of it – Shakespeare seems to have remembered and returned to phrases that had worked in the past. He was a reuser and a reviser, a point hardly worth making except that Heminges and Condell had said he was not.

There were ways other than blotting that playwrights could employ when working on what were called 'foul papers' – 'foul', because, as the very word suggests, it was in the nature of draft manuscripts to be messily blotched in appearance. If a writer were slightly undecided about a passage he had just completed, he could highlight it to be moved, or perhaps deleted later. The conventional way of doing this was to inscribe a vertical line along the side of the questionable section, singling it out without actually damaging the substance of the text, which might, perhaps, prove useful in another place or at another time.

Such passages, marked as debatable, but not physically crossed through, sometimes work their way into printed texts by mistake, for the compositors (typesetters) in the printing house did not always notice that a passage that had not been struck through had nevertheless been rejected.

Some printed Shakespearean texts show evidence that sections marked for excision have been mistakenly published. One occurs in *Love's Labour's Lost*. In that play, the King of Navarre and his young companions have sworn to live pure lives dedicated only to academic study; they also swear to forgo the company of women. When the Princess of France arrives in Navarre with her ladies, however, the King and all his followers are immediately smitten: each man falls in love, starts a flirtation and is, therefore, forsworn. Berowne, the most outspoken of the King's friends, takes it upon himself to defend and excuse what has happened.

The men should embrace the company of women, he maintains, for studying women is simply a variety of scholarly pursuit. As he puts it:

> From womens eyes this doctrine I derive,
> They are the Ground, the Bookes, the Achadems,
> From whence doth spring the true *Promethean* fire.
> (Q F2b, TLN 1652–4, 4.3.298–300)

And as he puts it a few sentences later:

> From womens eyes this doctrine I derive.
> They sparcle still the right promethean fier,
> They are the Bookes, the Artes, the Achademes,
> That shew, containe, and nourish all the worlde.
> Els none at all in ought proves excellent.
> (Q F3a, TLN 1701–5, 4.3.347–51)

Obviously only one version of this passage is supposed to have been retained but, as it is, both have worked their way into Shakespeare's printed text. In fact, the whole second half of Berowne's speech revisits the themes of the first half. What are editors to do with a text like this? Which of the passages should be kept and which rejected? What did Shakespeare intend? The answer is impossible to determine, and editors of *Love's Labour's Lost* always leave both of the above passages in the text and give Berowne his long, repetitive speech in full.[7]

This example is illustrative of the way Shakespeare sometimes wrote. It shows that he was capable of having second thoughts which he might mark for reconsideration rather than expunge. More significantly, it gives a brief glimpse of Shakespeare at a crux in the creation of his play. As it seems, he sometimes had an idea or a verbal image before determining what its final context should be. This is particularly clear in *Romeo and Juliet*, where Shakespeare appears to have settled on a passage to be spoken before deciding its speaker. At the end of 2.2 in the two surviving 'good' texts of *Romeo and Juliet*, Romeo realises that dawn is breaking.

Romeo   The grey eyde morne smiles on the frowning night,
　　　Checkring the Easterne Clouds with streaks of light,
　　　And darkness fleckted like a drunkard reeles,

> From forth daies pathway, made by *Tytans* wheels.
> Hence will I to my ghostly Friers close cell,
> His helpe to crave, and my deare hap to tell.
>
> *Exit.*
>
> *Enter Frier alone with a basket.*
>
> *Friar*   The grey-eyed morne smiles on the frowning night.
> Checking the Easterne clowdes with streaks of light:
> And fleckeld darkness like a drunkard reeles,
> From forth daies path, and *Titans* burning wheeles.
>
> (Q2 D4b; TLN 999–1009, 2.2–3.1.1–4)

Notice the slight variations in the passages spoken by Romeo and spoken by the Friar; 'darkness fleckted', becomes 'fleckeld darkness', 'daies pathway, made by *Tytans* wheels', becomes 'daies path, and *Titans* burning wheeles'. So the repeated segment is authorial: it is not the result of eye-skip or some other mistake in the printing house. As it seems, the substance of this passage was important to Shakespeare – but it did not matter who said it. When addressing 'characterisation', such examples should be borne in mind, for in this instance Shakespeare's characters are tools for a fragment of verse about the arrival of morning. Modern editors, looking at this repeated text in *Romeo and Juliet*, do not let it stand as they did Berowne's twice-spoken fragment in *Love's Labour's Lost*. Perhaps because the repetition is consecutive, or perhaps because the repetition is divided between two people, editors tend to print one version and not print the other, their choice – giving the passage to the Friar or giving it to Romeo – being random (though the fact that in the third surviving 'bad' text only the Friar speaks the speech should be borne in mind).[8]

   A Midsummer Night's Dream and *Julius Caesar* may both contain another variety of internal, local revision that has crept into the established texts. The passages marked for deletion are not repetitions, however, but alternatives. *A Midsummer Night's Dream* seems to have two endings one after another – a fairy masque (probably for private performance) and an epilogue spoken by Puck (probably for public performance). In *Julius Caesar*, the alternative passages relate to the character – and characterisation – of one of the play's protagonists. At the start of 4.3, Brutus already knows that Portia is dead; a few sentences later he discovers it to his

surprise. On each occasion he has a markedly different response
to the news. In the first instance he manfully faces up to sorrow,
as Macduff does in *Macbeth* when he hears of the death of his
wife and children. For the audience, this is the first time that we
learn that

Brutus   . . . *Portia* is dead.
Cassio   Ha? Portia?
Brutus   She is dead.
Cassio   How scap'd I killing, when I crost you so?
            O insupportable, and touching losse!
            Uppon what sickness?
Brutus   Impatient of my absence,
            And greefe, that yong *Octavius* with *Mark Antony*
            Have made themselves so strong: For with her death
            That tydings came. With this she fell distract,
            And (her Attendants absent) swallow'd fire.
Cassio   And dy'd so?
Brutus   Even so.
                        (TLN 2134–46, 4.3.147–57)

Later in the scene, Messala enters.

Messala   Had you your Letters from your wife, my lord?
Brutus   No *Messala*.
Messala   Nor nothing in your Letters writ of her?
Brutus   Nothing, *Messala*.
Messala   That me thinkes is strange.
Brutus   Why aske you?
            Heare you ought of her, in yours?
Messala   No my Lord.
Brutus   Now as you are a Roman tell me true.
Messala   Then like a Roman, beare the truth I tell,
            For certaine she is dead, and by strange manner.
Brutus   Why farewell *Portia*: We must die *Messala*:
            With meditating that she must dye once,
            I have the patience to endure it now.
                        (TLN 2175–88, 4.3.181–92)

This second version of the news takes a Brutus too weighed down
with sorrow and guilt to feel the additional blow. If he is Macduff

in version one, in version two he is like Macbeth, who responds
to the death of his wife with 'She should have dy'de heereafter;
/ There would have beene a time for such a word' (TLN 2238–9,
5.5.17–18). Shakespeare seems to be hesitating over a point
of characterisation here. Should he make Brutus sympathetic, or
stoical and detached? Macduff or Macbeth?[9] It is possible, of
course, that he wants to keep both options open and that the
repetition of the same matter in a different form is deliberate.
Editors always print both passages, and actors often act them; but
Shakespeare's habit of laying out alternative passages one after
the other on the same manuscript has already been illustrated.
He had a tendency to redraft while composing; indeed, flowing
effortlessly from one version to another is a product of that
comfortable ease and fluency in writing so criticised by Jonson.

Shakespeare's recycling of phrases across plays, combined
with what looks like a tendency to think and write in separate
'passages' without necessarily too much preimposed structure,
suggests an author who writes in blocks. Probably, like his Hamlet,
Shakespeare had a 'commonplace' or 'table' book in which he
stored observations and ideas for future use, some composed by
himself, some gathered from the writings of others. Hamlet says
the 'Tables' of his memory contain 'triviall fond Records' and
'sawes of [sententious sayings from] Bookes'. He adds an observation to his own commonplace book summarising what he has
newly discovered about his stepfather. 'My Tables', says Hamlet,
'my Tables; meet it is I set it downe, / That one may smile, and
smile and be a Villaine' (TLN 792–3, 1.5.106–7). 'One may smile
and smile – and be a villain' is the memorable phrase Hamlet
has created to be noted for rereading and, perhaps, reuse in the
future. In this play full of injunctions to 'remember' what has
happened, the tome full of insults that Hamlet so earnestly pores
over when talking to Polonius may well be his own table book.

A culture that works with commonplace books has a habit of
thinking in snippets, in pieces of removable text. Playwrights in
particular had a reputation for working from fragments, which is
why they were often known, critically, as 'playpatchers'.[10] So it is
no surprise to find suggestions that Shakespeare, as well as writing
spontaneously, also worked from separate pre-written pieces of
text. Nor, given that commonplace books were equally used for
storing the ideas of others, is it surprising to find that he gathered passages from the books he read for use in his plays. Sections

in *Antony and Cleopatra* closely adhere to Thomas North's translation of *Plutarch* (1579) and seem to do all they can to recall that
text. In particular, Shakespeare picks up not just what North says,
but the rhythms and vocabulary in which he says it. A famous
example is the depiction of Cleopatra's barge, which North
describes in these words:

> She [Cleopatra] disdained to set forward otherwise, but to
> take her barge in the river of Cydnus, the pope whereof was
> of gold, the sailes of purple, and the owers of silver, which
> kept stroke in rowing after the sounde of the musicke of flutes,
> howboyes, citherns, viols, and such other instruments as they
> played upon in the barge. And now for the person of her
> selfe: she was layed under a pavilion of cloth of gold of tissue,
> apparelled and attired like the goddesses Venus, commonly
> drawen in picture: and hard by her, on either hand of her,
> pretie faire boyes apparelled as painters doe set forth god
> Cupide, with little fannes in their hands, with the which they
> fanned wind upon her. Her ladies and gentlwomen also, the
> fairest of them were apparelled like the nymphes Nereides
> (which are the mermaids of the waters) and like the Graces,
> some stearing the helme, others tending the tackle and ropes
> of the barge, out of the which there came a wonderfull passing
> sweete savor of perfumes, that perfumed the wharfes side,
> pestered with innumerable multitudes of people. Some of them
> followed the barge all alongest the rivers side: others also
> ranne out of the citie to see her comming in. So that in thend,
> there ranne such multitudes of people one after an other to
> see her, that Antonius was left post alone in the market place,
> in his Imperiall seate to geve audience.[11]

Transmuting this passage into blank verse, Shakespeare added to
it a series of linked themes whilst nevertheless keeping much of
North's original language.

> The Barge she sat in, like a burnisht Throne
> Burnt on the water: the Poope was beaten Gold,
> Purple the Sailes: and so perfumed that
> The Windes were Love-sicke.
> With them the Owers were Silver,
> Which to the tune of Flutes kept stroke, and made

> The water which they beate, to follow faster;
> As amorous of their strokes. For her owne person,
> It beggerd all discription, she did lye
> In her Pavillion, cloth of Gold, of Tissue,
> O're-picturing that Venus, where we see
> The fancie out-worke Nature. On each side her,
> Stood pretty Dimpled Boyes, like smiling Cupids,
> With divers coulour'd Fannes whose winde did seeme,
> To glove the delicate cheekes which they did coole,
> And what they undid did. . . .
> Her Gentlewoman, like the Nereides,
> So many Mer-maides tended her i'th' eyes,
> And made their bends adornings. At the Helme
> A seeming Mer-maide steeres: The Silken Tackle,
> Swell with the touches of those Flower-soft hands,
> That yarely frame the office. From the Barge
> A strange invisible perfume hits the sense
> Of the adjacent Wharfes. The Citty cast
> Her people out upon her: and *Anthony*
> Enthron'd i'th' Market-place, did sit alone,
> Whisling to'th' ayre: which but for vacancie,
> Had gone to gaze on *Cleopater* too,
> And made a gap in Nature.
>   (TLN 902–31, 2.2.191–218)

The lovesick winds, the amorous water, the touches of the flower-soft hands are all Shakespeare's, flooding the passage with a sensuality lacking in North. He has added, too, a lyricism, taking repeated sounds, already a feature of North's writing, and playing on them so that they become a theme in themselves: the effect is a wealth, an extravagance of sound and image. What Shakespeare does is in no sense plagiarism, a term that did not exist at the time; it is *imitatio* ('imitation'), a variation on a pleasing theme and a homage to a writer greatly respected. North's *Plutarch* is said to have been the first English translation as famous for its translator as for its original writer (it was known as 'North's *Plutarch*', rather than just '*Plutarch*', even at the time). North, of course, was imitating Plutarch; Shakespeare was imitating North in a line of homage and inheritance.

Homages of this kind, combined with other borrowings – jokes that were around in London at the time, for instance – make up part of what Shakespeare does and expects the audience to recognise. The playwright Ben Jonson went a step further. He not only carefully edited his own plays for publication, excising the contributions of other playwrights ('this Booke . . . is not the same with that which was acted on the publike Stage, wherein a second Pen had good share: in place of which I have . . . put . . . mine own'); he also chose, sometimes, to print quotation marks around what he decided were the best or most memorable bits in his plays, singling key thoughts from the rest and, by so doing, highlighting them for removal into commonplace books.[12] In this way he broke his works back down into the separate fragments that had, presumably, made them up in the first place.[13] The urge to reduce texts to moments, to phrases or *sententia* was strong at the time; plays had the fragment firmly structured within them.

Throughout Shakespeare's canon there are revisions more wide-reaching and significant than discussed so far. These are revisions made over full and complete working plays, emendations made to works that have often already been performed. They relate to the policy of frequent adaptation that existed in the theatre of the time. London was too tiny to provide the audience for a 'run' of a single play, and even the same play could not be performed, unchanged, too many times. Title pages often claim to be, like the 1598 quarto of *Love's Labour's Lost*, 'newly corrected and amended' or, like the 1599 (quarto 2) of *Romeo and Juliet*, 'newly corrected, augmented, and amended' showing not just that plays changed regularly but that alteration was a prized quality. Even when plays themselves are not in reality altered, the claim that 'correction' has taken place continues to be made. Revisions to a text were seen to be a selling-point; an indication that in the playhouse a play was expected to be changed if it were to remain current.

Textual differences between two versions of the same play are of crucial importance, so what is meant by the words that often describe two different states of the text, 'quarto' and 'folio' should be explained. When two or more good texts of a Shakespeare play survive, at least one is going to be quarto and the other folio, so it is necessary to be absolutely clear what each implies, both in general and with respect to Shakespeare.

The terms 'quarto' and 'folio' simply denote the size of a book, and can be used to describe any published text. Paper could be printed on, folded and cut to produce books of various dimensions: if a sheet of paper were folded into quarters, it made a 'quarto'; folded into eight, it made an 'octavo'; into twelve it made a 'duodecimo'. Plays were usually printed in cheap, accessible quartos, and the only plays by Shakespeare published during his lifetime came out in this format (with the exception of *Richard Duke of York*, a 'bad' octavo). Shakespeare does not himself appear to have been responsible for selling any of his texts to publisher or printer, nor does he seem to have seen or made improvements to quartos before they were sent to booksellers. (Printing, publishing and bookselling were not then necessarily the separate trades they are today.)

Critics and editors divide extant quartos of Shakespeare's texts into 'good' and 'bad', though this process has of late come into disrepute.[14] Nevertheless, as the words are much used, and the concepts behind the words have not yet been fully reformed, it is important to describe what 'good' and 'bad' are used to imply. A 'good' quarto is any quarto containing a text that seems to be in some way authoritative, though 'authority' itself can mean a variety of different things. An authoritative text may originate in a Shakespearean rough draft ('foul papers'); in a scribe's neat copy of a Shakespearean draft; or in a playhouse manuscript used for prompting. So though a 'good' quarto is in some form traceable back to an authoritative Shakespearean text, as written or acted, it can have various different lineages.

A 'bad' quarto, on the other hand, is a quarto that contains a text so muddled and confused that it is judged not to have its basis in a straightforward authorial text (though it is not always apparent where a 'bad' quarto does come from). It is often said that 'bad' quartos consist of texts that were partially memorised and then semi-created by whoever supplied the manuscript to the printer. Sometimes a bad quarto is thought to be traceable to a particular actor who gave his 'part' to the printer and then remembered and rehashed as much of the rest of the play as possible. An alternative explanation is that a member of the audience who was skilled in stenography (a variety of shorthand) copied down as much of the play as he could and then made up the rest and gave it to the printer. Heywood claimed of his play *Queen Elizabeth* that 'some by Stenography drew / The plot: put it in print: (scarce one word trew:)'.[15] Perhaps a playwright, or a would-be playwright, produced the texts from a mixture of memory and invention. At the beginning of Shakespeare's folio Heminges and Condell claim that earlier quartos (they make no distinction between good and bad) were 'stolne, and surreptitious copies, maimed, and deformed by the frauds and stealthes of injurious impostors'.

Quartos, good and bad, were printed because publishers were prepared to gamble on their success. Legal fees of one kind or another meant that a printer/publisher would gain little money from issuing playtexts only once, but would profit considerably from reprints.[16] So it was that popular stage plays – the kind that might be assumed to lead swiftly to reprinting – were sought after. Why 'bad' quartos were printed as well as good is not entirely clear, but seems to relate to the way copyright worked at the time. Playwrights had no legal right over what they had written and textual ownership was, instead, accorded to whoever paid the stationers' guild a sum of money for the work in question. As soon as a play was acquired, it could be 'entered' (registered), sold and printed irrespective of its quality or of the feelings of its writer. Indeed, one of the reasons why 'authors' were so little thought of, and were often not named on quarto title-pages, is that they had no clear legal hold over their own creations.

A folio was the largest kind of book that could be published. To print it, sheets of paper were folded only once, and the result was a tome as expensive as it was imposing. The folio size was usual for bibles or the complete works of reputed classical writers. Thus, to have his works published in folio was a comment on Shakespeare's posthumous reputation. In 1616 Ben Jonson had been the first playwright who had dared publish his collected English plays and poems in folio, calling them *The Workes of Benjamin Jonson*, and, by so doing, implying that they were of equal status with the writings of classical authors. Many people found Jonson's attitude presumptuous in the extreme. In particular, they criticised his choice of the majestic term 'works' for what were in fact largely 'plays' (plays being, at the time, considered 'riffe raffes' and 'baggage bookes').[17]

To M. Ben Johnson demanding the reason, why he call'd his playes works.
Pray tell me Ben, where doth the mistery lurke,
What others call a play, you call a worke.

Thus answer'd by a friend in M. Johnson defence.
The authors friend thus for the author sayes,
Bens plais are works, when others works are plais.[18]

The collection of Shakespeare's plays published in 1623 after his death was in folio, following the example set by Jonson. Shakespeare's folio was, however, printed without recourse to the dangerous term 'works' or the demeaning term 'plays'; instead it was called, cumbersomely, *Mr. William Shakespeares Comedies, histories & tragedies*. That its contents are then divided into comedies, histories and tragedies is probably a necessity brought about by the title. Having Shakespeare's plays published in folio at all was nevertheless thought to be outrageous as the furious anti-theatricalist William Prynne makes clear. 'Some Play-books', he fumes, 'are growne from Quarto into Folio; which yet beare so good a price and sale, that I cannot but with griefe relate it, they are now new-printed in farre better paper than most Octavo or Quarto Bibles', adding in the margin, 'Shackspeers Plaies are printed in the best Crowne paper, far better than most Bibles'.[19] Shakespeare's folio was, however it dressed itself, potentially offensive simply as a book.

Mr. William Shakespeares Comedies, histories & tragedies came out seven years after Shakespeare's death, and contains thirty-six plays. All of these are by, or largely by, Shakespeare; other plays thought nowadays to be at least partially Shakespeare's but which are absent from the folio are *Pericles*, *Two Noble Kinsmen* and *Edward III*. Although all texts in the folio are 'good', it is hard to know what relationship they have with their dead author. Some appear to have come from foul papers, others from 'fair copies' of foul papers, others still from scribal manuscripts. Some may have come from prompters' books; some are set from already extant quartos which have themselves, to complicate matters further, been used as prompters' books – *Romeo and Juliet* is one such example. Folio plays set from quarto are *Love's Labour's Lost*, *A Midsummer Night's Dream*, *1 Henry IV*, *The Merchant of Venice*, *Much Ado About Nothing*. As only quartos and the folio survive – the few pages of *Thomas Moore*, perhaps, aside – the question as to what kind of text lies 'behind' a printed text cannot always be resolved.

Some texts survive only in folio and were never printed in quarto: *1 Henry VI*, *The Comedy of Errors*, *The Taming of the Shrew*, *The Two Gentlemen of Verona*, *King John*, *Julius Caesar*, *As You Like It*, *Twelfth Night*, *Macbeth*, *Measure for Measure*, *All's Well that Ends Well*, *Antony and Cleopatra*, *Timon of Athens*, *Coriolanus*, *Cymbeline*, *The Winter's Tale*, *The Tempest*, *Henry VIII*. Editing these texts is simple as there is no alternative text to muddle what is preserved; at the same time, as will be shown, these single plays often have internal indications that they once existed in variant, lost versions.

Other plays survive in more than one 'good' text: a quarto 'good' text and a folio 'good' text. And, often, these two 'good' texts are significantly different from each other, because they have different lineages and were written at different times. *Troilus and Cressida*, *King Lear*, *Othello*, *2* and *3 Henry VI*, *Richard III*, *The Merry Wives of Windsor* and *Henry V* all have two substantively different 'good' forms. *Hamlet* and *Romeo and Juliet* have two substantively different 'good' forms and each has a 'bad' form as well. Some other texts, while displaying minor differences between quarto and folio, are not significantly different. There is, for instance, one scene added to the folio text of *Titus Andronicus* that is not in the quarto: the 'fly-killing scene'. For the rest, the two texts are largely (but not entirely) the same. Other texts that display minor differences between quarto and folio are *Richard II* and *2 Henry IV*.

From about the turn of the last century up until the 1980s, editors confronted with two good-but-variant texts tended to argue that there had, presumably, been one perfect Shakespearean archetypal text that had been 'lost'. It was then suggested that the lost, perfect text could be recovered by conflating the remaining good texts together. Conflated editions of necessity provide the longest possible playtexts with the least possible 'authority' (a good quarto text, or a good folio text, may well have been performed in the playhouse; a combination of the two never was). Only in the 1980s did a group of scholars seriously reconsider the possibility that, when there is a good text from, say, 1604, and another good text from 1623, and both are different, what has probably happened is that the play has been revised over time. Comparing two texts, rather than welding them together, reveals something about the ways Shakespeare – or Shakespeare's theatre – emended playscripts.

Accounts show that it was normal to revise a play after it had already been performed. A simple example of post-performance Shakespearean revision emerges from Ben Jonson. In *Timber; or Discoveries*, Jonson picks up on a grammatical irregularity in Shakespeare's writing of *Julius Caesar*.

> Many times [Shakespeare] fell into those things, could not escape laughter: As when hee said in the person of Caesar, one speaking to him; Caesar, thou dost me wrong. Hee

replyed: Caesar did never wrong, but with just cause: and such like; which were ridiculous.[20]

So amused and infuriated was Jonson that he continued to harp on the one infelicitous phrase 'Caesar did never wrong, but with just cause' for the rest of his life: 'Cry you mercy' says his Prologue to *The Staple of News* (1640), 'you never did wrong, but with / just cause.'[21] But the single surviving text of *Julius Caesar* contains no such observation. The text as it now stands reads, 'Know, *Caesar* doth not wrong, nor without cause / Will he be satisfied' (TLN 1254–5, 3.1.48). Jonson, it would seem, made the criticism, and the text was changed – by Shakespeare or someone else – as a result.

Another post-performance revision was made to *1 Henry IV*. The character now known as Sir John Falstaff started life under the name of Sir John Oldcastle. But the Cobham family, descendants of the real Oldcastle, were offended by Shakespeare's scurrilous treatment of their ancestor, a famous Lollard martyr. Some time after the first performance of the play but before its publication, Oldcastle's memory was 'relieved' when the name of the fat rogue was altered to 'Falstaff' – although the change only effectively wronged a different family: 'Now as I am glad that Sir John Oldcastle is put out, so I am sorry that Sir John Fastolfe is put in, to relieve his memory in this base service, to be the anvil for every dull wit to strike upon.'[22] The surviving text of *1 Henry IV* retains leftovers of the earlier name of Oldcastle that no longer make sense, including Prince Harry's jocular address to Falstaff as 'my old Lad of the Castle' (TLN 148, 1.2.41–2). Some lines of the play seem to be metrically disturbed for the absence of the name's extra syllable, like 'Away good *Ned*, *Falstaffe* sweates to death' (TLN 844–5, 2.2.108).[23] The revisions in *1 Henry IV* may not have been absolute, however: the descendant of a noble family was insulted no matter which name was used, and it is possible that the company varied 'Falstaff' and 'Oldcastle' according to circumstance – late identification of 'fat John' with Oldcastle at least raises the possibility that the play was still sometimes performed using the old titles: 'I'me a fat man . . . I doe not live by the sweat of my brows, but am almost dead with sweating, I eate much, but can talke little; Sir John Old-castle was my great grand-fathers fathers Uncle . . .'[24] If the playhouse did retain the name 'Oldcastle' – or continue to hint at it – that may be because the revision itself was made unwillingly. But just because a writer does not want to alter his text does not make the changes invalid, though it does raise questions about what it means to be 'authorial' and how to define 'authorship' – especially as it is also possible that the person who changed the names in the text was not Shakespeare. Playwrights for the early modern theatre can be shown undertaking unwilling revision as well as willing revision – the one sometimes leading to the other.

Henry V, too, seems to have been speedily adapted in the light of the Earl of Essex's failure to subdue the Irish rebels. In the folio version of the play there is a chorus that declares that Henry V's successful return from the Battle of Agincourt will be greeted with the same rapture that would be accorded Essex were he 'As in good time he may, from Ireland comming, / Bringing Rebellion broached on his Sword' (TLN 2881–2, 5. 1. 29–34). This passage must have been composed between March and June 1599, a date that can be judged with some accuracy as the fact that Essex's journey was going to be a failure was obvious by July.[25] A later version of Shakespeare's *Henry V* (though published much earlier in a quarto of 1600) already lacks this Essex-promoting chorus; the text seems to have been almost immediately rewritten to take away the embarrassingly wrong prediction. Had Essex been successful, indeed, the text would still have needed to be changed simply to recognise the fact. Shakespeare's plays were a product of the time in which they were written and fully reflected its impermanencies.

When the Earl of Essex later tried to institute a coup in 1601 designed to replace Queen Elizabeth's counsellors with his own friends, that event also took its toll on a Shakespeare play. The Earl paid the Chamberlain's Men forty shillings to perform *Richard II* the day before his uprising. Presumably he chose to use the play because it presented an England weakened by bad leadership ('That England, that was wont to conquer others, / Hath made a shamefull conquest of it selfe', TLN 706–7, 2.1.65–6). The rebellion itself was, however, as unsuccessful as the Irish wars: the followers of Essex were arrested (they included Shakespeare's patron, Henry Wriothesley, Earl of Southampton); Essex was later executed. Under interrogation, the Chamberlain's Men claimed ignorance as to their own importance in the uprising. Yet as a shareholder ('sharer') in the Chamberlain's Men since 1599, Shakespeare must have sanctioned the resurrection of *Richard II* under circumstances that would have manipulated the audience's understanding of the play. If the plays were written to include changeable passages, they were also performed in situations that altered their meaning.

Richard II offers an example of post-performance revision that affects the printed text but may not have affected the playing text (the play was probably not performed again after its dangerous use in 1601). The folio and quarto versions of the text are relatively similar save for a single episode. In none of the first three quartos (one of 1597, two of 1598) is the 'deposition' scene of 4.1 published. This is the part of the play in which the King is made to hand his crown to Bolingbroke and renounce his kingship. It was probably because of Essex's uprising that the scene was subsequently excised from the text, remaining absent until the fourth quarto of 1608 which has, its title page boasts, 'new additions of the Parliament Scene, and the deposing of King Richard'. But though printings of *Richard II* reveal the loss and recovery of the scene, the alterations made to *Julius Caesar, 1 Henry IV* and even *Henry V* would probably not have been noticeable without external information alerting us to them. This has important ramifications, for it suggests that there were probably alternative versions of passages in Shakespeare plays that *have* been lost to time and that we do not know about.

Some plays that exist only in one form contain within their single texts hints of other sections that do not survive. The one folio edition of *Winter's Tale* includes, at the start of 4.1, a passage to be spoken by an actor playing Time. In it, Time enjoins the audience to 'Remember well I mentioned a sonne o'th'Kings, which Florizell / I now name to you ...' (*Winter's Tale*, TLN 1600–02, 4.1.21–2), but Time has not appeared before in the text in which this passage stands, and the audience is thus in no position to remember well or badly what he has said. Perhaps Time once had a larger role, like that of Gower in *Pericles*; possibly Time spoke a now-lost prologue. Meanwhile, *Measure for Measure* and *Twelfth Night* both have stories that take place in northern Europe, the first in Vienna, the second in Illyria (roughly situated between Albania and Greece). Yet all the characters have markedly Italian names, the protagonists of *Measure for Measure* including Isabella, Claudio, Lucio, Angelo and Mariana, those of *Twelfth Night* including Viola, Orsino, Olivia and Sebastian. It is possible, of course, that Shakespeare thought that everywhere abroad was a version of Italy. But, as he has a sense of Jewish and Roman names, it is equally possible that, at some point in the life of the two texts, either country or set of characters has been altered.

One reason why a play written before 1606 but performed after that date would have to be significantly revised was the 1606 'Act to Restrain the Abuses of Players' which stated

> That if at any tyme . . . any person or persons doe or shall in any Stage play, Interlude, Shewe, Maygame, or Pageant jeastingly or prophanely speake or use the holy Name of God or of Christ Jesus, or of the Holy Ghoste or of the Trinitie, which are not to be spoken but with feare and reverence, shall forfeite for everie Offence by hym or them committed Tenne Pounds.[26]

This act effectively outlawed all blasphemy on the stage, and much revision took place as a result of it: all swearing had to go from any pre-1606 play that was to be acted again. The law, however, did not extend to the publishing of texts; 'swearing' texts could be read but not seen. A simple example is offered by *King John*, for which only the folio version survives. The printed play itself, which seems to have been written in roughly 1595, is surprisingly free from swearing, and includes some awkward verse lines that are a beat or a couple of beats too long or too short. A couplet such as Philip the Bastard's 'O old sir Robert Father, on my knee / I give heaven thankes I was not like to thee' (TLN 90–1, 1.1.82–3) would obviously read better if the two-syllable 'heaven' yielded to a one-syllable word such as 'God'. 'Heaven' indeed seems to stand in for 'God' in much of the *King John*. This is a revised play, though it appears to be hamfistedly emended, perhaps by a prompter. Its swearwords have simply been replaced at the expense of the verse. Other texts in which swearing has been more or less competently removed are the folio texts of *Titus Andronicus*, *Richard III*, *Merry Wives of Windsor*, *1 Henry IV* and *Twelfth Night*.

Simply crossing out offending words would damage the verse of a text, as the above example illustrates; revision of this kind is unlikely to be authorial. Other plays show signs of having been returned to the author (or at least, to an author) for alteration. *Othello* offers an example. It exists in quarto (1622) and folio, the quarto being a 'swearing' text, the folio largely 'non-swearing' (the quarto text dates from before 1606 despite its late date of publication). In its two manifestations, the play begins like this:

(swearing pre-1606 text)
Rodrigo   Tush, never tell me, I take it much unkindly
   That you Iago, who has had my purse,
      As if the strings were thine, should'st know of this.
Iago   S'blood, but you will not heare me . . .
                                    (Q B1a, 1.1.1–4)

(non-swearing post-1606 text)
Rodrigo   Never tell me, I take it much unkindly
   That thou (*Iago*) who hast had my purse,
      As if ye strings were thine, should'st know of this.
Iago   But you'l not heare me:
                                    (TLN 3–5, 1.1.1–4)

It is touching to find that, together with taking out 'S'blood', a
corruption of the blasphemous expletive 'God's blood', the revising
author has carefully removed even the surely innocuous exclamation of contempt, 'tush'. Other slight changes have also been
made. Rodrigo's formal 'you' in the 'swearing text' has been
replaced by the familiar 'thou' in the non-swearing text. Perhaps
the close relationship between the two men had to be manifested
by modes of address once the casual familiarity implied by the
nonchalant swearing had been removed. Entire lines are rewritten
in slightly different form; while altering the text to remove the
blasphemy, other local revisions were made:

(swearing pre-1606 text)
Iago   It were not for your quiet, nor your good,
   nor for my manhood, honesty, or wisedome,
      To let you know my thoughts[.]
Othello   Zouns.
                                    (Q G3b, 3.3.152–4)

(non-swearing post 1606 text)
Iago   It were not for your quiet, nor your good,
   Nor for my Manhood, Honesty, and Wisedome,
      To let you know my thoughts.
Othello   What dost thou meane?
                                    (TLN 1764–7, 3.3.152–4)

'Zouns' or 'zounds' is a corruption of 'by God's wounds', and
a blasphemous swearword. What in the first text is Othello's

furious exclamation becomes, in the second, a question, a demand for more information. Othello has won back some articulacy in the folio; his descent into jealous madness is slower than it is in the quarto and more paced. In the folio, too, Othello concludes the five-beat ('iambic') verse line started by Iago: 'To <u>let</u> you <u>know</u> my <u>thoughts</u>. What <u>dost</u> thou <u>mean</u>?' The regularity of the verse completion again implies that he has not yet lost control as he has in the quarto, though it may also illustrate to what extent he is under Iago's sway: Othello completes Iago's lines. So alteration, whatever necessity brought it about, will often subtly (and sometimes less than subtly) change the tone of the play itself.

Other, additional, revisions have been made to *Othello*, revisions that suggest a Shakespeare who cannot leave his text alone once he has the chance to rework it (that 'Shakespeare' is the reviser is an assumption based on the quality of the revision). On one level simple substitution has taken place. There was, for instance, no legal or textual necessity to change the quarto's iambic 'And swiftly come to *Desdemona's* armes' (Q D4a, 2.1.80), to the folio's more torrid iambic 'Make loves quicke pants in *Desdemonaes* Armes' (TLN 844, 2.1.80), but that is the alteration. Perhaps, looking at the play again, Shakespeare decided to intensify the sexuality of the couple's love.

In addition, substantial passages appear in one text of *Othello* and not the other. They often work round certain themes, as though Shakespeare had a new connected series of ideas that he wove into the text. In the folio there are several passages that are absent from the quarto that suggest Othello used magic to win Desdemona's love. The characters that surround Othello in folio are, as a result, more implicitly racist than their counterparts in the quarto; the folio hero is more isolated. Shakespeare fiddled with his texts as he revised them, but, given the chance, he also could alter fundamental elements of the story – this is equally clear in *Hamlet* and *Lear*, in which 'good' texts differ so exceptionally as to constitute rather different plays.

Hamlet exists in three texts, two quartos and the folio. Of the quartos, one, the first, published in 1603, is designated 'bad' and is approximately 2150 lines long. The second, published in 1604/5, is designated 'good' and is considerably longer, extending to some 3600 lines. The folio text, also 'good', but manifestly later in composition than the good quarto, is 3500 lines long. The 'bad' quarto truly is a garbled form of the play. Rhyming couplets are

half-remembered: what in good quarto and folio is Claudius'
despairing 'My words flye up, my thoughts remain below, / Words
without thoughts, never to Heaven go' (TLN 2372–3, 3.3.97–8)
is, in the bad quarto, 'My wordes fly up, my sinnes remaine below.
/ No King on earth is safe, if Gods his foe' (Q1 G1a). Indeed,
God has, throughout the bad quarto, a much less ambiguous presence than in either of the good texts. The 'To be or not to be'
speech is rendered

> To be, or not to be, I there's the point,
> To Die, to sleepe, is that all? I all:
> No, to sleepe, to dreame, I mary there it goes,
> For in that dreame of death, when wee awake,
> And borne before an everlasting Judge,
> From whence no passenger ever returnd,
> The undiscovered country, at whoes sight
> The happy smile, and accursed damn'd.
> But for this, the joyfull hope of this,
> Whol'd beare the scornes and flattery of the world,
> Scorned by the right rich, the rich cursed of the poore?
>
> (Q1 D4b)

This speech certainly contains echoes of Hamlet's reflection on
death as an undiscovered country, but the undiscovered country
is unambiguously 'heaven' and is a place to which Hamlet has
the 'joyfull hope' of going. While in the 'good' texts the speech
is impelled by Hamlet's fears about an unknowable afterlife, here
in the bad text Hamlet has such a comfortable certainty of going
to Heaven that it is unclear what he is worried about. How 'bad'
this text actually is, is another question. Though the 1603 quarto
represents the play in a different state from either quarto or
folio ('Polonius' is here called 'Corambis'; 'Reynaldo' is called
'Montano'), it is not obviously a text that dates either from earlier
or from later than the two good texts.[27] It lies somewhere in
between the two; a bad version of a third state of *Hamlet*.
    In the story told by the 'bad' quarto, Gertrude, learning from
Hamlet that Claudius is a murderer, changes allegiance from her
new husband to her son. Her character may echo the equivalent
part of the Queen in the lost play of *Hamlet* (often called the 'Ur'-
Hamlet), perhaps by Kyd, from which Shakespeare took his story.
Maybe whoever constructed the quarto added elements remem-

bered from Kyd's play to flesh out the text. On the other hand, the moral dubiety of Gertrude in the two good versions of *Hamlet* could be seen as a textual alteration made by Shakespeare to something he had written. Just as Shakespeare added a layer of complexity to *Othello*, so his decision to complicate the role of Gertrude may have been carefully made; perhaps he wanted Hamlet to confront – but also to have inherited – two strands of 'villainy'.

So, as well as being a muddle, the bad quarto of 1603 is also a trace of a lost version of Shakespeare's *Hamlet*. This is no surprise: most plays, as has been shown, were somewhat 'fluid'. Other versions of *Hamlet*, entirely lost, are suggested by references and epitaphs. 'Ther are, as Hamlet saies,' writes Robert Armin, a performer of Fools for the Chamberlain's men, 'things called whips in store', a phrase that is absent from any of the three extant texts of *Hamlet*.[28] The line may be a misremembered version of *2 Henry VI*'s 'My Masters of Saint *Albones*, / Have you not Beadles in your Towne, / And Things call'd Whippes?' (TLN 882–4, 2.1.133–4) as is sometimes suggested, or it may relate to Hamlet's 'Whips and Scornes of time' (TLN 1724, 3.1.68). But given that it is written by an actor who had played in Shakespeare's *Hamlet* since its inception, the phrase might be from a version of *Hamlet* for which there is no other record. Richard Burbage, the actor, is particularly remembered for the way he 'but scant of breath' cried out 'Revenge for his dear father's death', an exclamation not present in any of Shakespeare's surviving *Hamlet*s.[29] Similarly, in a jest-book written by Richard Chamberlain in the 1630s, a section on 'Sundry mistakes spoken publickly upon the Stage' tells how an actor in *Richard III* reversed the names of Buckingham and Banister and said 'My Liege, the *Duke* of *Bannister* is tane, / And *Buckingham* is come for his reward'.[30] But in Shakespeare's play there is no character Banister, and there the words are 'My Liege, the Duke of Buckingham is taken, / That is the best newes' (TLN 3339–40, 4.4.531–2). True, the words may be from another popular play about *Richard III*, now lost – but they may equally be a testament to a different version of Shakespeare's text from either of the two that have survived.

Between the good *Hamlet* (1604) and the folio *Hamlet*, large-scale revision has taken place. The folio text includes about eighty lines that are not in the 'good' 1604 quarto, but it also omits about 230 lines that are. Was Shakespeare trying to create new audience interest in a tired play, or was he, once again, a victim of the practical demands of the censor? Perhaps both. 'Danish' jokes – the fact, for instance, that Danes are called drunkards and swine by other nations – are consistently revised out of *Hamlet*. Here is one of the passages later cut:

> This heavy headed reveale east and west
> Makes us tradust, and taxed of other nations,
> They clip us drunkards, and with Swinish phrase
> Soyle our addition.
>
> (Q2 D1a, 1.4.19–22)

This and similar observations seem to have been excised when King James came to the throne with a Danish wife in 1603. Has the play been altered so as not to offend royal sensibilities?

As with the emendations in *Othello*, the process of subtly but consistently changing *Hamlet* alters the nature of its hero. In the earlier good quarto, *Hamlet* seems to be closer to his revenge-play archetype. Important passages cut by the time of the later, folio text include the much-quoted section where Hamlet would, he says, trust Rosencrantz and Guildenstern, 'my two Schoolefellowes . . . as I will Adders fanged', and acidly declares that 'tis the sport to have the enginer / Hoist with his owne petar' (Q2 K3b, 3.4.202–7) – that is to say, that it is amusing to blow up the engineer with his own bomb. Without this malicious side, the later Hamlet is less vindictive, less of a standard 'revenger'.[31]

King Lear was once believed to exist in 'two *relatively corrupted* texts of a pure (but now lost) original'. These days it is thought instead to represent 'two *relatively reliable* texts of two different versions of the play'.[32] The two versions are the 'good' (but earlier thought 'bad') quarto of 1608, and the folio of 1623. There is also a second quarto of 1619 which is a reprint of the first quarto. The folio text, however, is thought to have been set from an annotated copy of quarto 2.[33] The *Lear* text is very different in the two versions and, because of this, *Lear* was made by critics the crucial example of undoubted authorial revision. Consideration of it set off the whole 'revision' controversy in the 1980s. Important essays showed changes to almost every character between quarto and folio. Michael Warren argued that the folio diminished the quarto role of Kent, Thomas Clayton that folio Lear was more dramatic in its final acts than the quarto, Beth Goldring that Cordelia was stronger in folio than quarto, John Kerrigan that the Fool was dramatically superior in folio.[34] John Jones argued that the quarto text represented a version of Lear filled with 'late play' devices – music, tears – and that the folio's was a harsher telling of the tale; Ioppolo that Cordelia was more powerful in the quarto.[35] But revision in *Lear* is actually unlike revision in any other play, a fact that is not taken sufficiently into account. In the case of almost all the plays discussed so far, one text relates to another. One is earlier, or one is later, with passages or sections reworked over time. In *Lear,* however, the two texts constitute two entirely different versions of the play, neither necessarily worse nor better than the other but both so minutely yet consistently varied that it is unlikely the same company performed them. One powerful example will serve: the death of Lear.

(Quarto text)
Duke.   all friends shall tast the wages of their vertue, and al foes
the cup of their deservings, O see, see.
Lear.   And my poore foole is hangd, no no life, why should a
dog, a horse, a rat [have] life and thou no breath at all, O
thou wilt come no more, never, never, never, pray you undo
this button, thanke you sir, O, o, o, o.
Edg.   He faints my Lord, my Lord.
Lear.   Breake hart, I prethe breake
Edg.   Look up my Lord.
Kent.   Vex not his ghost, O let him passe,
He hates him that would upon the wracke,
Of this tough world stretch him out longer.
Edg.   O he is gone indeed.

(Q1 L4a, 5.3.303–16)

(Folio text)
Alb.   . . . All Friends shall
Taste the wager of their vertue, and all Foes
The cup of their deservings. O see, see.
Lear.   And my poore Foole is hang'd: no, no, no life?
Why should a Dog, a Horse, a Rat have life,
And thou no breath at all? Thou'lt come no more,
Never, never, never, never, never.
Pray you undo this Button. Thanke you Sir,
Do you see this? Looke on her? Looke her lips,
Looke there, looke there.   *He dies.*

Edg. He faints, my Lord, my Lord.
Kent. Breake heart, I prythee breake.
Edg. Look up my Lord.
Kent. Vex not his ghost, O let him passe, he hates him,
    That would upon the wracke of this tough world
    Stretch him out longer.
Edg. He is gon indeed.

                  (TLN 3274–3290, 5.3.303–16)

As will be seen, the alterations here are not simply additions to the passage. The same words are given to different characters, and Lear dies at a different time. So in the first passage Lear expires just after begging his own heart to break, 'I prethe, break'. Edgar does not realise that the King's struggle is over ('Look up my Lord'); Kent does ('Vex not his ghost . . .'). Lear's final wish in the quarto has been to die, so that he is almost responsible for his death; the last word of the man who shattered the unity of his family and kingdom is 'break'. But in the second passage, Lear, in an addition, looks at the lips of Cordelia. Perhaps he dies in hope, thinking that his daughter is still breathing; perhaps he dies in anguish seeing that she is not. Either way, as the stage direction indicates, his death must occur at the end of the speech. Again, Edgar does not realise and tries to rouse the dead king ('my lord!') but now Kent, who understands all, wills his own heart to 'break I prithee . . .'. As a result, in the folio the hearty Kent wills death upon himself, begging his own heart to break – but it does not, just as nothing Kent has wanted or hoped for has worked in this play. When, a few lines later he relates that he has a journey to go on – and that his master has called him – his meaning is only too clear.

    Revision to a text did not stop with the death of the author. Plays that were, as has been shown, regularly reshaped during an author's life were, for the same reasons, regularly reshaped after his death. That means that by the time texts were gathered for Shakespeare's 1623 folio they may include developments instituted after 1616 (the date of Shakespeare's death). In several cases what has survived into the folio actually appears to be a later adaptation of the play made by another writer. So *Macbeth* has two stage directions, 'sing within. Come away, come away, &c.' and 'Musicke and a Song. Blacke Spirits, &c' (TLN 1466, 1572, 3.5.34.0, 4.1.44), both of which are cross-references to songs in scenes from Thomas Middleton's play *The Witch*. *Macbeth*, which is considerably shorter than any other Shakespearean tragedy, seems to be a cut-down version of a lost, longer text; its reviser may well be Middleton, who was himself a playwright for the King's Men. May 'Middleton' have added other passages to *Macbeth*? It is quite possible that the trochaictetrameter 'Double, double, toil and trouble', a form of verse not used elsewhere by Shakespeare, may also be a reviser's interpolation.[36]

What quartos and folio seem to offer are fixed moments in the fluid life of a text, some more 'authorial' than others, though perhaps it is wrong to use the sense of an 'author' as a way of deciding what constitutes a good or bad text. Certainly 'Shakespeare' appears to have accepted revision even if unwillingly, and emerges as a writer capable of changing his mind in ways that alter characters and affect plots. He seems prepared to accept passages into his plays that censorship, circumstance or current events are responsible for. He also appears to have chosen to erase lines that have subsequently been designated 'immortal'. Revision, invisible to the reader of edited texts, and alien to anyone who wants to think that Shakespeare wrote with the permanence his lines are now accorded, is a basic feature of the early modern repertoire.

4
Rehearsal, Performance and Plays

Though 'Shakespeare's' London was the largest city in the country, it was only a mile or so square: the entirety of early modern London would fit into Hyde Park now. As the city was so small, the potential audience for any theatre was also small – there were not enough people to supply a daily audience for the same play if it were repeated too frequently. So throughout Shakespeare's lifetime theatres put on different plays every day: there were no 'play runs'. Every acting week, then, consisted of a variety of new and old plays interspersed, an 'old play' being a play that the company had acted before. An unpopular new play, a play that was 'damned' or 'hissed' after first performance, would not be performed again. A reasonably popular play could expect up to twelve performances in all spread over two years; an extremely popular play might become 'stock' and be performed on a regular basis for a number of years.

What does it mean to share a large number of plays amongst the same small number of people? This chapter explores the way a theatrical company dealt with the quantity of texts they had to learn and relearn. It considers the designation of certain roles within playing companies, and how Shakespeare's plays reflect this. The process of putting a play on is discussed, with a look at actors' preparation from the moment when separate scripts ('parts') were received, through to brief collective rehearsal. Are Shakespeare's texts a product of the way they were disseminated and learned? How is the playhouse context reflected in the texts of the plays themselves?

Here are some concrete examples of a regular weekly playing schedule for an acting company performing at the Rose playhouse in the 1590s, taken from the *Diaries* of the theatrical entrepreneur Philip Henslowe.[1] The Admiral's Men (the company that played at Henslowe's Rose theatre) performed six days a week during 1594/95, and offered thirty-eight plays in all, of which twenty-one were new. Few of those new plays remained in the repertory for more than a year. In January of the next year, 1595/96, the Admiral's Men played on every day except Sunday and presented fourteen different plays. Of these, six were only ever given one performance – and that is for January alone.

To put this in context, consider one week of that January (between the 18th and 25th) from the perspective of Edward Alleyn, the main actor of the Admiral's men. The plays were *The Jew of Malta*, *The Famous Victories of Henry V*, *Barnado and Phiameta*, *Chinon of England*, *Seven Days of the Week part 2* and *Pythagorus*. Alleyn would, probably, have had to play Barabas one day, Henry V the next, Barnardo the day after, followed by Chinon, whichever character starred in the lost *Seven Days*, and Pythagoras. So he had no opportunity for the kind of reflective rehearsal that we have today, or for delving into the problems of motivation in the manner of a modern actor: he would have had little time to do more than learn or relearn his lines. Yet parts written for performers acting inside this system are often dense, complicated and richly obscure. Why – and how – were texts written in so complex a fashion when they were going to be treated in what appears to be such a cavalier manner?

The answer, of course, is that they were not regarded cavalierly. Preparation for performance was thorough, though very different from the way plays are made ready now. Actors' texts of the period reflect and are a testament to the kind of work involved.

The early modern theatre had a system of typecasting in the original sense of the word: it cast along the lines of personality 'type', so that fat jolly men had fat jolly parts, and lean melancholic men played lean melancholic types. This is broader than modern typecasting: a lean melancholic man could, for instance, be a villain or a hero – his parts were not always the same, but his real-life character type always shaped them. As players seem to have been cast in similar kinds of role during a theatrical season, and were generally cast in parts that matched their actual personalities, there was less need for any actor to work on issues of characterisation: kingly types would usually be kings, 'braggarts' (proud, boasting types) would play braggarts, and the clown would be the clown. This helped actors perform different parts on a daily basis, while also making those parts 'make sense' not just to the actors playing them but also to the watching audience.

'Types' had names and characteristics – king, braggart, fool, old man – and each probably had a regular set of clothes as well as a verbal designation. Given that actors played to type, it is clear that plays written for a particular set of players must also have been designed for a limited number of types. In *Hamlet*, the Prince refers to the way plays are constructed out of set characters. When he meets the players, he knows what parts they can offer before he learns their specific repertory, both because he knows the company and because he knows theatre. He says:

> He that playes the King shall be welcome; his Majesty shall have Tribute of mee: the adventurous Knight shal use his Foyle and Target: the Lover shall not sigh *gratis*, the humorous man shall end his part in peace: the Clowne shall make those laugh whose lungs are tickled a'th' sere: and the Lady shall say her minde freely; or the blanke Verse shall halt for't.
>
> (TLN 366–72, 2.2.319–25)

Hamlet sees the players – and their plays – as a distillation of the range of parts the company seems to offer.

Bearing character types in mind when looking at the plays of Shakespeare can be very instructive. A speech-prefix or stage direction in an early printed playtext often varies between using a character's name (for instance, 'Lancelot'), and a character's generic type (for instance, 'Clown'). What this suggests is that Shakespeare did not always create fictional characters with personal names. Instead, he may have started by writing a play for, say, King, Queen, Bastard, Fool, Braggart, Clown, Old Lady, Friar, Nurse, adding individual names later. There follow some examples of generic names from speech-prefixes and stage directions of early texts (their modern designation – what is found in edited texts – is given in parentheses afterwards):

> Enter Clowne (Lancelot) and Jessica, folio, *Merchant of Venice*, 3.5.0

> Enter two Clownes (Gravediggers), Q2 (1604/5), M1b, *Hamlet*, 5.1.0

> Enter Bastard (Philip) with Austria's (Richard's) head, folio, *King John*, 3.2.0

> Enter a Bragart Gentleman (Osric), Q1 (1603), I2a, *Hamlet*, 5.2.80.1

> Enter Braggart and his Boy (Don Adriano; Moth), Q (1598), C3b, *Love's Labour's Lost*, 3.1.0

> Enter Lady of the house and Nurse (Lady Capulet, Nurse), Q2 (1599), K1b *Romeo and Juliet*, 4.4.0

And here is a section of dialogue exactly reproduced from the folio text of *King Lear*, showing that the speech-prefix 'bastard' is used for Edmund, even though within the text itself he is addressed by his name:

Edg.   How now Brother *Edmond*, what serious contemplation are
  you in?
Bast.   I am thinking Brother of a prediction I read this other day,
  what should follow these Eclipses.
                                        (TLN 467–70, 1.2.138–41)

Some of these generic names are familiar. Most, however, are not. This is because modern editors usually 'discover' a character's name, and use it in speech-prefixes, opting to ignore the other, 'generic', name. A present-day reader, trained up on novels, is naturally interested in the individual. But in some plays only 'types' are provided for characters, and then modern editors have to use those generic types for titles. So even in modern edited texts the nurse in *Romeo and Juliet* is known only as 'Nurse', and the Fool in *King Lear* is 'Fool'. Macbeth in the play of that name has a title of his own, but his wife has only his name feminised – 'Lady' Macbeth (compare other tragic wives who *do* have names of their own, such as Desdemona in *Othello*, and Hermione in *The Winter's Tale*, and others who do not, such as the bad Queen in *Cymbeline*). Characters who are generally identified by their generic type in the speech-prefixes of early editions, but who are actually addressed by name in the text, have their names extracted by modern editors. One example is the Bastard in *King Lear*, to whom editors always give the name Edmund (confusingly, the Bastard in *King John*, who also has a name, is usually called Bastard by them). The fool in *Measure for Measure* is called 'Clowne' in speech-headings of the Folio, but Pompey (his 'name') in modern editions. Similarly, modern editions of *Measure for Measure* prefer Thomas and Peter to '2 Friars'.

A different kind of example is offered by *Hamlet*. In the quartos and folio of that play, the King and Queen are called just that – King, Queen – despite the fact that the Queen is referred to as Gertrude in the text. So the second quarto (1604/5) provides the following exchange:

King   How is it that the clowdes still hang on you.
Hamlet   No so much my Lord, I am too much in the sonne.
Queen   Good Hamlet cast thy nighted colour off . . .
(Q2 B4b; 1.2.66–8)

A modern edition individualises the King and Queen in literary, novelistic fashion, giving the Queen her name of 'Gertrude' and the King his name 'Claudius'. In fact, though Gertrude is called by her name in the play, the name Claudius is never used in any of the texts of *Hamlet* itself: it is a redundant or 'dead' name, a name that exists *only* in a speech-prefix. An audience in Shakespeare's day, and indeed now, never learns that Claudius is the king's name. Another 'dead' name is that of the prince in *Romeo and Juliet*, who is, it would seem, called 'Prince Eskales', but, again, only in the speech-prefix. To the audience, would those characters be individualised – or would one be 'king' and one 'prince'? In opting to flesh out characters in this distinctive way wherever possible, modern editors lose what they do not want to recognise: the mass-produced qualities of many of Shakespeare's characters; the way one king is often like another, because frequently he is written for the same actor.

Knowing the way Shakespeare wrote can help explain why it is that some characters seem to exist in more than one play: there are across-play types traceable to actors' personalities. This is particularly easy to see in the case of the clown. The Chamberlain's Men, had, in the early days, a clown by the name of William Kempe, who performed light, humorous roles. He was also a noted morris dancer, and in 1600 famously danced a nine-day trip from London to Norwich (he wrote about it in *Kemp's Nine Days' Wonder*, 1600). The parts Shakespeare appears to have written for Kempe reflect his nature, which is probably why 'Fools' and 'Clowns' in Shakespeare's early plays share certain qualities: they are ridiculous and slow-witted. Dogberry in *Much Ado*, Launce in *Two Gentlemen of Verona*, Launcelot Gobbo in *The Merchant of Venice* and Constable Dull in *Love's Labour's Lost* seem to have been Kempe characters, and can be compared to stories told of Kempe himself:

> Will[iam] Kempe by a mischance was with a sword run quite through the leg, a Country Gentleman comming to visit him, asked him how he came by that mischance, he told him, and withal, troth saith he, I received this hurt just eight weekes since, and I have laine of it this quarter of a yeare, and never stirr'd out of my Chamber.[2]

Kempe eventually left the company for which Shakespeare was writing, perhaps under a cloud – it has been suggested that Hamlet's exceptions to clowns who 'speake . . . more then is set downe for them' (TLN 1887–8, 3.2.39–40) is a reference to Kempe and his habit of extemporisation. For whatever reason, Kempe set off in 1599 first to dance his morris to Norwich (see Plate 4.1), then to dance over the Alps to Rome.[3]

A new Fool was acquired for the Chamberlain's Men to fill the gap left by Kempe. His name was Robert Armin, and his character was markedly different from that of his predecessor. He was lean, intelligent, articulate, played the lute and sang, and from the point at which the company acquired him the 'fool' parts in Shakespeare plays change their nature. Professionally Armin what was known as an 'artificial' or 'wise' fool, a different variety from 'natural' (meaning 'born') fools. While natural fools were stupid by nature, 'artificial' fools were foolish by design and through study. Armin, the Globe's new 'wise' fool, wrote a book on the

Plate 4.1 Illustration from the title page to William Kempe's *Kemp's Nine Daies Wonder* (1600). Reproduced by permission of the Bodleian Library.

nature of fooling called *Foole Upon Foole* (1600), which he later revised as *A Nest of Ninnies* (1608); it commends the artificial over the natural fool because

> Naturall Fooles, are prone to selfe conceipt:
> Fooles artificiall, with their wits lay wayte
> To make themselves Fooles, liking the disguise,
> To feede their owne mindes, and the gazers eyes.[4]

No one would accuse Armin of really being a fool as they had Kempe:

> To honest-gamesome Robin Armin,
> That tickles the spleene like an harmeles vermin.
> Armine, what shall I say of thee, but this,
> Thou art a foole and knave? Both? Fie, I misse;
> And wrong thee much, sith thou in deede art neither,
> Although in shew, thou playest both together.[5]

Armin was also a poet and a playwright. So the profusion of 'wise' fools in the plays of Shakespeare after 1600 – the Fool in *Lear*,

Touchstone in *As You Like It*, Feste in *Twelfth Night*, Lavache in *All's Well that Ends Well* – seem to be a reflection of a playhouse change. That said, Armin did also inherit the parts of Kempe that were still in repertory: he has, he tells his readers, been 'writ downe for an Asse' in his time, indicating that he succeeded Kempe as Dogberry in *Much Ado About Nothing*.[6]

One picture of Armin survives at the front of the printed text of his play *The Two Maids of Moreclack* depicting the clown in character, and bearing about him props that comment both on John of the Hospital (the role he played) and on the man (Plate 4.2). Hanging from Armin's belt in the picture is a long black object: an inkhorn. The inkhorn's visible presence indicated someone who

Plate 4.2 Illustration from the title page to Robert Armin's *The History of the Two Maids of More-Clacke* (1609). Reproduced by permission of the Huntington Library, San Marino, California (RB 56220).

was in constant need of writing materials (a strong statement in an age in which many people were illiterate); it signified that its wearer was erudite – or pretentious.

Unsurprisingly, roles written for 'women', played by boys, were altered more frequently than any other roles. Boys change, they go through growth spurts, their voices break, they finally cease to be able to be 'women' any more and have to start playing male roles (Henry Glapthorne writes a poem to 'Ezekiel Fen at his first Acting a Mans Part'.)[7] 'What, my yong Lady and Mistris?' says Hamlet jestingly to the boy player, 'Byr lady your Ladiship is neerer Heaven then when I saw you last, by the altitude of a Choppine' (a 'chopine' was a shoe with a monstrously high cork heel). He adds the hope that 'her' voice has not yet broken: 'Pray God your voice like a peece of uncurrant Gold be not crack'd within the ring' (*Hamlet*, TLN 1402–4, 2.2.424–7). Perhaps a growth spurt explains the muddle in *As You Like It* where Celia is described as being 'the taller' woman (TLN 440, 1.2.262), though later it is Rosalind who calls herself 'More then common tall' (TLN 580, 1.3.111). Sometimes voice-breaks seem to be hastily accommodated in texts, as when, in *Cymbeline*, Arviragus and Guiderius are about to sing a song but Guidarius suddenly decides he will instead 'weepe, and word it with thee' (TLN 2553, 4.2.240). *Twelfth Night*, too, which only exists in one text, seems also to bear the leftovers of a voice-revision. Viola, when first met stranded on the Illyrian shore, is unsure what to do. She eventually settles on dressing as a boy and going to join Orsino's court. She is sure she will be accepted by the Duke 'for I can sing, And speake to him in many sorts of Musicke, / That will allow me very worth his service' (TLN 109–11, 1.2.57–9). At this point, the role of Viola is written for a singing heroine, which works well with the structure of the narrative. Orsino indulges in music-fed love-melancholy; Viola will, over the course of the play, sing him into real love. But whether because the boy playing Viola lost his voice or was replaced with a worse singer (or whether the company wished their new Fool, Armin, to sing the songs instead), Viola's songs are given to Feste. Here is a passage in which Viola (dressed as a boy, Cesario), is asked to sing:

Duke   Give me some Musick; Now good morrow frends.
    Now good Cesario, but that peece of song,
    That old and Anticke song we heard last night;

Me thought is did releeve my passion much,
More then light ayres, and recollected termes
Of these most briske and giddy-paced times.
Come, but one verse.
Curio He is not heere (so please your Lordshippe) that should
sing it?
Duke Who was it?
Curio *Feste* the Jester my Lord, a foole that the Ladie *Oliviaes*
Father tooke much delight in. He is about the house.

(TLN 885–96, 2.4.1–13)

Basic revision seems, here, to have removed Viola's songs and
given them to Feste, necessitating Feste's unlikely presence in the
house of Orsino for this scene. The song that Feste sings, 'Come
away, come away death', would have made Viola, had she sung
it, subject to the same moody melancholy as Orsino and so could
have linked the two through the medium of music. In the mouth
of Feste the song is an ironic commentary on what is going on.
Of course, the song Viola sung might have been different from
Feste's, for plays were reshaped to accommodate company
changes, and the nature of the change will have dictated the variety
of the rewriting.

We can trace through the plays one particular singing boy
in the Chamberlain's Men, although it is unclear who he was.
Shakespeare's tragedies alter to follow the singing skills of, it would
seem, one especially talented young man. Of the two versions of
Othello, one, the quarto, is without music, the other, the folio, contains a song – the 'willow song' – for Desdemona to sing. Though
it is hard to date the writing of the two *Othello* texts, the difference
probably relates to the fact that major Shakespearean heroines sing
between 1601 and 1604, and that they then all stop until 1609
(when the company moved to the Blackfriars theatre and there was
a general increase in the music used for plays).[8] Ophelia and the
musical Desdemona, it seems, are part of a general proliferation of
singing women traceable to an accomplished singing boy. But the
'willow song', present or absent, makes a fundamental difference
to the play. Its pathos but also its homeliness counterbalance
the chaos of the drama with a wistful gesture towards folk song
and country values; the symbolism of a willow song, a formula
traditionally used to describe the sorrowings of a rejected or
dejected lover, also sounds an ominous warning to the audience.

Spectators in the early modern theatre regularly saw the same actors perform in a host of different plays. Unsurprisingly, particular performers soon came to be recognised as celebrities. John Manningham, writing in 1602, tells an anecdote about a starstruck woman who 'grew . . . far in liking' with Richard Burbage. She was particularly taken by Burbage's portrayal of Shakespeare's Richard III – so taken, in fact, that she requested Burbage to 'come that night unto her by the name of Richard the Third'. As it was, the story goes, Shakespeare 'overhearing their conclusion' turned up slightly earlier at the woman's house, and was 'at his game' by the time Burbage arrived. 'Message being brought that Richard the Third was at the door, Shakespeare caused return to be made that William the Conqueror was before Richard the Third.'[9] Young gallants started to imitate Burbage's Richard III, and the various traits with which he glamorised the tyrant king. As one contemporary poem had it: '*Gallants*, like *Richard* the usurper, swager, / That had his hand continuall on his dagger.' Years later, during the civil war, frightened politicians were still described as being 'in such a perpetuall bodily feare of their owne shadowes . . . that like cruell Richard, their hands are always upon their Dagers'.[10] Another poem tells how a tavern-keeper recounting the historical story of what happened in the battle of Bosworth Field, 'when he would have said, King *Richard* dy'd, / And call'd a Horse, a Horse, he *Burbage* cry'd'.[11] Other parts that Burbage played include Hamlet, Othello, and Lear in the plays of those names, and Heironymo in Kyd's *Spanish Tragedy*. On Burbage's death, what is particularly bemoaned is that the parts he played have expired with him – at that time, parts were so closely associated with the actors who 'owned' them that it was not necessarily thought possible to put on plays once their performers had died:

> No more young Hamlett, ould Heironymoe
> Kind Leer, the greved Moore, and more beside,
> That lived in him; have now for ever dy'de.[12]

In fact Burbage's parts were inherited by two members of the company, John Lowen and Joseph Taylor, whose performances were themselves said to have been inherited by the great Restoration actor Thomas Betterton: 'Burbage' was thus thought to have lived on through preservation of his acting techniques.

As this illustrates, Burbage's performances were, and continued to be, famous for the man as much as for the plays. Shakespeare had to write bearing 'Burbage' in mind.

An audience, having come to watch a particular performer as much as a play, could not automatically be relied on to see a story through to its conclusion. The playwright Glapthorne, in his *Ladies Privilege* (1640), refers to spectators who make the author 'end his Play before his Plot be done': the onlookers had a disturbing tendency to go away before the play was fully over.[13] In the eighteenth century the audience would sometimes leave the theatre when the lead actor in a tragedy 'died', even though the play itself was not finished; it is certainly possible that playwrights of the early modern period feared the same and that this is why almost all major actors' tragic deaths are grouped together in the last act, a feature of what have come to be called 'revenge tragedies' such as *Hamlet* or John Webster's *Duchess of Malfi*.[14]

It is often useful to see what parallels in character type can be drawn between one play and another, particularly when looking at plays written closely together. Shakespeare is writing for the same performers. Is he exploring different aspects of the same character type over time? The same variety of feisty heroine is, after all, presented in Kate (*Taming of the Shrew*) and Beatrice (*Much Ado About Nothing*); the same kind of compellingly destructive villain in Iago (*Othello*), Edmund (*King Lear*) and Iachimo (*Cymbeline*); the same plump rogue in Falstaff (*1* and *2 Henry IV, Merry Wives of Windsor*) and Sir Toby Belch (*Twelfth Night*); the same well-meaning but misdirected old man in Polonius (*Hamlet*), Menenius (*Coriolanus*) and Gloucester (*Lear*). Rather than looking at these separate characters inside their separate texts it can be telling to see them in terms of a continuum carrying over from one text into another.

The fact that actors played to character-type affects more than speech-prefixes. When an actor stepped on to the stage he may have done so replete with all the other, similar, characters he had played on that stage. Just as areas of the stage, like the trap, had a composite nature built out of its use in many plays, so actors may have had a series of composite character types built up over years of performance which affected every play they were in by every author. Indeed, sometimes Shakespeare writes passages in which an actor pointedly links himself from within one play with some of the parts that he has played in other plays. The Fool in *Lear* sings a snatch of the song 'The rain it raineth every day':

> He that has and a little-tyne wit,
> With heigh-ho, the Winde and the Raine,
> Must make content with his Fortunes fit,
> Though the Raine it raineth every day.
>   (TLN 1729–32, 3.2.74–6)

That same song, with different words, is the epilogue to *Twelfth Night*, presumably sung by the same performer, Robert Armin, Shakespeare's wise-fool actor:

> When that I was and a little tine boy,
> with hey, ho, the winde and the raine:
> A foolish thing was but a toy,
> for the raine it raineth every day . . .
>   (TLN 2560–3, 5.1.389–92)

'The rain it raineth' is Armin's across-play song, and it is possible that, on occasion, it was sung also in other company plays. In making one play gesture towards another, Shakespeare upsets the difference between one separate text and another. Here, indeed, Shakespeare muddies the distinction between a tragical history set in England (*Lear*) and a fictional comedy set in Illyria (*Twelfth Night*). Why so? Partly, perhaps, because he is creating out of the wise fool type an 'everyman' character who can make universal comments that are not play-specific or specific only for a particular variety of fictional world. 'The rain it raineth', a melancholy song about the humdrum sameness of life in a raining world, is one of them. The song also breaks down the boundaries that separate play from play, reminding the audience that it is watching a character it has seen before: one that can die or disappear in one play, and live again in another. On one level this lessens the tragedy of tragedy and the comedy of comedy by disturbing the completeness of the play world; on another it extends the stories into the world of the audience, setting up a series of questions about the relationship between reality and fiction.

Another example of one play gesturing towards another can be found in *Hamlet*, which contains several references to *Julius Caesar* (both were originally performed at about the same time, between 1600 and 1601). Possibly these references can be traced to the fact that Shakespeare wrote *Hamlet* just after – or perhaps while – writing *Julius Caesar* in around 1599. But the references may serve another purpose too. One particular account of *Julius Caesar* occurs only in the earlier 'good' quarto of *Hamlet* (published 1604/5). By the time of the folio (1623), a later text, it has been removed. The passage in question is spoken by Horatio standing on the battlements having just seen the ghost of Hamlet's father for the first time. It is then that he starts, for no particular reason, to relate in lurid detail what happened in Rome before Caesar's murder:

> In the most high and palmy state of Rome,
> A little ere the mightiest *Julius* fell,
> The graves stood tenantless, and the sheeted dead
> Did squeak and gibber in the Roman streets . . .
> (Q2 B2b, 1.1.113–16)

This can be read as a promise of ghoulish pleasures in the other play if the same audience chooses to come back to the theatre. In other words, it might be an advertisement. That, at any rate, would explain the loss of the passage from the later folio text: by the time that the later version of *Hamlet* was in performance, *Julius Caesar* had dropped out of the repertory and was no longer relevant. Another possible advertisement for *Julius Caesar*, perhaps good enough as a joke in its own right to be kept as part of the body of the play, occurs in a dialogue between Polonius and Hamlet. It is both in second quarto and in folio. Polonius recalls that he once acted at university and, when asked who he performed, replies 'I did enact *Julius Caesar*. I was killed i'th'Capitol. *Brutus* killed me.' Hamlet replies in one of his characteristic puns 'It was a bruite part of him, to kill so Capitall a Calfe there' (TLN 1960–1, 3.2.102–6). Again, the exchange is unnecessary to the plot, and seems rather to relate to the fact that the actors now playing Polonius and Hamlet also perform Julius Caesar and Brutus in the other production. One *fiction* refers to another *fiction*. There is also there, perhaps, an aside to the audience who are shrewd enough to pick up on it: Brutus, played by the Hamlet character, killed Caesar, played by the Polonius character; Hamlet will in due time also kill Polonius. Here, too, is further information about character 'types'. The connection between Brutus and Hamlet, if both were indeed played by the same actor, is intriguing: both despite their careful reflection are led to perform actions they largely regret. As for Caesar and Polonius, does the link imply that Caesar, continually presented in the play as physically weak – infertile, epileptic and a

bad swimmer – was also played by a performer famous for his presentation of fatuous and slightly ridiculous old men?

The epilogue to *2 Henry IV* is a third text that refers beyond
itself, promising yet another play with Falstaff in it and apolo-
gising for Falstaff's earlier designation 'Oldcastle' (discussed in
Chapter 3). This epilogue not only recalls the history surrounding
the name-change in *1 Henry IV*, it is also carefully subversive: in
naming 'Oldcastle', it usefully reminds the audience that Falstaff
and Oldcastle are one and the same, and so prevents the Oldcastle
designation from being forgotten.

> One word more, I beseech you: if you be not too much cloid
> with Fat Meate, our humble Author will continue the Story
> (with Sir John in it) and make you merry, with faire Katherine
> of France: where (for any thing I know) Falstaffe shall dye of
> a sweat, unlesse already he be kill'd with your hard Opinions:
> For Old-Castle dyed a Martyr, and this is not the man.
>
> (TLN 3344–8, epilogue)

Plays were rather less individuated than they seem now in separately bound and edited editions, and it is useful to think of texts
not so rigidly as separate entities but as part of a series containing
all the other plays performed by the same actors.

Typecasting limited the amount of preparation necessary before
performance – and, in a system where different plays were put
on each day, every way of reducing preliminary work had to be
used. Rehearsal, in particular, was organised around the principle
of a little time and a large number of plays. So the way actors
came into contact with new plays, and the amount of information they were given to learn, needs to be explored to show how
rehearsal practice shaped the texts of Shakespeare.

When an author had completed his new play he would read
it to the actors. Actors thus had a chance to hear the story of the
play and to decide whether they liked the text and the writing.
But only actors who had a financial interest in the acting company
attended such a reading.[15] Those actors were called 'sharers'
because they held shares in the company's wealth and received
a regular portion of the theatre's daily revenue. Lesser actors may
never have heard in full the text of the play in which they were
to perform. Thomas Killigrew, for instance, who was a child in
the 1620s, recalls being outside the Red Bull theatre 'when the

man cried to the boys, "Who will go and be a divell, and he shall see the play for nothing?"'.[16] He joined the throng and went on stage to perform that same day – he knew no more of the play he was in than his walk-on role.

After the reading, the actors would be given their separate parts to take home and learn. These parts consisted of their own lines only: actors were never given the full text of a play to study, they simply received their personal speeches. They knew when to speak, however, because they were also given the last few words of the speech that preceded their own to listen out for. They would wait until they heard these last few words – called 'cues' – and then say the relevant passage that they had learned followed it. An actors' part of the time (that of 'Orlando' in Greene's *Orlando Furioso*), shows the full text the actor is to speak, and the number of words that made up the cue-lines. Note, in the fragment provided, how the number of cue-words given is varied when cues are similar; note too the stage direction giving the actor additional information on the right-hand side (that he is to beat A[rgulius]).

I pray the tell me one thing, dost thou not
knowe, wherfore I cald the

——————————————————————— neither

why knowest thou not, nay nothing thou
mayst be gonne, stay, stay villayne I tell
the Angelica is dead, nay she is in deed

——————————————————————— lord

but my Angelica is dead.

——————————————————————— my lord
and canst thou not weepe   he beat*es*. A.
——————————————————————— Lord[17]

The whole process of distributing and receiving separate parts can be seen in convoluted form in *A Midsummer Night's Dream*. First Quince, who is the reviser if not the author of the mechanicals' play *Pyramus and Thisbe*, tells the actors what characters they are to play and a tiny bit about their roles:

Quince   You *Nicke Bottome* are set downe for *Pyramus*.
Bottom   What is *Pyramus*, a lover, or a tyrant?
Quince   A Lover that kills himselfe most gallantly for love.
                              (TLN 289–92, 1.2.21–4)

Then Quince hands each actor what he calls their 'scrip' or 'scroll', the rolled-up sheet of paper on which their individual part is written. All performers are sent away to memorise their parts: when they next meet together, the parts must already be fully learned. Learning happened in isolation from the rest of the text.

> *Quince*   ... But masters here are your parts, and I am to intreat
> you, request you, and desire you, to con them by too morrow
> night ...
>
> $\qquad\qquad\qquad\qquad$ (TLN 359–61, 1.2.99–101)

So it was in the professional theatre. An actor, having received the roll of paper on which his separate part was written, learned his lines separately. Minor actors did not necessarily know details of the story in which they were performing until they entered on to the stage itself. Edmund Gayton, one of the followers of the playwright Ben Jonson (a member of what came to be called the 'school of Ben'), tells an anecdote about a university production that illustrates very plainly the effect this can have. He recalls how two separate actors had both independently learned the parts of ghosts. Neither, however, was prepared to see the other on the stage.

> Two Scholars there were ... whose parts were two Ghosts
> or Apparitions ... These two at the Repetitions [individual
> rehearsals] spoke their lines very confidently, insomuch, that
> the Judges thought they would be very good Ghosts; but
> when the tryall night came that the Play was to be presented
> to some few friends ..., and ... these two Scholars were put
> ... into white long robes ... just as they put their heads
> through the hangings of the Scene ... they ... were so
> horribly frighted at one another's ghastly lookes that no force
> of those behind them, could get them to advance a foot
> forward toward the stage, or speak a word of their Parts.[18]

The two actors had completely established their roles away from the rest of the play, and without necessarily being very clear about the story told by the text in full. Testimony that this was true also of London players comes from the opening of Marston's *Antonio and Mellida*. In the Induction to that play, the actors enter still holding their parts. They are about to perform, but they claim not to know what parts the others are playing:

Galeatzo   Come sirs, come: the musique will sounde straight for entrance.
Are yee readie, are yee perfect?
Piero   Faith, we can say our parts: but wee are ignorant in what mould we must cast our Actors.
Albert   Whome doe you personate?
Piero   Piero, Duke of Venice . . . whome act you?
Albert   The necessitie of the play forceth me to act two parts . . .
Galeatzo   Wel, and what doest thou play?
(Antonio and Mellida, 1602, Induction)[19]

Antonio and Mellida is, of course, exaggerated, but a parody works only if it has a core of truth in it. As it seems, not only did actors play to character type; they also played without access to the full text of the play and with only hesitant knowledge of the story of that play.

In the professional theatre, there were usually 'instructors' to help actors through their isolated learning-process. Instructors were, in the case of lesser actors, superior actors, and in the case of superior actors, the author – or nobody.[20] But what precisely was established during instruction was what the actor would have to say and do, not what other characters would say and do. Neither actor nor instructor generally had access to the full play, for the prompter kept it locked away – full plays were the playhouse's most treasured possessions. They did, however, occasionally have 'parts' written that were for more than one player – two-player parts for the eighteenth century survive in the Folger Shakespeare Library, and evidence from the plays of Shakespeare show that a boy player and his master often have dialogue strictly with one another, meaning that they can rehearse whole scenes with each other away from the rest of the company.[21] Trying to sort out how to perform their 'part' well, actors in Shakespeare's day were not primarily concerned with the story they were telling. Instead they were looking inwards at their parts, determining what the emotions required by their roles were, and how best to manifest them using gesture and pronunciation.

Which 'passion' was being exhibited, and at what moment, was easily identifiable in a part and so was seen to be one of the most important aspects of acting; a term often used to describe the art of acting at the time was 'passionating'. When Hamlet decides to test one of the players' skills he demands 'a passionate speech' in order to give the court 'a tast of your quality' (*Hamlet* TLN 1476–7, 2.2.431–2). 'Passion' was not the vague word then that it is now. 'The passions' were the emotional extremes. Passions featured in Shakespeare plays include joy and grief – Kent's heart 'twixt two extremes of passion, joy and greefe, / Burst smilingly' (*King Lear* TLN 3161–2, 5.3.198–200); love – Orsino suffers from 'the passion of my love' (*Twelfth Night* TLN 274, 1.4.24); fear – Joan La Pucelle [Joan of Arc] believes 'of all base passions, Feare is most accurst' (*1 Henry VI* TLN 2420, 5.2.18). The passions and other emotions (arguments raged as to whether there were seven or more identifiable passions) had fairly regular significations, so the actor had only to recognise which emotion was indicated in a text to know how to display it appropriately.[22] Falstaff in *1 Henry IV* makes fun of this process when, preparing to play-act the part of Henry IV in a game with Hal, he asks for 'a Cup of Sacke to make mine eyes looke redde, that it may be thought I have wept, for I must speake in passion, and I will doe it in King *Cambyses* vaine' (TLN 1341–4, 2.4.383–7). When Hamlet gives advice to the players, he gives particular attention to the best (and worst) ways to exhibit the passions:

> in the verie Torrent, Tempest, and (as I may say) the Whirle-winde of Passion, you must acquire and beget a Temperance that may give it Smoothnesse. O it offends mee to the Soule, to see a robustious Pery-wig-pated Fellow, teare a Passion to tatters.
>
> (TLN 1853–8, 3.2.5–10)

Visible transitions from one major passion to another within a speech were highly thought of – and so were written into texts. In Shakespeare's plays they may occur when prose gives way to verse, when simple language gives way to complex language or when long, singing lines give way to short, staccato sentences. These are some of the features that an actor would identify in his part as he worked together with his instructor. A change of passions is clearly indicated in Leontes' part (*The Winter's Tale*) for 1.2. The text is presented as the actor playing Leontes will have received it, though possibly with a 'cue' longer than the actor could have hoped for.

Why, that was when
Three crabbed Moneths had sowr'd themselves to death,
Ere I could make thee open thy white Hand:
And clap thyselfe my Love; then didst thou utter,
I am yours for ever.

——————————————————————————— while a friend.
Too hot, too hot:
To mingle friendship farre, is mingling bloods.
I have *Tremor Cordis* on me: my heart daunces,
But not for joy; not joy.

(TLN 172–84, 1.2.101–11)

Leontes conceives a sudden and irrational jealousy. His emotions,
his 'passions', change here as jealous anger overwhelms him. The
text reveals the altered emotion, the contained jealousy manifest-
ing itself in Leontes's second speech, where the obsessional repetition of words and phrases 'too hot, too hot', 'mingle . . . mingling',
'not . . . joy, not joy' tell the player to work himself into a stammering rage. In texts of the time, one passion often yields to another
with enormous rapidity, partly because passions were thought to
overtake the intellect by their speed and violence, and partly
because skill in showing a quick 'transition' of passions was highly
valued. In *Richard III*, the Second Murderer, preparing to kill
Clarence, is struck by a sudden fit of conscience: what he calls a
'passionate humour'. He apologises: 'I hope this passionate humour
of mine will change, / It was wont to hold me but while one tels
twenty.' Twenty seconds, then, for a significantly changing passion.
In fact, the change of mind comes more quickly than that:

1 Mur.   How do'st thou feele thy selfe now?
2 Mur.   Some certaine dregges of conscience are yet within mee.
1 Mur.   Remember our Reward, when the deed's done.
2 Mur.   Come, he dies: I had forgot the Reward.

(TLN 954–60, 1.4.120–6)

Or, as the second murderer will have received the passage:

——————————————————————————— thy selfe now?
Some certaine dregges of conscience are yet within mee.
——————————————————————————— the deed's done.
Come, he dies: I had forgot the Reward.

Reading a part in terms of passions goes some way towards explaining the high emotional charge of plays at the time, and the speed with which one strong emotion surrenders to another: Othello's and Leontes' sudden jealousy (*Othello, Winter's Tale*); Lear's sudden rage and sudden madness (*King Lear*); Olivia's and Romeo's sudden love (*Twelfth Night, Romeo and Juliet*). 'Unlikely' transitions are not unusual in such a system. Oliver's sudden alteration from bad to good man (*As You Like It*), Orsino's 'love' for Viola on learning that she is not a boy Cesario (*Twelfth Night*) are written in a system that allows for – and indeed encourages – violent transitions.

So an actor would need to break his speeches down into passions that could then be exhibited using gestures and tones, a process that observers watched for as Thomas Wright explains in his *The Passions of the mind in General*: 'passion . . . by gestures passeth into our eyes, and by sounds into our ears'.[23] Pronunciation was matched by weighty, telling gestures that were a physical way of illustrating the passions. Othello in his rage bites his lower lip ('Alas, why gnaw you so your nether-lip', TLN 3290, 5.2.43); as does Wolsey in *Henry VIII*:

> . . . He bites his lip, and starts,
> Stops on a sodaine, lookes upon the ground,
> Then layes his finger on his Temple: straight
> Springs out into fast gate, then stops againe,
> Strikes his brest hard, and anon, he casts
> His eye against the Moone: in most strange Postures
> We have seene him set himselfe.
> (TLN 1974–80, 3.2.113–19)

That there were conventions for exhibiting certain emotions can be seen from the texts that try to define them. The 'country man' who wrote *The Cyprian Conqueror* (*c*. 1633) gives a preface explaining the requisite gestures for his play: 'in a sorrowful parte, ye head must hang downe; in a proud, ye head must bee lofty; in an amorous, closed eies, hanging downe lookes, & crossed armes, in a hastie, fuming, & scratching ye head &c'.[24] Moth, in *Love's Labour's Lost*, describes to Don Andriano di Armado how to bear himself when he is in love. The crossed arms of the quotation above must have been important, for Armado should have his 'armes crost on your thinbellie doublet, like a Rabbet on a spit' (TLN 787–8, 3.1.18–19). Ophelia, describing the moment when Hamlet came into her room and affrighted her, depicts Hamlet in a state of dishevelment that seems to her like the traditional dress of a distracted lover: 'his doublet all unbrac'd, / No hat upon his head, his stockings foul'd, / Ungartred, and downe gived to his Anckle' (TLN 974–6, 2.1.75–7). It is Hamlet's appearance that seems to have misled both Ophelia and Polonius as to the root cause of his madness. The Prince has given out the wrong visual signals: he has wordlessly deceived Ophelia.

'Correct' action and gestures continued to be taught for the next two centuries, though it is never easy to sort out exactly what was involved, for the 'rules' get muddled in with the 'conventions'. Some of the gestures simply mimicked social behaviour; others were contrived and required an audience capable of reading them. The two are separated in a couple of linked books written in 1644 by John Bulwer: *Chirologia*, which shows the 'Natural' (instinctive) language of the hand, and *Chironomia*, which shows the 'Art' or rules that govern 'Manuall Rhetorique'. Both books were designed to teach deaf people a way of communicating. *Chirologia* is thought to be an exaggerated depiction of socially recognisable hand-gestures such as might also have been used on the stage and shows how words and concepts – anger, love, friendship – had physical manifestations. The playwright Heywood shows the importance of gesture as an element of communication when he writes that the actor should 'fit his phrases to his action, and his action to his phrase, and his pronuntiation to them both'; Hamlet similarly recommended 'Sute the Action to the Word, / the Word to the Action' (TLN 1865–6, 3.2.17–18).[25] In the theatre in particular, large gestures will have been very important, for corrective spectacles for short sight did not exist and subtle inflections of the face would not have been visible to most of the audience. How important hand-movements were is illustrated by a passage in *Titus Andronicus* in which Titus explains the difficulty he has in fully expressing his feelings. It occurs at a point in the play when Titus has rashly cut off his hand, and is therefore unable to emphasise his words with the requisite gestures: 'how can I grace my talke', he laments, 'Wanting a hand to give it action' (TLN 2301–2, 5.2.17–18).

Pronunciation, too, was very important, and actors spent much preparation time establishing the correct 'emphasis' in a sentence. A famous elegy on Burbage relates the way the great actor died:

he lost the art of speaking first so that death could not to be charmed away from his purposes by speech in which 'not a word did fall, / Without just weight, to ballast itt with all'.[26] There were, in addition, clear and important vocal differences in the way verse and prose were spoken. Nowadays at the theatre it is often hard to tell whether an actor performing a Shakespearean text is speaking verse or prose. But Shakespeare often wrote parts that switched from one to the other, because a different vocal register was used for each. Low language had one 'tone', high language another. Heightened language needed heightened enunciation. The beat of a verse was often punched out in none-too-subtle a fashion (speaking verse too brutally in declamatory fashion was called 'ranting'; verse written too brutally was 'fustian' or 'bombast'). Modern-day Russians speaking verse do so in a rhythmical, cadenced manner that brings it somewhat nearer to music, and this is probably much closer to the Shakespearean manner of verse-speaking, for verse was often linked to music. Some telling Shakespearean verse–prose transitions will feature in the next chapter.

The 'instruction' an actor received on his separate part did not involve discussing character or motive – indeed it often did not involve asking the actor to think at all. It was a system merely in place to help the actor establish what the emotions – the 'passions' – were in his part, and how best to show them, tonally and with action. Sometimes, therefore, the process of instruction was completely dictatorial. One university play from the time shows Richard Burbage 'instructing' a student for the part of Heironymo in *The Spanish Tragedy*: 'I thinke your voice would serve for Hieronimo: observe how I act it', he says, 'and then imitate me' (*Return from Parnassus* (1606), 4.3).[27] Instruction often took this form: a superior actor or the playwright recited the part to the actor concerned in the way it should be spoken. The actor then learned that method – and that was the rehearsal. And when Hamlet instructs the actors, he does it in just this way. He has composed an extra speech of 'some dosen or sixteene lines' (TLN 1581, 2.2.541–2) to be added into their play *The Murder of Gonzago*, and, as it appears, he then goes on to teach the actor exactly, syllable-for-syllable, how to say it – through imitation. 'Speake the Speech', he cautions, '. . . as I pronounc'd it to you' (TLN 1849–50, 3.2.1–2). Actors were not free to act as they wished; they were free only to act as the text wished them to – with help from overseers who could aid in interpreting a text's demands.

A 'part', once learned, was supposedly fixed. When an actor became too old to perform his part, he handed it on to his successor in a very literal way. He gave that successor the written 'part' on which the text was inscribed, and he taught him the 'correct' way of speaking and acting it – the emphases and the gestures. The new actor would then be rated by his ability to mimic the old one: anything he altered was likely to be frowned on. Japanese Noh plays are still passed on in a similar fashion, each performance an echo of earlier performances. In Britain, parts continued to be handed down from one actor to another in this way, with mannerisms learned and reproduced for the next two hundred years. John Downes, a Restoration prompter, claimed that his players had directly inherited Shakespeare's 'action', and traced the performance of certain roles back through Betterton to Davenant to Lowen to Shakespeare himself.[28] Those same performances were handed on again, broadly in the same form, for the next hundred years, acquiring local additions on the way – Powell in the 1690s mimicked Betterton's Falstaff so closely that he included in it Betterton's 'acute pains of gout' and the characteristic wince they occasioned.[29] Originality was far from being the goal of any production of the time: each one strove to imitate the first ('real') production of the play.

Actors' separate texts contain all the information necessary for that actor to perform his 'part' well. These include, together with 'passions' and humours, whatever personality traits are features of the character. Such traits are often easy to pick up when examining a text that contains only a single actor's lines with cues, but easy to miss when looking at the whole play as a unity. Probably personality traits related to the real character of the actor who was to perform the part in question; possibly some of them were, indeed, added by the actor concerned. Hamlet in quarto 2 (1604/5) and folio (1623) has a particular verbal tick that no performer other than, significantly, the Ghost possesses – he repeats himself a lot. 'O God, O God! / How weary, stale, flat, and unprofitable / Seemes to me all the uses of this world?' (TLN 315–17, 1.2.132–3); 'Thrift thrift *Horatio*' (TLN 368, 1.2.180), 'What do you read my Lord?' 'Words, words, words' (TLN 1230, 2.2.192); 'You cannot Sir take from me any thing, that I will more willingly part withal, except my life, my life' (TLN 1258–60, 2.2.216–17) (Q2 F1b: 'except my life, except my life, except my life').

This tells the player something about the way Hamlet thinks. Repetition suggests a combination of nerves and obsessiveness; it shows a man thinking faster than he can speak and stammering to get out his sense. Against such verbal awkwardness, Hamlet also uses certain fragile, sensitive, emotional words repeatedly, which is one of the features that gives him a spiritual edge, for all his self-obsession and murky sexuality. One Hamlet word is 'soft!' used as an exclamation meaning 'look there'. 'But soft, behold: Loe, where it comes againe' (TLN 126, 1.1.126); 'But soft, me thinks I sent the Mornings Ayre' (TLN 743, 1.5.58); 'Soft you now, / The faire *Ophelia*' (TLN 1741–2, 3.1.87–8); 'Soft now, to my Mother' (TLN 2263, 3.2.392). Another very Hamlet characteristic is to substitute the word 'soul' for 'mind': 'Since my deere Soule was Mistris of my choyse' (TLN 1914, 3.2.63); 'it offends mee to the Soule' (TLN 1856, 3.2.8); 'My soule is full of discord and dismay' (TLN 2629, 4.1.45). The obsession with the 'soul' as against the mind may show a man applying religious terminology to his own thought-process: perhaps he has elevated his own thinking into a religion. Or perhaps the point is that he has rationalised away his religion, turning instead to the classical idea that the soul, *anima*, is the seat of judgement. Either way, these repeated words are acting clues inside texts that, carefully read, can offer clear direction to the actor. One role in Hamlet in particular shows how an obsession with a couple of words – in this case, 'my lord' – is made absolutely obvious when looking at the play in parts, but is not necessarily visible when looking at the full text. It is the entire part for Reynaldo, and to the actor it would have looked something like this:

```
                                      ———— these notes Reynoldo.
I will my Lord.
                                      ———— Of his behaviour.
My Lord, I did intend it.
                                      ———— marke this Reynoldo?
I, very well my Lord.
                                      ———— youth and liberty.
As gaming my Lord.
                                      ———— goe so farre.
My Lord that would dishonour him.
                                      ———— of generall assault.
But my good Lord.
```

	you doe this?
I my Lord, I would know that.	
	man and Country.
Very good my Lord.	
	did I leave?
At closes in the consequence:	
At friend, or so, and Gentleman.	
	have you not?
My Lord I have.	
	fare you well.
Good my Lord.	
	in your selfe.
I shall my Lord.	
	plye his Musicke.
Well, my Lord.	*Exit.*

(TLN 860–969, 2.1)

This in some way 'advises' the actor, for Reynaldo's obsequious deference to Polonius is undercut by the repetition. Plays look different when seen in 'part' terms, a point that will be returned to in Chapter 5.

So the learning of parts, what was called 'study', was a solitary business, and happened alone or in the company of an instructor. Shakespeare wrote jokes around the fact that actors knew well only their studied parts, not the full text. Gibing at Petruchio and accusing him of play-acting, Kate in *Taming of the Shrew* asks him 'Where did you study all this goodly speech?' (TLN 1141, 2.1.262) as her way of suggesting she does not believe or recognise what he says. Viola, in *Twelfth Night*, has 'studied' a speech of love that Orsino taught her. When she is asked a question for which she has learned no response she does not know how to reply – 'I can say little more then I have studied, & that question's out of my part' (TLN 472–3, 1.5.178–9).

How, then, were all these separately prepared actors gathered together in such a way that, in the end, a play actually worked on the stage? *A Midsummer Night's Dream* gives something of an idea. There was, usually, a full rehearsal of some kind before performance, which all actors were supposed to attend. This would smooth over problems with complicated stage-action (fights, dances, slapstick), and make sure each actor had a sense of the broad outline of the story. If, however, the rehearsal could not go ahead or was called off, performance could follow anyway: group rehearsal was one of the less important elements in the preparation of a play. So in *A Midsummer Night's Dream* the actors' bitty rehearsal is stopped part way through because Bottom has – literally – become an ass. Most of the mechanicals' play has not been rehearsed, but that does not prevent them from putting on their show. Bottom, transmuted back into himself again just in time to go on stage, draws attention to what he considers the most important aspect to precede performance. He reminds his fellow actors to gather up their costumes and take a last look over their separate parts to be sure that they know them: 'Get your apparell together, good strings to your beards, new ribbands to your pumps, meete presently at the Palace, every man looke ore his part: for the short and the long is, our play is preferred' (TLN 1780–3, 4.2.35–9). The unit of play that concerned the actor – even the moment before performance – was his separate part, not the full text.

With plays prepared in this fashion, the prompter, or 'book-keeper' as he was sometimes called, was very important. He was responsible for more than simply setting on the right track an actor who had missed his cue – though he was of course in charge of that. Romeo refers to the occasions ('out of such prolixity') when the entirety of the prologue was 'faintly spoke / After the Prompter' *Romeo and Juliet* (Q1 only, C1a). But, much more importantly, the prompter also managed the entrances and exits, arranged the basic blocking on the stage, and saw to it that the timing was right *during performance*, rather like a modern musical 'conductor'. Medieval pictures of prompters show how sometimes performances really were 'conducted', the prompters clutching batons in their hands to indicate which actor is to speak. Renaissance prompters still performed a similar task, though by then they had retreated behind stage, and were no longer visible to the audience.[30] They did, however, continue to control timing ('Were it my Cue to fight', says Othello, 'I should have known it / Without a prompter', TLN 302–3, 1.2.83–4); 'What would he [the player] doe,' asks Hamlet, 'Had he the Motive and the Cue for passion / That I have?' (TLN 1601–3, 2.2.561–2) (Q2 H4b 'and that for passion').

But the major difference between performances now and then was that in Shakespeare's time plays had no director. Modern rehearsal, conversely, takes the form it does largely because the director is in charge of productions. This figurehead, who came to be a regular part of production at the turn of the nineteenth century, is now considered artistically in charge of the play he or she puts on: theatre critics refer to Peter Brook's *Midsummer Night's Dream* (rather than Shakespeare's); cinema critics write of another new Steven Spielberg film (rather than naming the author). But in the days before the director, no single person was exactly artistically in charge of a play, and a play therefore spoke for itself. It was not overlaid with a concept, it *was* its concept – which is why clues to its performance are wrapped inside the parts themselves.

Receiving texts and performing them in the manner described meant that actors performed without ever really losing their sense of 'part'. There are, for instance, indications that actors in performance often did not maintain their fictional character while another actor was on the stage. Burbage was congratulated for continuing to hold his role on the stage even when he was not saying anything (Flecknoe praises him for 'never falling in his Part when he had done speaking; but with his looks and gesture, maintaining it still').[31] Big-headed actors might even self-consciously direct their performances away from the players they were with, rather than towards them 'for applause-sake', like the player described by John Stephens who 'When he doth hold conference upon the stage; and should look directly in his fellows face . . . turnes about his voice into the assembly.'[32]

Sometimes it seems that a line or so was simply added by the actor into his part even if it did not always make sense in the fuller context of the play. One particular example occurs when Hamlet dies. In the good second quarto text of 1604/5, Hamlet's death ends with the silence he has foretold, 'the rest is silence' (O1b), so that there follows the silence of death and eternal nothingness begins. In the 1623 folio's later good text, Hamlet's death is like this: 'the rest is silence, OOOO. *Dyes*' (TLN 3847, 5.2.358). Could it be that Burbage, playing Hamlet, wanted a more glamorous death-scene than the one the text gave him? As it appears, Burbage has frustrated the wishes of the author for a reflective, silent death, by imposing on to his part a noisily vocal deathrattle, though it ruins the tenor of the last lines. It has further been suggested that Burbage added revenge-play motifs to Shakespeare's subtle *Hamlet*, perhaps trying to bring it more in line with other revenge plays, or to give back to it some of the best moments from the lost 'Ur'-*Hamlet*. One other line thought perhaps to be an actor's interpolation is the free-standing 'Oh Vengeance' that is added to the middle of one of Hamlet's blank-verse set pieces in folio and is not present in either of the earlier quartos.[33]

> Remorseless, Treacherous, Letcherous, kindles villaine!
> Oh Vengeance!
> Who? What as Asse am I? I sure, this is most brave,
> That I, the Sonne of the Deere murthered,
> Prompted to my revenge by Heaven, and Hell,
> Must (like a Whore) unpacke my heart with words . . .
> (TLN 621–7, 2.2.580–5)

Shakespeare's actors by their personalities, their acting quirks, and also by the way they received and responded to their texts, are all features of the way the plays were written in the first place – and are responsible for some of the ways plays were subsequently changed.

5
Props, Music and Stage Directions

The two guards at the opening of *Hamlet* are surrounded by darkness so intense that they cannot see each other, as the nervous dialogue they exchange reveals.

Bernardo	Who's there?
Francisco	Nay answer me: Stand & unfold your selfe.
Barnardo	Long live the King.
Francisco	*Barnardo*?
Barnardo	He.
Francisco	You come most carefully upon your houre.
Barnardo	'Tis now strook twelve, get thee to bed *Francisco*.
Francisco	For this releefe much thankes: 'Tis bitter cold,
	And I am sicke at heart.

(TLN 4–13, 1.1.1–9)

That last line gives a context to the kind of darkness the play is dealing with. The reference to the lack of light and the cold set the scene 'realistically', but the indefinable grief that strikes Francisco describes the inside of the *Hamlet* world. Hamlet, later, will declare in similar vein that 'all's ill about my heart' (Q2 N3b, F reads 'all heere a-bout my heart' TLN 3661, 5.2.212–13) –

again, something is wrong, but the wrong is unattached to any direct cause, just as 'something', again not quite definable, 'is rotten in the State of Denmarke' (TLN 678, 1.4.90). *Hamlet* is full of vagaries, ambiguous senses of wrong that are so far from having identifiable cause that they cannot even be properly articulated: in a sense, everything is 'dark' in *Hamlet*. So the kind of night the play opens on is a night of the soul, a metaphorical night, though it is also a fictional night: the clock in the passage above has just struck twelve. Perhaps because this variety of night is more than just scene-setting, the actors *articulate* it to the audience (verbally) rather than manifest it physically with the use of torches, lamps or other 'night-time' props. It may, indeed, be important for the story that the stage should be without the comfort of torchlight at this point, for the kind of darkness that stops Bernardo seeing Francisco needs to be impenetrable. The themes of this chapter are the nature and uses of verbal props and, in contradistinction, physical props.

As 'scenery' was not used on the early modern stage, verbal descriptions that explain where a character is are very important. They are not, however, trustworthy, and, when a place is envisioned only verbally, the depiction given is not always supposed to be understood in a straightforward fashion. So when Gonzalo and his dishonest companions look at the island of *The Tempest*, each perceives a different place. Gonzalo sees a rich, fertile land of delicate air, and abundant foliage; Antonio and Sebastian see a barren desert, with only a few strands of greying grass:

Gonzalo   How lush and lusty the grass looks? How green?
Antonio   The ground indeed is tawny.
Sebastian   With an eye of greene in't.
Antonio   He misses not much.
Sebastian   No: he doth but mistake the truth totally.

(TLN 727–30, 2.1.53–8)

Neither observation tells the audience what the place is really like; but then the island is 'magic', and can, like Ariel, take any form it pleases. The characters are in fact describing their inner emotions rather than the world they see. The absence of stage furniture in the early modern playhouse meant that plays were not situated and could dictate and redictate perceptions to the audience. The island in *The Tempest* is of the mind, and collapses, as the play-world collapses, when the story comes to an end: 'These our actors . . . Are melted into Ayre . . . like the baselesse fabricke of this vision' (TLN 1819–22, 4.1.148–51). The absence of realistic scenery is, therefore, important.

The same is true of *Macbeth*. In creating an oppressive stage castle for Macbeth to live in, a set designer can obscure the play's ambivalence. The castle is, like the island of *The Tempest*, a manifestation of the characters who look at it. Duncan and Banquo, two of the heroes of *Macbeth*, have a conversation about Macbeth's habitat. They say

King Duncan   This Castle hath a pleasant seat,
　　The ayre nimbly and sweetly recommends it selfe
　　Unto our gentle sences.
Banquo   This Guest of Summer,
　　The Temple-haunting [M]arlet does approve,
　　By his loved Mansonry, that the Heavens breath
　　Smells wooingly here: no Jutty frieze,
　　Buttrice, nor Coigne of Vantage, but this Bird
　　Hath made his pendant Bed, and procreant Cradle . . .
　　　　　　　　　　　　　　(TLN 434–42, 1.6.1–8)

Descriptions spoken by characters onstage should not be assumed to take the place of scenery, or to be about environments that are often designedly unclear and carefully uncharacterised. Even what the audience *can* see is sometimes reinterpreted by the characters on stage. After the Ghost in *Hamlet* has walked off the stage in full view of the audience (his stage direction in folio is '*Exit the Ghost*', TLN 66) Marcellus describes how he 'faded on the crowing of the Cocke' (TLN 156, 1.1.157). Similarly, when the king in *King John* regrets commanding Hubert to kill the young Prince Arthur, he blames Hubert's ugly face (his 'abhorred aspect'), for inspiring murderous thoughts. But Hubert explains that he has not carried out the King's instructions and that Arthur still lives. Overjoyed, John apologises:

King John   Doth *Arthur* live? O hast thee to the Peeres,
　　Throw this report on their incensed rage,
　　And make them tame to their obedience.
　　Forgive the Comment that my passion made
　　Upon thy feature, for my rage was blinde,

> And foule immaginarie eyes of blood
> Presented thee more hideous then thou art.
> (TLN 1986–91, 4.2.260–6)

The audience, who will have had a full view of Hubert throughout, might well have felt that the true changeable hideousness was in the mind of King John himself.

As words do so much to complicate appearances, actual straightforward physical props are used carefully. Their heavy realism is countered by the fact that they are generally used neither imaginatively nor realistically, but symbolically.

Plays, though staged with a minimum of bulky scenery, were lavishly produced with rich clothing and, contrary to what is often thought, many and varied props. But visual signs – clothes, props – were 'read' symbolically rather than, as now, naturalistically. They were in many ways the physical versions of metonyms ('metonymy' is the action of substituting for a word denoting an object, a word or phrase denoting a property of the object or something associated with it): just as the word 'crown' or 'throne' can represent kingship, so, similarly, a stage crown or stage throne could represent kingship, abnegating the necessity of (what could not be staged) a rich palace. Often stage directions show which single, relevant items were brought on stage to symbolise place, person or event. Directions, for instance, that tell the actor to 'enter, as at night' are explained with the addition 'with torches' or 'softly'.[1] This was used for a darkness that was less complicated than that in the opening of *Hamlet*. The torch shows that, otherwise, without the torch, the player would be unable to see: at the time there was no changeable lighting on the stage. But, naturally, the physical torch, already in itself a symbol, easily takes on a symbolic role in the plays that use it. When King Claudius guiltily starts up in the middle of the *Hamlet* play-scene demanding 'Give me some Light. Away' (TLN 2140, 3.2.269), he is stating a practical need and making a symbolic point. Claudius needs torches to light him as he leaves the room, a reminder that the play is set at night in an ill-lit castle, full of hidden things; he is also seeing to it that the actors of *The Murder of Gonzago* are deprived of their light, which means that they cannot continue with their performance: now no one can see what happens next in a play that promises to incriminate Claudius. But the need for light is also part of the theme of darkness on which the play opened:

Claudius' inner darkness ('Oh bosome, blacke as death!', TLN
2343, 3.3.67) is highlighted in his yearning, when confronted with
his guilt, for illumination.

Torch-play is also used for its semi-symbolic potential in
Macbeth, where Banquo's murder is preceded by the extinguishing
of the torch: 'Who did strike out the Light?' (TLN 1246, 3.3.19).
Again, this is a practical prop that also makes a symbolic point.
Literally, the light is extinguished; in story terms, putting out the
light was 'not the way' for the darkness allows Banquo's son
Fleance to escape. Symbolically, Banquo's life is ended and darkness possesses the *Macbeth* world – for a while. Othello spells out
the connection when he extinguishes the candle in Desdemona's
room prior to killing her: 'put out the Light,' he tells himself, 'and
then put out the Light' (TLN 3246, 5.2.7). The verbal metaphor
is met by the brutal physicality of the action; in *Othello*, a play
obsessed with white and black, with light and darkness, Othello
has let his dark triumph. Symbol and metaphor, verbal and physical prop, merge.

The same to-and-fro between words and stage furniture
occurs in *Antony and Cleopatra*. The language of the play strongly
associates the two protagonists with the props that will finally kill
them. So Cleopatra reveals that the infatuated Antony has a pet
name for her: 'Hee's speaking now, / Or murmuring, where's my
Serpent of old Nyle, / (For so he cals me)' (TLN 553, 1.5.24–6).
Cleopatra's connection with a snake may be suggestive of the fall
of Eve (the Egyptian queen will bring about Antony's destruc-
tion); or it may be phallic, implying that Cleopatra has already
'unmanned' Antony. Only at the end of the play, however, comes
the irony: Cleopatra dies with a 'Poore venomous Foole' (TLN
3557, 5.2.305), an asp, at her breast; she has, the play visually
suggests, died because of what she is. Antony in the same play is
strongly linked to his sword, another phallic symbol. The sword
is what he trusts to and swears by:

Antony   Now by [my] Sword.
Cleopatra   And Target.
    (TLN 399–400, 1.3.82)

Tellingly, Cleopatra recalls the time when she took the sword
from Antony and, in exchange, dressed him in her clothes: 'I
drunke him to his bed: / Then put my Tires and Mantles on

him, whilst / I wore his Sword Phillippan' (TLN 1049–51, 2.5.21–3). The sword, that has symbolised the strength (and weakness) of Antony, is finally what the hero learns from the pointedly named 'Eros' to plunge into his own body. Antony's death too was foretold in what he lived by if he had but known it.

Illustrated title pages to plays and ballads show some of the other signs that may have been used on stage. Kyd's *Spanish Tragedy* in its 1615 edition is embellished with a woodcut illustrating moments from the play (Plate 5.1). Examining the title page with the eyes of an early modern theatre spectator (the person most likely to choose to buy *The Spanish Tragedy*), it is possible to gather information conveyed by the construction of the image. The picture, of course, may not itself describe the actual staging of the play, nevertheless, it uses a set of symbols anticipating that they will be understood.

In the woodcut, Heironymo holds a lighted torch (signifying that it is night) while the boots of the hanged Horatio are spurred (signifying that he has been riding). The bower or arbour in which Horatio is hanging, meanwhile, is symbolic in itself: it is a

Plate 5.1 Illustration from the title page to Thomas Kyd's *The Spanish Tragedy* (1615). Reproduced by permission of University of Cambridge Library.

lattice-work arch but its leafy coverage shows it to represent a tree. Hieronymo in the play talks of 'the tree' he planted ('I set it of a kernel . . . Till at the length / It grew a gallows and did bear our son').[2] This leafy arch is probably reminiscent of a theatrical prop – there is no other reason for the artist to envisage a representative rather than a realistic tree. Pictures could, at the very least, be understood 'emblematically' as a collection of symbols revealing time, place and activities passed; props in plays had a similar function.

More clues as to the type and nature of playhouse props can be seen in the inventory that Henslowe kept for the Rose theatre. The actual manuscript of this inventory is now lost, but an eighteenth-century transcription of it was printed by the theatre historian and editor Edmund Malone. Here is an extract, illustrating the props that a theatre of the 1590s used in production.

> The Enventary tacken of all the properties for my Lord Admeralles men, the 10 of Marche 1598:
>
> *Item*, j rock, j cage, j tombe, j Hell mought.
> *Item*, j tomb of Guido, j tomb of Dido, j bedsteade.
> *Item*, viij lances, j payer of stayers for Fayeton.
> *Item*, ij stepells, & j chime of belles, & j beacon.
> *Item*, j hecfor for the playe of Faeton, the limes dead.
> *Item*, j globe, & j golden sceptre; iij clobes.
> *Item*, ij marchepanes and the sittie of Rome.
> *Item*, j gowlden flece; ij rackets; j baye tree.
> *Item*, j wooden hatchet; j lether hatchete.
> *Item*, j wooden canepie; owld Mahemetes head.
> *Item* j lyone skin; j beares skyne; & faetones lymes, & Faeton charete; & Argosse heade.
> *Item*, Nepun forcke & garland.
> *Item*, j crosers stafe; Kentes woden leage.[3]

The list raises as many questions as it answers. What was 'the city of Rome'? Was it, perhaps, a curtain for the back of the stage, the *frons scenae*, with a picture on it? Is this, then, one of the ways that plays indicated 'place'? Certainly the hangings were often pictorial, for John Taylor, a Thames sculler who frequented all the southbank theatres and was also a poet (so called Taylor 'the water poet') describes a tragic scene in which the stage is 'all hang'd with the sad death of Kings, / From whose bewailing story sorrow springs'; Shirley, the playwright, describes a semi-empty theatre in which 'The benches then / Were all the grave spectators, but that here / Some cruell Gentlemen in your hangings were'.[4] When a tragedy was to be performed plain black hangings were sometimes substituted. In the anonymous play *A Warning for Fair Women* of 1599, personifications of Tragedy, Comedy and History contest for superiority, until History observes: 'Look, Comedy, I mark'd it not till now, / The stage is hung with blacke, and I perceive / The auditors prepar'd for tragedie'; 'Hang all your house with black', goes an elegy for Burbage, 'May nought but Tragedyes afflict your sceane'.[5] Even before a play started, and before any actor spoke, then, the tragic theme could already have been visually symbolised, undercutting any moments of comedy with its dark unspoken symbolism. Hamlet, a walking tragedy in his own person, never casts off his black suit of mourning. Colour could 'speak' though its specific language can be remote from us.

Other features on Henslowe's list are equally suggestive. Why is there more than one tomb – was each tomb separately inscribed, and was this normal? Could the dead-limbed heifer or the golden fleece be used in any other productions? How big was the steeple and did it contain the bells – or was it simply a representation of a steeple, like the tree in the woodcut for *The Spanish Tragedy*? An item referred to amongst Henlowe's clothing inventories is one 'cloak for to make you invisible': again, this must have been a cloak that the audience could 'understand'. Perhaps it had shut eyes on it: in quarto *2 Henry IV* the character representing Rumour enters 'painted full of Tongues' (A2b), presumably wearing a cloak decorated with tongue images. The Globe will have had a similar list of props – indeed one or two of its regular props can be determined by careful reading of the plays. The company had, for instance, a lion's skin. It crops up on the shoulders of Austria in *King John* ('Thou weare a Lyons hide, doff it for shame, / And hang a Calves skin on those recreant limbs', TLN, 1054–5, 3.1.131), and on the back of Snug in *A Midsummer Night's Dream*'s play-within-a-play, *Pyramus and Thisbe* ('halfe his face must be seene through the Lyons necke, and he himselfe must speake through, saying thus . . .', TLN 847–9, 3.1.36–7). They also had a throne, of course, and a tomb, a bed, books, weapons and some way of indicating the interior of a court-house.

Plate 5.2, also from the title page to a play, suggests the way a 'study' might have been symbolised, showing how a few items of stage furniture could have sufficed to construct an academic magician's room. The woodcut features an armillary sphere (the metal-worked sphere that hangs on the wall, for telling the stars), and a shelf-full of books (note the fact that books were, in the early modern period, shelved with the spine to the wall and the leaves outward, probably a leftover from the days when books were chained to a wall by their spines). The title page image is matched by one to the prose history *The famous historie of fryer Bacon*, published in 1627 by Francis Grove, and later, in 1630, used for the play *Friar Bacon and Friar Bungay*. That woodcut also includes the sphere and the shelf of books; indeed, the two illustrations may consciously recall one another – each story concerns an academic who is also a conjurer or magician – but the fact that a

Plate 5.2 Illustration from the title page to Christopher Marlowe's *The Tragicall History of the life and Death of Doctor Faustus* (1631). Reproduced by permission of The Huntington Library, San Marino, California (RB 62484).

study in Wittenberg (*Dr Faustus*), and Brasenose College, Oxford (*Friar Bacon and Friar Bungay*), are depicted so similarly also points towards a consensus as to what a stylised 'study' should contain.

Even the way hair was arranged was visually telling. One stage direction in the 'bad' quarto of *Hamlet* (1603) requires Ophelia, on her first mad entrance, to come in 'playing on a Lute, and her haire downe singing' (Q1 G4b). The folio at the same point has: 'enter Ophelia distracted' (TLN 2766). Distraction, as this suggests, was represented in the unbound hair. Extreme grief verging on the edge of madness, and madness itself, stemming from grief, was symbolised by letting the hair hang down – sane women kept their hair bound and ordered.[6] So, in *Troilus and Cressida*, mad Cassandra enters 'with her hair about her ears' (TLN 1082, 2.2.100.0); in *Richard III*, the grief-stricken Queen enters also 'with her hair about her ears' (TLN 1306, 2.2.33.0). A character's tresses are loosened as a way of giving sorrow a physical and, in stage terms, visually powerful manifestation. Constance in *King John* deliberately chooses to free her hair to demonstrate the grief she feels at losing her son Arthur. King Philip, seeing Constance, is horrified into thinking that his mother has actually gone mad with sorrow. But Constance inveighs against the very appearance she has given herself: she has used the convention of the loose hair to force Philip to listen to her, if only to make her put up her hair again:

Constance   I am not mad: this haire I teare is mine,
      My name is *Constance*, I was *Geffreyes* wife,
      Yong *Arthur* is my sonne, and he is lost: . . .
Philip   Binde up those tresses . . .
      Binde up your haires.
Constance   Yes that I will: and wherefore will I do it?
      I tore them from their bonds, and cride aloud,
      O, that these hands could so redeeme my sonne,
      As they have given these hayres their libertie:
      But now I envie at their libertie,
      And will againe commit them to their bonds,
      Because my poore childe is a prisoner.
                      (TLN 1429–60, 3.4.45–75)

Unable to work her will through feigned madness, Constance shackles her hair once more, to illustrate her son's imprisonment.

Plate 5.3 accompanies a ballad printed in 1654 telling the tale of *Titus Andronicus*. Again, it is a woodcut that either reflects the staging of the play, or shows conventions consonant with it, for it links itself carefully with the theatres of the 1640s and before. Published during the interregnum when all playhouses had been forcibly closed, to the top right of the ballad's woodcut is a section that shows where the play *Titus* was acted: a round theatre with its flag up. The theatre may be specific – is it, perhaps, the Globe? – although it is more likely to be an all-purpose representation of a playhouse of the past. Either way, the picture accompanying the ballad, as well as the story told in it, is linked with staged productions of *Titus Andronicus*.

In the top centre of the woodcut is the raped Lavinia with her symbolically unbound hair a sign of her grief. She is writing the names of her accusers in the sand: writing, because at this point in the play/ballad her tongue has been cut out and her hands lopped off (unlike her counterpart in the play, however, this Lavinia holds the stick in her stumps rather than her mouth). At the bottom centre of the picture the two well-dressed rapists are in the process of having their throats cut. They had come to visit Titus in disguise, claiming that they were Rape and Murder, but the picture shows that they arrived wearing the spurred boots that

Plate 5.3 Woodcut illustration accompanying ballad of *The Lamentable and Tragical History of Titus Andronicus* (*c.* 1655–65). Reproduced by permission of The British Library.

link them to the time when, earlier (top left), they went out hunt-
ing and caught Lavinia, whom they raped, and Bassianus, her
husband, whom they killed. The woodcut suggests that the boys,
when enacting Rape and Murder, look as they did when performing those crimes: they *are* 'rape' and 'murder', then, and, indeed,
are killed for their actions in the same clothes, a satisfying irony.
Does this relate to costuming in the staged production of *Titus
Andronicus*? To the far left of the picture is Aaron the Moor buried
'brest-deep' in earth as the play gives out will be his punishment:

> Set him brest deepe in earth, and famish him:
> There let him stand, and rave, and cry for foode:
> If any one releeves, or pitties him,
> For the offence, he dyes. This is our doome:
> Some stay, to see him fast'ned in the earth.
>   (TLN 2683–7, 5.3.179–83)

At the end of the play there is a general exit, except, presumably, for Aaron, 'fastened in the earth'. In the picture he makes
lamentation with his hands, the rest of his body being under-
ground. Perhaps, again, this hints at the staging of *Titus Andronicus*
– 'burial in sand', almost certainly consisted of standing in the
trap on the stage: the trap that was the gate of the stage's 'hell'.
Seeing Aaron in the trap is to see the character already in Hell,
a comment to the audience about the state of Aaron's soul and
his fate. On the bottom right of the picture, set apart in a box,
Tamora and Saturninus prepare to eat the meal Titus has cooked
them, consisting of a pie made from Tamora's sons, the rapists.
Saturninus in this picture wears a crown, yet in the play he is a
Roman emperor, not a king. Almost certainly, however, the same
clothes often furnished both in the playhouse, for, again, the
symbol is what is important: indeed, if 'emperor' did not resemble
'king' the audience might have had no way of interpreting Roman
clothes in hierarchical terms. This is clear from the other, far
more famous, *Titus Andronicus* drawing from the time (Plate 5.4).

The drawing, seemingly penned by Henry Peacham the
draughtsman, is dated 1595 (though the date and ascription may
be the work of the Victorian forger John Payne Collier). The
picture itself is genuine however, and seems to depict a medley
of moments in the play all of which may relate to a production.
Tamora, queen of the Goths, here wears a crown symbolising her

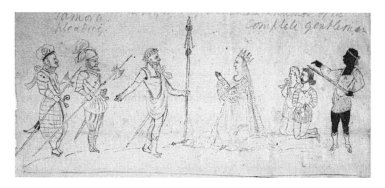

Plate 5.4 Henry Peacham (?), drawing from William Shakespeare's *Titus Andronicus* (? 1595). Reproduced by permission of the Marquess of Bath, Longleat House, Wiltshire.

status, which is also signalled by her sophisticated dress. That dress, however, appears to be Elizabethan. To the left of the drawing are two soldiers symbolised as such by their halberds; again, they are Elizabethan in appearance. Aaron the Moor is obvious by his colour: his dress is ambiguous, and may be all-purpose 'ethnic'. Only Titus in the centre makes a half-hearted show of being Roman by wearing a toga slung over one shoulder; the sword at his side is worn in Elizabethan fashion. He, perhaps, is also the only symbol that the play is set in Rome at all. Who or what symbolised 'Rome' in *Julius Caesar*? A decorated curtain? Certainly not Caesar himself, who appears to have been dressed as an Elizabethan would-be monarch, wearing a 'doublet' and hoping for a 'crown': 'when he perceiv'd the common Heard was glad he refus'd the Crowne, he pluckt me ope his Doublet, and offer'd them his Throat to cut' (TLN 367–70, 1.2.263–6). It is rare even in paintings of the period to find 'classical' costume actually represented: most 'history' was depicted as happening in modern-day Elizabethan or Jacobean dress. Cleopatra, feeling faint in *Antony and Cleopatra*, asks Charmian to loosen the strings of her bodice – 'cut my lace, Charmian' (TLN 386, 1.3.71). This, and other similar examples also show to what extent one play was staged like another – a further aspect of the across-play continuum described in the last chapter.

Clothes were read symbolically: they were, in many ways, simply other versions of 'props'. If a character wore a blue coat and a flat cap, he looked like (and therefore was) an apprentice – unless the text told a different story. Similarly, if he wore rags he was a beggar. So clothes could denote the character but, more than that, character could denote place. Alan Dessen has suggested that

> At the Globe or Fortune or Blackfriars, place was signalled primarily by means of costume. For example . . . a forester or woodsman would signal a forest; a host or vintner, an inn; figures in nautical costume, a ship. In such an onstage vocabulary, distinctive properties or costumes serve as visual clues: . . . the forester's green garments or weapons; the vintner's apron or handheld glasses.[7]

Clothes, then, are another kind of visual prop and in the same way have both a straightforward representation and, often, a symbolic subtext.

Though clothes are not generally described, sometimes it is possible to work out how they may have been used to enhance the action of certain plays. Juliet in *Romeo and Juliet* wears her 'best Robes' (TLN 2405, 4.1.110) when she takes Friar Laurence's potion, but these, presumably, are also the clothes she married in and perhaps, too, the clothes she wore for the Capulets' masked ball. Dying in her wedding-clothes on a stage tomb (situated, presumably, in the same place as the wedding bed in the marriage scene), Juliet links sex and death – the connection between the two running through and under the text of the whole play: 'Do thou but close our hands with holy words' says Romeo to the Friar, 'Then Love-devouring death do what he dare' (TLN 1398–9, 2.6.6–7). Those themes are revisited in *Othello*: in that play Desdemona pointedly asks that her wedding sheets be laid out on the bed in which she will later be killed. *Othello*, moreover, has a repeated visual theme of disturbed sleep that will culminate in the final bedchamber death scene; the play continually stages muddled and vulnerable characters raised in their nightgowns and misunderstanding what is going on around them. Brabantio, woken in the night by Iago and Rodrigo, appears in the first scene 'in his night gowne' according to the 1622 quarto (B3a); Othello and then Desdemona are roused from sleep in 2.3 by Cassio's drunken brawling – as the text suggests, they are in their night clothes and have been disturbed from consummating their marriage: 'All's well, Sweeting: / Come away to bed' (TLN 1376–7, 2.3.251–2). Later, an intimate scene has Desdemona prepare for bed helped by Emilia ('Give me my nightly wearing', TLN 2985, 4.3.16); she dies in her night clothes in bed, shortly followed by Emilia who has herself been roused from slumber by the sounds of the killing. Montano, Gratiano and Iago rising in the night when they hear what Othello has done may, indeed, all be in their night clothes; Iago has, like Macbeth, 'murther'd Sleepe' (*Macbeth* TLN 699, 2.2.39).

Shylock in *The Merchant of Venice* is obviously dressed in special clothes that identify him as a Jew. He makes this plain when he rails against the Christians who 'spit upon my Jewish gaberdine' (TLN 440, 1.3.112). Presumably he wore the dark red dress and yellow cap traditionally associated with Jews: at any rate, he wore a stage costume that visually separated him from non-Jews. This raises questions about the important court case at the end of the play. When Portia, disguised as a learned doctor, enters the court and asks 'Which is the Merchant here, and which the Jew?' she cannot actually be requesting information, as she can tell who is whom by looking – in addition to the Jewish gabardine, Shylock probably had a proboscis or 'visage (or vizard) like the artificiall Jewe of Maltaes nose'.[8] Portia, however, raises one of the primary questions of the play: who is the buyer precisely, and who the seller? Who is being truly 'Jewish' (at that time 'jew' was a name of opprobrium for a grasping person who drove a hard bargain)? Both merchant and Jew emerge badly from the play that had as its title in the Stationers' Register (a book in which ownership of texts was recorded) 'The Marchaunt of Venyce or otherwise called the Jewe of Venyce'; the shared financial concerns, the misplaced love, even the reliance on Portia, consistently link merchant and Jew throughout the play. Perhaps, the text may suggest, the two are not as different as we would like to think.[9]

Having an audience trained to 'read' clothes in a very literal way also allows the playwright to play games with people's expectations. When a boy plays a girl, the audience may 'understand' that he *is* a girl. But suppose he dresses as a girl who then disguises herself as a boy, as does Viola in *Twelfth Night*, Rosalind in *As You Like It*, Julia in *Two Gentlemen of Verona*, Jessica, Portia and Nerissa in *Merchant of Venice*. The spectators then *recognise* that they are seeing a girl dressed as a boy, although what they are *actually* seeing is a boy dressed as a boy. No doubt one reason why girls

are so frequently dressed as boys in Shakespearean dramas is that
it is easier for a boy to play a boy than a girl. But, from the audience's point of view, the confusion has interesting gendered
ramifications. Sebastian, Viola's twin brother, is described in
Twelfth Night as being a boy who looks exactly like Viola: Viola
being a 'girl' dressed as a boy. But given the similarity of appearance, it may have been hard for the spectators to know when
they were seeing Viola and when Sebastian; when what they were
watching was to be understood as a real boy and when it was
not: they would have had the same genuine difficulty as the characters in the play who also cannot tell the difference.

Then again, there were more subtle games that a playwright
could introduce. Doubling was common in the theatre of the
time – 'Albert' in Marston's *Antonio and Mellida* explains to his
fellow actors, 'The necessitie of the play forceth me to act two
parts' – and there was a convention that if a character changed
clothes then he was someone else, though often someone else
of similar rank and position.[10] It is fairly likely, for instance, that
the actor who was Brabantio, Desdemona's father in the first act
of *Othello*, also played Gratiano, Brabantio's brother, in the last
act. If that were the case, then he had the poignant task of
announcing his own death: 'Poore Desdemon: / I am glad thy
Father's dead, / Thy Match was mortall to him: and pure greefe
/ Shore his old thred in twaine' (TLN 3492–5, 5.2.204–6). How,
then, of characters who stay themselves, but change clothes?
Usually they articulate that fact so the audience knows what is
going on. Kent in *Lear* decides to shave off his beard and change
his voice so that he can continue to serve the king who has
banished him:

> If but as [well] I other accents borrow,
> That can my speech defuse, my good intent
> May carry through it selfe to that full issue
> For which I raiz'd my likenesse.
>   (TLN 531–4, 1.4.1–4)

But sometimes the playwright chooses that an actor, though
dressed differently, will continue to represent the same person –
and does not 'tell' the audience. At the beginning of *As You Like It*
Oliver was an evil man with an irrational hatred of his good
brother Orlando. In the fourth act, Oliver enters the play in new

clothing and 'reformed', having been rescued from the mouth of a hungry lion by his kind brother's aid. He does not, however, immediately reveal who he is, with the result that the audience learns Oliver's identity at the same time as the characters in the play:

Celia   O I have heard him speake of that same brother,
  And he did render him the most unnaturall
  That liv'd amongst men.
Oliver   And well he might so doe,
  For well I know he was unnaturall.
Rosalind   But to Orlando: did he leave him there
  Food to the suck'd and hungry Lyonnesse?
Oliver   Twice did he turne his backe, and purpos'd so:
  But kindnesse, nobler ever then revenge,
  And Nature stronger then his just occasion,
  Made him give battell to the Lyonnesse:
  Who quickly fell before him, in which hurtling
  From miserable slumber I awaked.
Celia   Are you his brother?
Rosalind   Was't you he rescu'd?
Celia   Was't you that did so oft contrive to kill him?
Oliver   'Twas I: but 'tis not I: I doe not shame
  To tell you what I was, since my conversion
  So sweetly tastes, being the thing I am.
                    (TLN 2272–90, 4.3.121–37)

The spectators fool themselves beyond the remit of the text: they both actually see that the actor is Oliver, and, presumably, take it that he is someone else: a good man. In fact Oliver's changed clothes are here a sign of a changed personality. Whereas he was before 'bad', he is now 'good' ('Twas I, but 'tis not I'): he *is*, therefore, someone else as he says, and this is illustrated by his altered dress and appearance.

Music also was used symbolically; the idea of 'atmospheric' music had not yet come about. So, for instance, no Shakespearean ghost's entrance is flagged by sinister music – or by music of any kind – as would happen in a modern film. The ghost of Hamlet's father, the ghosts of Banquo and of Caesar, all enter and depart without musical accompaniment. Nevertheless, music is important to the meaning of various moments in Shakespeare's plays, for the kind of music and the type of instruments played made certain symbolic statements out to the audience. Hautboys, the ancestors of the oboe, with their reedy, nasal sound, were taken to symbolise the fact that something bad was about to happen, like the oboes under the stage when Antony's god Hercules leaves him in *Antony and Cleopatra*. They are present too in *Macbeth* sounding out a warning note when Duncan arrives at Dunsinane; present when the witch's cauldron sinks; and behind the players' dumb-show in *Hamlet*.[11]

Conversely, music in *Twelfth Night* and *Troilus and Cressida* is rich and self-indulgent. There, characters *use* music rather than respond to its dictates: Orsino elects to suffer love-melancholy and forces the music to back him up, as did Cleopatra, who demanded music because it was the 'moody foode of us that trade in love' (*Antony and Cleopatra* TLN 1025–6, 2.5.1). *Twelfth Night* begins before its words do: it starts with Orsino's 'food of Love', music; ending on the Clown's song *'for the raine it raineth every day'*. The play, however, 'teaches' Orsino, through the medium of pointedly ironic songs, to turn his attentions away from the world of emotional indulgence and to concentrate on the world of real emotions instead. Helen in *Troilus and Cressida* similarly gluts herself with songs about what she calls love but is in fact sex: 'Let thy song be love: this love will undoe us al. / Oh *Cupid, Cupid, Cupid.*' The song that follows is

> *Love, love, no thing but love, still more:*
> *For O loves Bow,*
> *Shootes Bucke and Doe:*
> *The Shaft confounds not that it wounds,*
> *But tickles still the sore:*
> *These Lovers cry, oh ho they dye;*
> *Yet that which seemes the wound to kill,*
> *Doth turne oh ho, to ha ha he:*
> *So dying love lives still,*
> *O ho a while, but ha ha ha,*
> *O ho grones out for ha ha ha – hey ho.*
> (TLN 1588–98, 3.1.114–26)

The decadent impropriety of the song is on one level simply amusing, but it also illustrates a Helen who is indulgent, coarse and bored. That the song is about dying for love – dying, here, meaning to have an orgasm – is pointedly ironic: the sore, the wound, the killing, and the groans are sexual in the song, but are also reminders of the Trojan war in which Helen has no interest, and that is being waged for her.

Music at the time was understood to relate to ideas about divine order, and so could be read two ways by the audience: as a comment on the state of divine harmony or disharmony in the play-world; and as a rhetoric of the emotion. The old Pythagorean concept of the universe had held it that the planets were fixed in their place by harmonic law, sometimes called the music of the spheres, or 'musica mundana'. This dictated to or was reflected by 'musica humana', the music of men.[12] When men's nature was in tune with celestial music, all was well; but out of tune with their universe, and all was ill. Themes of musical order or disorder run through many Shakespearean plays. 'Take but Degree away, un-tune that string,' warns Ulysses in *Troilus*, 'And hearke what Discord followes' (TLN 568–9, 1.3.109–10). When music is ill-used in Shakespeare, or when, more sinisterly, it goes wrong, the bad music often reflects or suggests divine disorder in the larger world. The young instrumentalist who has fallen asleep in *Julius Caesar* wakes up from a bad dream and says what in the story of the play is a fact – but to the audience is prophetic: 'The strings my Lord, are false' (TLN 2305, 4.3.291). Kate in *Taming of the Shrew* breaks a lute over the head of her tutor with 'Frets call you these?' (TLN 1020, 2.1.152). The broken or mutilated instruments seem to be employed at times when 'harmony' has been in some way shattered.

Music can make one set of statements to characters in the play, and another to the watching audience. It does so in *Antony and Cleopatra*, when the boozy Antony and Caesar make an uncertain and over-drunken peace. Portentously they sing a drinking-song that begins 'Come thou Monarch of the Vine, / Plumpie Bacchus, with pinke eyn' (TLN 1466–7, 2.7.113–14). To the watching audience this was almost a blasphemous parody of 'Veni Creator Spiritus', a Whit Sunday hymn. The transmutation of a hymn meant for the holy spirit to one intended for the ears of the god of drunkenness and immoral revelry would have been an ominous indication that the concord represented by the song had a corrupt foundation – and that tragedy would follow.[13]

When Pericles is finally reunited with his daughter Marina and his world resolves itself, he hears the divine music of the spheres. The text, however, does not indicate that actual music should be played, so it seems that the heavenly bounty is for Pericles only:

Pericles   I embrace you, give me my robes.
   I am wilde in my beholding, O heavens blesse my girle,
   But harke what Musicke tell, Hellicanus my Marina,
   Tell him ore point by point, for yet he seemes to doat.
   How, sure you are my daughter; but what musicke?
Helicanus   My Lord I heare none.
Pericles   None, the Musicke of the Spheres, list my Marina.
Lysimachus   It is not good to crosse him, give him way.
Pericles   Rarest sounds, do ye not heare?
Lysimachus   Musicke my Lord? I heare.
Pericles   Most heavenly Musicke.
   It nips me unto listning, and thicke slumber
   Hangs upon mine eyes, let me rest.

(Q I1b, 5.1.221–35)

Music had, earlier on in the play, awakened Pericles' wife Thaisa, thought dead, though that music could be heard by all ('The Violl once more,' demands Cerymon, 'The Musicke there . . . give her ayre', Q E4a, 3.2.90). The redemptive power of music, music showing harmony both earthly and heavenly, is a theme in this play; and the bounty of the harmony extends out to the watchers with the happy ending: 'New joy' says Gower to the audience in the last line, 'wait on you' (Q I3b, 5.3.102).

   Thaisa's awakening recalls an important textual moment in *King Lear* where Lear, according to the quarto, returns to sanity, partly through being allowed to sleep, partly through being played curative music. So Cordelia prays that Lear's own music be set on the right course, that his strings be retuned:

   O you kind Gods cure this great breach in his abused nature,
   The untund and hurrying senses, O wind up
   Of this child changed father . . .

(Q K1b, 4.7, not in Riverside)

   In answer, as it were, the Doctor rouses Lear to the sound of gentle music; and the old man wakes up weeping and sane.

Doctor   Please you draw neere, louder the musicke there [.]
Cordelia   O my deer father, restoration hang thy medicine on my
   lips
   And let this kis repaire those violent harms that my two sisters
   Have in thy reverence made.

(Q K2a, 4.7.24–8)

This is one of the passages significantly revised out of what is
thought to be the later text (the folio text) of *Lear*. In the harsher
folio *Tragedy of King Lear* there is none of the saving grace of music.
Much of the verbal lyricism is gone in that play, replaced by
heavier, more muscular, brutal language; and in the same way
the tragedy is less relieved – there is less room for hope. This
second *Lear* is darker than the first, and in it Cordelia's prayer is
not met with as unambiguous an answer, and there is no doctor
to help cure the muddled king:[14]

Cordelia   O you kind Gods!
   Cure this great breach in his abused Nature,
   Th'untun'd and jarring senses, O winde up,
   Of this childe-changed Father.
Gentleman   So please your Majesty,
   That we may wake the King, he hath slept long?
Cordelia   Be govern'd by your knowledge, and proceede
   I'th'sway of your owne will: is he array'd?

(TLN 2763–70, 4.7.13–19)

Another use of music is, of course, the songs themselves. Here
it is noticeable that Shakespeare frequently supplies words for the
songs that occur in his plays: many other playwrights do not. The
presence of the words to the songs shows that the actual substance
of the texts was important. Traditionally, moreover, there had
been few or no songs sung in tragedies, so Shakespeare, in intro-
ducing the tragic song supplement, was bringing something quite
new to the theatre.[15]

Hamlet relies considerably on the use of the tragic song. In the
play one point continually illustrated by staging is that the world
has gone topsy-turvy and that everything keeps happening the
wrong way round: there is 'mirth in Funerall, and . . . Dirge in
Marriage' (TLN 190, 1.2.12); the flowers that should have decked
Ophelia's bridal bed are instead placed on her grave. The music

also mirrors – or helps create – this upside-down world. Ophelia is buried without anyone singing a requiem for her, because, as the 'churlish' priest holds, 'Her death was doubtful . . . We should profane the service of the dead / To sing a requiem' (TLN 3426–7, 5.1.227–37). And yet Ophelia has had songs sung for her; songs that seem to amount to a pagan requiem. Preparing Ophelia's grave, the gravedigger sings 'In youth when I did love, did love' (TLN 3251, 5.1.61), a song about tiring of love and being ready for death that also parodies the themes of Ophelia's mad songs: sexuality and the grave.

One particularly ironic use of music occurs at the end of the play and contributes to the play's bleak conclusion. As Hamlet dies, Horatio says a blessing over him: 'Goodnight, sweet Prince, / and flights of Angels sing thee to thy rest' (TLN 3850, 5.2.359–60). The audience, hearing this for the first time, would have been primed for ethereal music like the 'celestial music' that Pericles hears. But the next line explains what actually then happens. 'Why' exclaims the anguished Horatio, 'do's the Drumme come hither?' (TLN 3851, 5.2.361). The expectation of singing angels yields to the harsh intrusion of a martial drum: the *Hamlet* world is still disordered, confused and essentially back-to-front in a way that the play has not been able to solve. Perhaps this is an acknowledgement of the havoc Hamlet has wrought. Denmark, powerful and confident at the beginning of the play, has been reduced to a client of Norway by the end, and largely as the result of Hamlet's activities; one of the broader topsy-turvy *Hamlet* themes. But perhaps, also, there is a suggestion that the intervention of Fortinbras is not the happy conclusion to the play that is sometimes suggested, but is as dark as all the other happenings. The Kenneth Branagh film of *Hamlet* concentrating on the cruelty and singlemindedness of the Norwegian prince favoured this interpretation.[16]

Colour, props, music, stage-hangings and words themselves had layers of meaning, some of which made statements out into the audience that were not to be understood by the characters in the play, and some of which were proleptic, their full meaning to be recognised only retrospectively. Denying a text its theatre symbolism, confining it to the page, is to remove layers of potential meaning from it. To read the text alone and take that to be the play itself is to ignore the visual and aural commentary that shaped it in the theatre.

6
Prologues, Songs and Actors' Parts

When you look at a folio or quarto version of a Shakespeare play, or any other early modern play, the use of different typefaces for certain bits of the playtext will be immediately apparent. Specifically, it will be clear that parts of the text are nearly always differentiated from the rest by being printed in larger or different type. Those bits of a play are the prologues, the epilogues, the songs and the letters; all four tend to be visibly separated from the body of the text. In its original form, the printed text does not look homogeneous, a feature that is easily lost when looking at a modern, regularised edition.

Why did the playhouse give a different worth to different bits of text? This chapter will look at how an assemblage of textual pieces comes seen to be a solid dramatic work. It will then pare some of Shakespeare productions back into the discrete sheets of paper that made them up, showing how printed plays relate to theatrical manuscripts.

It has already been shown that a published play reflects in some form the state of the manuscript behind it. But why might the playhouse manuscript have given special treatment to prologues, epilogues, songs and letters? To answer the question it is necessary to see in what other ways those same sections of

text are printed differently from the text around them. Here are
some examples, transcribed to show the layout and typeface of
the passages in their various folio versions:

> *THE PROLOGUE.*
> *I Come no more to make you laugh, Things now,*
> *That beare a Weighty, and a Serious Brow,*
> *Sad, high, and working, full of State and Woe:*
> *Such Noble Scoenes, as draw the Eye to flow*
> *We now present.*
>   (*Henry VIII* TLN 2–6, prologue)

> THE EPILOGUE.
> *Tis ten to one, this Play can never please*
> *All that are heere: . . .*
>   (*Henry VIII* TLN 3449–51, epilogue)

> *Duke.*   I prethee sing.   *Musicke*
>   *The Song.*
> *Come away, come away death,*
> *And in sad cypresse let me be laide . . .*
>   (*Twelfth Night* TLN 939–41, 2.4.50–2)

> *Lad.*   What have we heere?
> *Clo.*   In that you have there.   *exit*

>   *A Letter.*
> *I have sent you a daughter-in-Law, shee hath recovered the King, and*
> *undone me.*
>   (*All's Well*, TLN 1418–22, 3.2.17–19)

As the above makes clear, in these instances 'the prologue', 'the
epilogue', 'the song', 'a letter' have their own generic headings,
although what they are is quite obvious from the context. The
titles are removed by modern editors, but when present they isolate
sections of play as varieties of literature in their own right; it is
as though prologue, epilogue, song and letter are not entirely part
of the texts to which they are attached.

   A brief look at some songs in plays by Shakespeare and other
writers will reveal what must sometimes be happening in the
playhouse to account for the different type and the seemingly

unnecessary headings. The printed plays of James Shirley will be
found often to have moments like this from his *The Duke's Mistress*
(1638):

> *Du.*   Musicke, the minuits
> Are sad i'th absence of *Ardelia*,
> And moove too slow, quicken their pace with Lutes,
> And voices.
>
> *A Song.*
> *Du.*   No more; we will be Musicke of our selves,
> And spare your Arts . . .[1]

Here the heading of 'a song' is present, but the ditty itself, music,
words and all that 'quickened the pace', are absent. This can be
matched by similar examples in Shakespeare. In *Julius Caesar*
Lucius plays the troubled Brutus a song, but falls asleep while
performing it. The tune, says Brutus, was played for 'slumber',
but 'slumber' has in turn murdered the player with the 'leaden
mace' of sleep. This is, of course, a passage more about the mind
of Brutus than about sleep or the tune, nevertheless the violence
of the observation is movingly flanked by the love Brutus obviously has for the boy singer. Love, violence and despair combine,
and the nature and words of the 'sleepy tune', whatever they were,
will have given a further contrast as well as a context to this
passage. And yet here is the moment exactly as it looks in the
one surviving folio text of the play.

> *Luc.*   I have slept my Lord already.
> *Bru.*   It was well done and thou shalt sleepe againe:
>   I will not hold thee long. If I do live,
>   I will be good to thee.
>   *Musicke, and a Song.*
>   This is a sleepy Tune: O Murd'rous slumber!
>   Layest thou thy Leaden Mace upon my Boy,
>   That playes thee Musicke? Gentle knave good night:
>   I will not do thee so much wrong to wake thee:
>   If thou do'st nod, thou break'st thy Instrument,
>   Ile take it from thee, and (good Boy) good night.
>   (TLN 2273–85, 4.3.263–72)

The substance of the sleepy tune is lost, just as the words to the song from Shirley's *Duke's Mistress* have disappeared. *Pericles*, too, contains such a moment. Marina has been sent by Lysimachus to try to rouse Pericles with her 'sweet harmonie, and other chosen attractions'. She starts with a song:

Lys.   Come, let us leave her, and the Gods make her prosperous.
                                 The Song.
Lys.   Marke[d] he your Musicke?
Mar.   No nor lookt on us.

(Q H3b, 5.1.79–81)

Marina is Pericles' long-lost daughter, but at this point in the play neither she nor Pericles realise that. What was in her song? Was it about relations or relationships? Was it about love or loss or childhood? Did it send out obscure messages to the audience? As Emilia puts it in *Othello*, 'What did thy Song boad Lady?' (TLN 3545, 5.2.246). We cannot know, however, for the song is gone.

The same is true of *1 Henry IV*:

Hotsp.   Peace, shee sings.
    Heere the Lady sings a Welsh Song.
Hotsp.   Come, Ile have your Song too.
          (TLN 1789–91, 3.1.244–5)

Of course, the fact that the song in *1 Henry IV* was in Welsh, a language that most of the audience would not understand, renders the value of the words that much less relevant. Nevertheless, the fact of the loss is revealing, and can be added to the one or maybe two lost songs in *Love's Labour's Lost*. In that play the boy Moth enters on to the stage together with Don Adriano his master. What then happens is unclear:

                    Song.
Bra.   Warble childe, make passionate my sense of hearing.
Boy.   Concolinel.
Brag.   Sweete Ayer ...

(Q C3b and F 770–5, 3.1.1–4)

The scene certainly begins with a lost song – but the meaning of Moth's response to 'warble child' ('Concolinel'), has long puzzled commentators. It is quite possible, given the context of the play, that that term, too, is the heading for a song (the Irish 'Can cailin gheal' – sing maiden fair – has been suggested, as has the French 'Quand Colinelle' – 'when Colinel') and that this scene contains two lost songs. Alternatively, 'song' and 'concolinel' are the same single lost song – we cannot know because nothing besides the puzzling title remains.

Lost songs raise a number of issues. They show that sometimes simply the title 'song' was supplied in the text, while the ditty itself must have been written on a separate piece of paper. This may explain the title 'the song' that heads so many songs in Shakespeare texts, and may explain, too, why those texts are in varied type: they looked 'different' from the rest of the play because they were different in manuscript. A number of early modern plays have their songs separately printed, gathered either at the front or the back of the edition, illustrating the separate nature of the songs from the playtext. Often, it seems, songs were not written directly into the playhouse 'book'.[2] But why might songs have been transcribed aside from the playtext?

For actors, who had a different play to put on every evening, there was very little time to learn scripts. Anything, therefore, that could reduce the learning load was very useful. Bits of play that could be written out on separate pieces of paper and read on stage rather than learned in advance were always helpful. With songs there was the added advantage that a separate sheet could provide the music as well as the words. So, it would seem, the pieces of paper on which songs were written were commonly kept outside plays as well as (and sometimes instead of) in them.

Various textual issues arise from this. If the song in the playhouse is kept separate from the rest of the play, then it can easily be lost while the body of the dialogue survives (as illustrated) or easily be taken away or moved from one character to another. Consider how many of the examples of revision already discussed happen around or in connection with songs. The willow song is present in folio *Othello* and absent in the quarto; Viola's songs in *Twelfth Night* appear to have been given to Feste; two songs are added to *Macbeth* out of Middleton's *The Witch*. *Measure for Measure* has been revised for performance at the Blackfriars theatre (it is a play to which act breaks have been added), and it has a song added between Acts 3 and 4, 'Take o take those lips away'. As Shakespeare usually wrote his own words to songs in plays, the suggestion is, in the latter two instances where the full song text is not supplied, that someone else has revised the plays and made the additions. A play is simply more flexible wherever songs are. For the same reason, songs are less likely to be written by the author than other bits of text: some of Shakespeare's songs are in fact common early modern songs. The willow song is one such example; 'o mistress mine' (*Twelfth Night*) another.

A play thus has particular sections that are less 'fixed' and less 'authorial' than other sections. The fact of the 'lost' songs means that surviving songs should be looked at carefully. If the words to a song have survived, that may mean that the text itself is of especial significance. As Shakespeare's plays generally do supply the words to songs, then the songs are directly relevant to the body of the text (rather than being, like the Welsh song, more important for sound than meaning). It is significant, also, that many songs do seem in fact to have been written especially for the play in which they appear.

As with songs, so letters, too, may also have been read on stage by actors rather than being committed to memory. Even in the nineteenth century, the player Edward Cape Everard writes of opening a long letter to be read in the first scene of a play and finding it 'a mere blank!'. He continues, with some pride for his foresight, 'Luckily for me, I had always made it a rule to study my Letters, as well as my character; it was well I did.'[3] There may be lost letters in the plays of Shakespeare, just as there are lost songs; certainly not all letters received are read aloud as we might expect.

As with songs and letters, so with prologues and epilogues. They also tend to be printed in italics and given a heading; in the layout of some early modern texts they follow on from one another, although in performance one opens the play and the other concludes it. Sometimes the same prologue is given to more than one play, like the prologue that boasts about the playwright's 'wonne grace' in the theatre previously, which opens both Rowley's *All's Lost by Lust* (1633), and Dekker's *Wonder of a Kingdom* (1636).[4] This suggests that stage orations, too, were kept together on different pieces of paper from the play itself. Moreover, many Shakespeare texts have survived without prologue or epilogue, though they seem originally to have had one or the other. Time in *Winter's Tale*, it was suggested in Chapter 3, may refer to a lost prologue when he asks us to 'remember well' the son of the king he previously mentioned – even though we have not heard of him in the text as it stands. Falstaff describes kissing and embracing as being 'the prologue of our Comedy', meaning, of course, the preliminaries to the desired event; the comedy in which he makes the observation, *Merry Wives*, now lacks a prologue (TLN 1744–5, 3.5.75); in *2 Henry VI*, which also has no prologue, Gloucester describes his own death as simply 'the Prologue to their Play' (TLN 1451, 3.1.151); 'We are cast,' observes Antonio in *The Tempest*, another play without a prologue, 'to performe an act / Whereof, what's past is Prologue' (TLN 947, 2.1.252–3). Each play seems to think a prologue normal to a production; each play nevertheless has no prologue. On the other hand, a prologue thought to be by Shakespeare survives in a commonplace book. It is not play-specific, and is not printed with any play: 'As the diall hand tells ore.'[5] But then, plays that exist in more than one version often include one text with and one text without prologue or epilogue. *Romeo and Juliet*, for instance, appears in the folio without the 'star-crossed lovers' prologue; *Henry V* in its 'bad' 1600 quarto has neither prologue nor chorus; the *Troilus* prologue is absent from the quarto and early printings of the folio. Conversely, a prologue does survive for Shakespeare's *Richard III*, though it is not by Shakespeare and is never printed with the text. It is a prologue by Heywood and is written for a little boy who was in Queen Anne's Men and played Richard III at the Red Bull playhouse some time between 1605 and 1619: 'If any wonder by what magick charme, / Richard the third is shrunke up like his arme . . .'[6] Prologues were not only quickly lost, but were also quickly replaced as circumstance dictated.

Like songs and, perhaps, letters, textual fluidity and change can be expected around prologues and epilogues, and we might suspect that Shakespeare plays that now have neither originally had at least one. Prologues and epilogues were thought to be disposable, as the textual history of the prologue to *Troilus and Cressida* reveals. *Troilus* was first published in quarto in 1609; that same quarto was twice produced, the second version containing introductory material absent from the first (that reissued quarto is, for this reason, described as 1609b). Neither quarto version contains a prologue. When *Troilus* was first set for printing in the folio it was similarly prepared for publication without a prologue, and early sheets from the first setting of the play show the text starting immediately on the verso, the back, of the last page of *Romeo and Juliet*. But then the publishers of the folio ran into difficulties securing rights to print *Troilus* legally. They stopped typesetting *Troilus* after they had already printed the first few pages of the play.

By the time the legal problems had been resolved, the space after *Romeo* had been filled with a different play, *Timon of Athens*. So *Troilus* was set again and placed after *Henry VIII*. It was such a late inclusion that it has no page numbers and is not mentioned in the 'catalogue of the severall Comedies, Histories, and Tragedies contained in this Volume' at the start of the folio. Some sheets that had previously been printed for the play, however, had been preserved and were bound into folio texts with the tail end of *Romeo* on the recto, the front of the page, as a crossed out or 'cancelled' sheet (a 'cancellans'). The newer sheets needed a layout equivalent to the old sheets if all were to be used, so a piece of text was acquired to supply the page no longer occupied by the end of *Romeo*: the prologue. This prologue, which had not featured in either 1609 quarto of *Troilus*, would otherwise have been lost to history. In other words, prologues and epilogues were not part of a unified text, sharing the same rights and lasting qualities. They were ephemeral and were not thought of as having the importance or the permanence of the text of the play itself, though they often had an alternative existence. Many prologues and epilogues are separately preserved in books of poetry and jests.

Why? At first the separation of prologue and epilogue from text seems surprising, for, unlike songs and letters, they were not read on stage, but learned off by heart. In the 'bad' quarto of *Romeo and Juliet* there is a reference to a prologue that is 'faintly spoke / After the prompter' (Q1 C1a), and two boys at the start of Ben Jonson's play *Cynthia's Revels* quarrel because each has learned the prologue and wants to say it.

The reason for the division of prologue or epilogue from play seems to be that prologues and epilogues were not permanent features of a production. Some of them are specifically designed for court performance – if so, they are, of course, to be spoken only on a single occasion. But, reading public theatre prologues and epilogues of the period *en masse*, it becomes obvious that all share the same themes. They are, for instance, always unclear what the spectators will think of the play. Will the audience, they all ask, 'approve' the performance or 'dismiss' it? The prologue to *Henry V* requests the audience 'Gently to heare, kindly to judge our Play' (TLN 35); the *Troilus and Cressida* prologue is bolder on the same question: 'Like, or finde fault, do as your pleasures are' (TLN 31); while the prologue to *Henry VIII* hopes that 'the play may passe' (TLN 12), but also lists the types of spectators likely to dislike this kind of production. Epilogues, meanwhile, seem pointedly to demand applause whilst fearing to be hissed, booed or 'mewed at'. Prospero ends *The Tempest* with an epilogue in which he expresses a fear that his project (to please the audience) will fail unless everyone agrees to release him 'from my bands / With the helpe of your good hands' (i.e. applaud the play) (TLN 2331). At the end of *A Midsummer Night's Dream*, Puck asks the audience not to 'reprehend' him but 'Give me your hands, if we be friends' (TLN 2221, 5.1.429–37); Rosalind, concluding *As You Like It*, hopes that 'the play may please' (TLN 2791) and, again, suggests brashly that the audience 'for my kind offer, when I make curt'sie, bid me farewell' (TLN 2795–6). As prologues and epilogues for public performance repeatedly show, then, they are for an audience that is 'judging' the play and deciding whether or not to award it approval.

When did the audience have the chance to show their opinion of a play? They judged it on its first performance, an occasion that cost more than any other performance and that was often described as the 'trial' of the play itself.[7] Whatever the reader of Shakespeare's folio chooses to think, write Heminges and Condell bluntly in their introduction to the book, the plays 'have had their triall alreadie' (A3a). Hamlet discusses a play that was disliked by an audience and therefore did not survive beyond its first day. He recalls that the play was good, but too sophisticated – like caviar – so that it appealed to those few with fine taste, and was objectionable to the rest: 'the Play I remember pleas'd not the Million, 'twas *Caviarie* to the Generall: but it was (as I receiv'd it and others, whose judgement in such matters, cried in the top of mine) an excellent Play' (TLN 1479–82, 2.2.434–9). A play recently rejected by the audience (a 'damned' play) is referred to by the epilogue to *2 Henry IV*. The performer playing the epilogue recounts how he was 'lately heere in the end of a displeasing Play, to pray your Patience for it, and to promise you a Better' (TLN 3332–3). Other playwrights famously had their plays damned on the first performance. They include Ben Jonson, whose *New Inn* (1631) was censured by the 'hundred fastidious impertinents . . . present the first day', John Fletcher, whose *Faithful Shepherdess* (1609?) was 'scornd' by its first audience, and Peter Hausted, whose *Rival Friends* (1632) was 'Cryed downe by Boyes, Faction, Envie, and confident Ignorance', though 'approv'd by the judicious'.[8]

So the purpose of prologue and epilogue alike was to woo the first-performance audience which was judging or auditioning the play and to petition the spectators, begging them to be indulgent rather than unkind. A play, having survived its first day and been 'passed' by the audience, seems to have shed its stage orations which could then float free of the text, and so were easily lost before publication.[9] First performances of a play will, then, have been different from any subsequent performance. They will, on the other hand, have been similar to all other first performances, the presence of prologue or epilogue in itself linking all new plays (whoever they are by) with one another – particularly as the actors playing prologues and epilogues usually wore the same black cloak. In Heywood's *Four Prentices of London* the Prologue wears a 'long blacke velvet cloake'; in Edward Phillips's *The Mysteries of Love and Eloquence* 'Prologues' are described as 'set and starcht speeches to be gravely delivered ... by the man in the long cloak with the coloured beard'.[10] A picture of a prologue is provided in a book by George Wilkins which tells a tale closely connected to the story of the play *Pericles*. Wilkins's *The Painful Adventure of Pericles* (1608) has a picture of Gower on the title page, wearing a cloak and holding a staff, hinting at the way 'Gower' was staged. Laurel or 'bay' wreaths were also standard for prologues: 'A Prologue in Verse is as stale, as a black Velvet Cloake, and a Bay Garland' says a Beaumont and Fletcher prologue.[11] But a cloak represents scholarship and 'bays' an award for poetic creativity: prologues are dressed like 'authors' but are played by actors. In other words the playhouse takes over 'authorship' on the first performance, which queries the 'ownership' of a play from first performance onwards. Plays may even have been given in over-long form on their first day, so that the moments clapped or hissed by members of the audience could be enlarged on or cut – at any rate, some textual shortening between first and second performance seems regularly to have taken place.[12] A play in performance was by no means textually fixed.

For the playhouse, then, 'the play' may have consisted of one book containing the dialogue, some sheets of paper containing the songs, some other sheets of paper containing letters, and finally some sheets on which were written the prologue and/or epilogue (fashion seems to have dictated whether to have one, the other or both). This was not, however, always the case. If Shakespeare, for instance, writes a song while writing a play and transcribes the whole into his foul papers, and if those foul papers then become the prompter's 'book', the words of the song survive into the playtext. If, on the other hand, he either writes the song later or simply requests that any old song, or a popular song from elsewhere, be acquired, the song may not make its way into the prompter's book. There are other variations on these two options, of course – but the point is that a play easily resolves into fragments that have separate lives from the body of the text and only a hesitant relationship to the play itself. What do we mean, then, when we talk about 'the text', and about 'textual unity'? The way actors received and responded to their parts shows that the whole notion of 'the play' as a single entity may itself be slightly misguided.

Plays themselves were disseminated to actors in segmented form, in 'parts', as Chapter 4 showed. The 'part' did not relate strongly to the play in narrative terms, for the full story is not clear from looking at a part. Each actor received what he was to say and a cue; to him, the play will have consisted of his role and the few words that led into it. Much theatrical by-play is made of the idea of 'cues' and 'parts' within Shakespeare's plays. In *A Midsummer Night's Dream* Flute has difficulty understanding how his 'part' of 'Thisbe' works. According to Peter Quince, Flute muddles in his cues with his own lines and speaks the whole lot.

Flute   Most radiant *Piramus*, most Lilly white of hue,
      Of colour like the red rose on triumphant bryer,
      Most brisky Juvenall, and eke most lovely Jew,
      As true as truest horse, that yet would never tyre,
Quince   Ile meete thee *Piramus*, at *Ninnies* toombe.
      Ninus toombe man: why, you must not speake that yet; that you answere to *Piramus:* you speake all your part at once, cues and all. *Piramus* enter, your cue is past; it is never tyre.
Flute   O, as true as truest horse, that yet would never tyre:
Bottom   If I were faire, *Thisby* I were onely thine.
                                        (TLN 906–17, 3.1.93–104)

But the further joke is that the actual actor, playing Bottom playing 'Pyramus', will have received a real cued part for this same moment in the scene that must have looked something like this:

———————————————————————— never tyre:
If I were faire, Thisby, I were onely thine.

As the cue 'never tyre' repeatedly occurs in the above scene, it could be that the real actor actually starts to speak three times, for the very words with which Quince (the prompter) chides Bottom for neglecting his cue ('your cue is past; it is *never tyre*') give him a false cue. After Quince's 'never tyre', both Thisbe and Pyramus, who both now have 'never tyre' as their next cue, may start speaking simultaneously. The whole section is, of course, dedicated to making jokes about country mechanicals who do not understand the theatre and cannot work out the cueing system.

The term 'part' used for the script actors received (and still used today to describe the role an actor plays) arises, of course, from the fact that actors were not given the full text of the play but only 'part' of it, the part with their lines and cues. Similarly the term 'role', it has been suggested, originates in the roll of paper on which the 'part' was written: your 'part' or 'roll' was your bit of the play, consisting of your lines to be spoken and your cues to be listened for. Terms such as 'part' or 'parcell', both used to describe the script in the form received, indicate that the fragment was thought of as being just that, 'part' of something larger.

Why did actors receive their texts, their 'parts', in this way? There are several obvious reasons. One is that all parts had to be written by a scribe (probably the prompter), and there would not have been the time, or the paper, or the incentive to pen a full version of the play for each separate actor. Moreover, the more copies of a play in existence, the more likely it was that one of them might end up in the hands of a printer. Not that that was entirely a bad thing: printing a play was a good way of advertising it and playhouses seem selectively to have released their texts for publication, particularly over periods when they could not perform – for instance, when the theatres were closed because of plague. Plays were not generally released to the printing houses until approximately two years after they reached the stage, however.[13] The fewer people with access to a 'new' play – a play never performed before – the more would have to pay the theatre to hear the story.

As a result, it was as usual to come across a play in its separate bits as to come across it as a whole: texts had a strong part-based life. The 'bad' quartos may show the result of this. Editors examining 'bad' texts believe they can sometimes tell if an actor was responsible for stealing the text, for there often seems to be one consistently 'good' part running through the bad text, and lines can be seen to be relatively 'more' good (when that actor is on stage) and 'less' good (when he is not). The conclusion is that the actor contributed his part and his memory to recreating the text. So in the 'bad' Quarto of *Henry V*, the actors (or actor) who may have been responsible for pirating the text were, perhaps, the players of Gower and Exeter.[14]

How would an actor in the theatre use his part? In performance he would listen for his 'cue', and then say the speech that he had learned would follow it. These cues, however, were extremely short. As the example from *A Midsummer Night's Dream* showed, Pyramus had a two-word cue, 'Never tyre'. From the surviving 1590s professional part of 'Orlando' in *Orlando Furioso*, quoted in Chapter 4, it seems that cues of one to three words were normal, and that it was equally normal not to name the cue speaker. During the Restoration, similarly, actors were given parts (or lengths, as they were then called) with up to three cue words and without the name of the cue speaker supplied (a 1662 part survives for the character 'Trico' in a play called *Ignoramus*). During the eighteenth century, as the many extant professional parts from that period illustrate, cued parts continued to be presented in the same way; even nineteenth- and twentieth-century parts (then called 'sides') did not look much different. French and German parts for the medieval and early modern period, of which there are many, also show the use of exceptionally brief cues: in France, cues do not seem to have extended beyond one word.[15] Hardly surprisingly, the fact of the cue becomes a source for metatheatrical references: 'your speech being ended, now comes in my cue' (Heywood, *The Royal King and the Loyal Subject*); 'Your qu. / . . . 'twill be spoken quickly / Therefore watch it' (Middleton and Rowley, *A Fair Quarrel*); 'Speak count, tis your Qu' (Shakespeare, *Much Ado*, TLN 704, 2.1.305).[16]

There follows a recreation of the opening of the 'part' for Olivia in *Twelfth Night*, 1.5. Slightly generous cues of three words have been given.

———————————————————————— which is she?
Speake to me, I shall answer for her: your will.
———————————————————————— least sinister usage.
Whence came you sir?
———————————————————————— in my speech.
Are you a Comedian?
———————————————————————— of the house?
If I do not usurpe my selfe, I am.

(TLN 462–80, 1.5.167–87)

The first 'cue' is 'which is she?' (or, perhaps, 'is she?') after which Olivia knows to reply 'Speake to me, I shall answer for her will'. The next cue is 'sinister usage' for which the response is 'Whence came you sir?' As is obvious, the cues do not tell the actor much about the story of the scene he is in, though they may, like the ominous 'sinister usage' of the passage above, help him define what emotions to exhibit. Actors largely had to build their performances and sense of character out of the words they themselves were given to speak and their cues; they might not hear the context of their words until very late in the preparation process, perhaps not until performance.

The fact of working with a short cue line of three or fewer words meant that giving an actor 'premature cues' may, on occasion, have been used purposefully in the action of the play. Shylock's part in *Merchant of Venice* seems to offer a useful example of this, for it is one of Shylock's characteristics to become fixed on certain verbal formulae, his main figure of speech being repetition. The cued-part effect of this, however, seems to be that he is continually interrupted by the other characters.

Scene 3.3 in *The Merchant of Venice* is one in which Solanio, Shylock and Antonio are on stage with Shylock. Read in 'full text', Shylock rants, Antonio then interjects to demand that Shylock hear him speak, Shylock refuses, and finally Solanio chimes in to call Shylock an impenetrable cur. But, in part form, the scene takes on a different momentum. Provided below is the part for Solanio in that scene. If given a 'long' cue of three words he is listening out for 'have my bond'. If given an even longer cue, he is listening for 'I'll have my bond'. When he hears the cue, he is to respond, 'It is the most impenetrable curre / That ever kept with men'. His 'part' at this stage in the action will have looked something like this:

———————————————————— have my bond.
It is the most impenetrable curre
That ever kept with men.

Now here is Shylock's speech:

Shylock   Ile <u>have my bond</u>, [Solanio: It is the most impenetrable
curre . . .] speake not against my bond,
I have sworne an oath that I will <u>have my bond</u>: [It is the
most impenetrable *curre* . . .]

Thou call'sdt me *dog* before thou hadst a cause,
But since I am a *dog*, beware my phangs . . .
Ile <u>have my bond</u>, [It is the most impenetrable *curre* . . .] I
will not heare thee speake,
Ile <u>have my bond</u>, [It is the most impenetrable *curre* . . .] and
therefore speake no more.
Ile not be made a soft and dull ey'd foole,
To shake the head, relent, and sigh, and yeeld
To Christian intercessors: follow not,
Speaking, I will <u>have my bond</u>.
Solanio   It is the most impenetrable curre
That ever kept with men.

(TLN 1690–1705, 3.3.4–19)

In 'part' terms, what seems to be happening is that Shylock, while
addressing himself to Antonio, repeatedly throws out Solanio's
cue early. So Antonio makes two forlorn attempt at interjection
('I pray thee heare me speake') and gives up, while his indignant
friend continually attempts to break Shylock's flow – but whenever he tries, he is told to be quiet. By the time Solanio gets a
chance to speak, he is truly angry. Antonio, resigned, chivvies his
friend: 'Let him alone, / Ile follow him no more with bootlesse
prayers'. Is this scripted babble? Does Solanio's 'impenetrable
curre' speech, which looks on paper to happen only once, actually partially happen four additional times? Were that the case,
then the reference to curs might also be important, enraging
Shylock anew with the recollection that Antonio before had been
ready enough to label him 'dog'; hence, perhaps, his sudden
change of direction: '*Thou* call'sdt me dog *before* thou hadst a cause,
/ But since I am a dog, beware my phangs' (my italics). Something
of the same kind seems to happen again when Shylock gives a
complicated reply to the Duke's request for a 'gentle answer' (4.1):

You'l aske me why I rather choose to have
A weight of carrion flesh, then to receive
Three thousand Ducats? Ile not answer that:
But say it is my humor; Is it <u>answered</u>?
What if my house be troubled with a Rat,
And I be pleas'd to give ten thousand Ducates
To have it bain'd? What, are you <u>answer'd</u> yet? . . .
[I can] give no reason, nor I will not,

> More then a lodg'd hate, and a certaine loathing
> I beare Anthonio, that I follow thus
> A loosing suite against him? Are you <u>answered</u>?
> *Bassanio*   This is no answer thou unfeeling man . . .
> (TLN 1945–68, 4.1.40–63)

This is indeed more rhetoric than 'answer': from being asked to answer a question, Shylock has talked himself into a position where he is asking a question instead. The argument contains three parts as though it has a kind of logic that it does not: each part consists of a blustering question as to whether the answer has now been supplied, but the reasons given – whim, humour – are no answers to Bassanio, who is looking for something more rational than blind hatred. Does Bassanio three times (or twice depending on the length of the cue) point this out? 'This is no answer' and '*This* is no answer'? It is, similarly, possible that Salarino (3.1) breaks in at each of Shylock's 'to his bond' to query *why* Shylock is so obsessed with his bargain:

> *Shylock*   There I have another bad match, a bankrout . . . who
> dare scarce shew his head on the Ryalto . . . let him look
> <u>to his bond</u>, he was wont to call me Usurer, let him looke <u>to</u>
> <u>his bond</u>, he was wont to lend money for a Christian curtsie,
> let him looke <u>to his bond</u>.
> *Salarino*   Why I am sure if he forfaite, thou wilt not take his flesh
> . . .
>
> (TLN 1260–4, 3.1.43–51)

One other, more general example is when Shylock is talking to Tubal (3.1) about the loss of his daughter and his money. At this stage he is overwrought, excitable and full of repetitions; as an emotional pointer, the actor will have recognised the fact and worked on it. But the effect seems to be, as ever, that Shylock is throwing out premature cues so that he is continually interrupted by his interlocutor. His part for this moment will have been something like:

> What, what, what, <u>ill lucke, ill lucke</u>.
> ———————————————————— from Tripolis.
> I thanke God, I thanke God, <u>is it true, is it true</u>?
> ———————————————————— escaped the wracke.

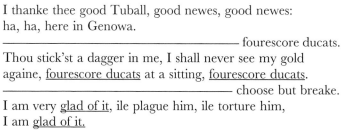

I thanke thee good Tuball, good newes, good newes:
ha, ha, here in Genowa.
——————————————————————— fourescore ducats.
Thou stick'st a dagger in me, I shall never see my gold
againe, <u>fourescore ducats</u> at a sitting, <u>fourescore ducats</u>.
——————————————————————— choose but breake.
I am very <u>glad of it</u>, ile plague him, ile torture him,
I am <u>glad of it.</u>

$$\text{(TLN 1311–28, 3.1.98–117)}$$

Performed from parts, the interlocutor, Tubal, will, it appears, spend most of this scene talking half over the friend whom he is enraging with his mischievous 'comfort'. So though a full text is always linear, the spoken text underlying it could have been a vibrant scripted confusion of interwoven voices – and all because of the way actors received their parts.

The part-based actor has scripted and in his possession everything he says, but *not* everything that is said to or about him. If something is said about him in a scene when he is not even on stage, he may not know about it, just as, years later, the famous Mrs Pritchard was accused of having performed Lady Macbeth from her part without reading the tragedy through: 'She no more thought of the play out of which her part was taken, than a shoemaker thinks of the skin, out of which he is making a pair of shoes.'[17] Could this mean that the actor playing Lear in *King Lear* does not know Regan's startling insight, 'he hath ever but slenderly knowne himselfe' (TLN 318–19, 1.1.293–4), and cannot, therefore, use that observation as a character-note? True, major actors will have heard a 'reading' during which the story of the play as it then stood was related to them. But the tale may well have gone through several changes since that point, and, anyway, the reading will have been some weeks before first performance, and between it and the actual production there will have been performances of many other plays. What can a term like 'characterisation' mean when looking at actors who learn only what their character says?

Obviously performers responded in a particular way to texts that obscured some basic features of the play – but revealed others. This can be seen by returning to Olivia's part in *Twelfth Night*. Olivia's cues are both telling and reticent: the (male) actor playing Olivia who received this part would not necessarily have

understood exactly the conversation he was having. He would,
however, have understood the shift in passions that he undergoes
two-thirds of the way down the scene. What happens is not simply
that in the text the actor stops bantering; it is also that the actor
stops speaking prose. At this stage in the play Olivia is talking to
Viola for the first time. Viola is dressed as a boy, Cesario, and
Olivia does not know his or her real sex. In the following passage
Olivia lifts her veil and she and Viola (Cesario) see one another
properly for the first time.

———————————————————————————— see your face.
Have you any Commission from your Lord, to negotiate
with my face: you are now out of your Text: but we
will draw the Curtain, and shew you the picture.
Looke you sir, such a one I was this present: Ist not
well done?
———————————————————————————— God did all.
'Tis in graine sir, 'twill endure winde and weather.
———————————————————————————— world no copie.
O sir, I will not be so hard-hearted: I will give out
divers scedules of my beautie. It shalbe Inventoried and
every particle and utensile labell'd to my will: As, Item
two lippes indifferent redde, Item two grey eyes, with
lids to them: Item, one necke, one chin, & so forth.
Were you sent hither to praise me?
———————————————————————————— non-pareil of beautie.
How does he love me?
———————————————————————————— sighes of fire.
Your Lord does know my mind, I cannot love him
Yet I suppose him vertuous, know him noble,
Of great estate, of fresh and stainlesse youth;
In voyces well divulg'd, free, learn'd, and valiant,
And in dimension, and the shape of nature,
A gracious person; But yet I cannot love him:
He might have tooke his answer long ago.
———————————————————————————— not understand it.
Why, what would you?
———————————————————————————— should pittie me.
You might do much:
What is your Parentage?
———————————————————————————— am a Gentleman.

Get you to your Lord:
I cannot love him: let him send no more,
Unlesse (perchance) you come to me againe,
To tell me how he takes it: Fare you well:
I thanke you for your paines: spend this for mee.
———————————————————————— Farwell fayre crueltie.
Exit [*Viola*]
(TLN 462–583, 1.5.230–88)

After the cue 'non-pareil of beautie' there is a line that may be
in verse: 'how does he love me?' from which, looked at in the
part, the next line spoken follows on in one long stream of thought:
'how does he love me? Your <u>Lord</u> does <u>know</u> my <u>mind</u>, I <u>cannot</u>
<u>love</u> him'. It is from 'Your Lord does know' onwards that Olivia
speaks only verse. This prose/verse alteration will have been visible
to the actor even before he read a word of the text; he will have
seen it, thus, as a visual stage direction, a sign that his conversation is changing its nature in some way. What takes place in this
scene, as the part manifests, is that Olivia has fallen in love; could
it be that the stage direction about when to do so is embedded
in the very layout of the part? Is it possible that Olivia falls for
Viola while denying the possibility of ever loving Orsino? The
suddenness with which love overtakes Olivia is no surprise from
the perspective of the early modern stage. Thomas Killigrew's *The
Princess* (1664), 2.2 contains the stage direction 'Virgilius spyes
Cicilia and falls in Love with her', similarly in a stage direction
to John Marston's *Insatiate Countess* 'Isabella falls in love'.[18] If a stage
direction can tell the actor to fall in love, then 'falling in love'
must somehow have been visible – probably gestural – so that
the change-of-text in Olivia's part may also tell the player the
'action' to be performed. This is, of course, all conjectural, but it
is certainly always important to be aware of changes of tone and
pace within specific actors' parts as well as over whole texts or
scenes. Viola, for instance, in this scene has an entirely different
verse/prose pattern, seemingly using verse when employing the
'heightened language' Orsino has taught her, and prose when she
is speaking for herself.

  There are many illuminating prose/verse transitions in the plays
of Shakespeare when a major emotional change is signified. In
Much Ado About Nothing, Beatrice speaks only prose until she hears
her friends declare that Benedict loves her. Having done nothing

but throw prose insults at Benedict hitherto, she now falls in love
and starts speaking verse. Looking at the full play, the 'moment'
of changed emotion is not particularly obvious: there is one scene
in which Beatrice insults Benedict in prose; later there is another
in which she listens to her friends talking of Benedict's affection
for her and responds in poetry. But the actor playing Beatrice
will have received a part that collapsed the distance from one
scene to another, showing a sentence in argumentative prose
followed by a section in poetry:

> Yea just so much as you may take upon a knives point,
> and choake a daw withall: you have no stomacke signior,
> fare you well.
> ——————————————————————————— some with traps.
> What <u>fire</u> is <u>in</u> mine <u>eares</u>? can <u>this</u> be <u>true</u>?
> (TLN 1076–199, 2.3.254–6; 3.1.107–8)

Again, the actor might have read the layout of the part as a way
of approaching the emotional activity within the part.

Before the time at which Shakespeare was writing, plays had
traditionally been composed in verse only. Indeed, the usual title
by which the writer of a play was known while Shakespeare was
alive was 'poet'; the word 'playwright' was only introduced around
or just after Shakespeare's death (it is first recorded in poetry in
1617).[19] Sometimes Shakespeare bows to this: *Richard II* is written
entirely in verse. But, as with so much else, Shakespeare was bold
and experimental. He took to using prose regularly, though traditionally it had been spoken only by fools, clowns and low-down
characters. In his earlier plays the traditional distinctions are more
likely still to pertain: the prose is often casual and the verse is
reserved for high matter like love or reflection. Tragic heroes'
soliloquies, for instance, are always in verse in the earlier plays,
though a 'low' character such as Launcelot Gobbo in *Merchant of
Venice* may be given a soliloquy in prose. But, roughly the same
time as the company started to perform at the Globe playhouse,
Shakespeare starts varying verse and prose in a more complex
ways. These moments will have been clearer to an actor playing
from 'parts' than to a modern reader. For instance, the full text of
Hamlet (probably written in 1600) seems to be composed in a medley of prose and verse.[20] Divided into parts, however, distinctions
between the two in 'good' quarto and folio alike start to make sense.

Hamlet begins his part speaking in verse. Then, after he has seen the ghost, he determines (as he explains) to 'put an Anticke disposition on' (TLN 868, 1.5.172). The next time he speaks he acts the fool with Polonius ('y'are a Fishmonger', TLN 1211, 2.2.174) and he talks in prose. Indeed, whenever he is fooling, he seems to speak prose: in this way, the actor himself, and all who perform with him, can see that he is 'mad'. When he is not fooling – generally in the soliloquies, where he reveals to the audience his rational side – he returns to verse. The actor of Hamlet thus has a text in which his character never loses the ability to address the audience (and close friends such as Horatio) in 'sane' verse: Hamlet appears to be exactly what he says he is, a sane man pretending to be mad. The verse–prose crux comes in the burial scene. Hamlet, by this stage, has learned on board ship that his uncle, Claudius, has planned to have him put to death on his arrival in England. This is, in fact, Hamlet's first direct proof, outside the ghost's testimony, that Claudius truly has a murderous nature (the audience has heard Claudius confess his guilt in soliloquy, but Hamlet has not). Hamlet manages to escape the death that Claudius had planned for him, jumping aboard a pirate ship, and imposing what was to have been his fate on Rosencrantz and Guildenstern. He has confronted death, rejected it and chosen to live, consciously saving his own life by not going to England. Now Hamlet finds himself back in Denmark and in a graveyard just as Ophelia, whom he belatedly realises he loved, is buried. Having insisted to the court of Denmark that he was mad, Hamlet now has to prove that he is sane. From the entrance of Ophelia's coffin, he speaks only verse in public until the time he dies, though he exchanges frivolous banter in prose with Osric. Ophelia, conversely, speaks only rational verse until going mad: from then until she dies she speaks prose. Actors, following hints in their parts, might not be absolutely clear about the 'story' of the play but were very cognisant of mood and mood-change.

Difficult as it is to contemplate, actors continued to create spectacular and complex performances from knowledge of cued parts – and not much concern with 'meaning' or the full play – even last century: parts or 'sides' as they were often called, were used in repertory up until the 1950s. 'I believe that learning the part and each cue with a postcard over the page, which I do relentlessly, is the most horrible drudgery', said Noel Coward. 'I don't worry about whether I'm getting at the right meaning at this

point. When I get up on the stage, the words give me the meaning:
you can't know it better than the words.'[21]

Within parts and along their length, the register or tone used
tells the actor about the kind of relationship he has with the person
he is addressing – and when that relationship changes. He can
observe whether he favours the familiar 'thou' form of speaking,
the more formal and distant 'you' form, or varies between the
two.[22] Informal and formal modes of address can, for instance,
be seen to vary in frequency and use in the 'part' belonging to
Lady Macbeth. Early in the play, Lady Macbeth refers to Macbeth
as 'thee'; she does this both when alone on her first entrance and
when later joined by her husband. When Macbeth seems unwilling
to perform the murder she takes on a tone of command: 'when
you durst do it, then you were a man' (TLN, 528, 1.7.49) before
switching back to the familiar 'thee' to wheedle him round. But
there is an unalterable change in her tone later on in the play.
From 3.3 onwards Lady Macbeth loses her power. As Macbeth's
guilt and bloodlust cuts him off from conversation or understanding with anyone else, so Lady Macbeth ceases to be privy
to his thoughts or plans. She dare no longer use the familiar
shared 'thee' form to her husband, and her part shows that her
language becomes increasingly formal: she calls Macbeth 'you',
'sir', 'My Royall Lord'. This can be illustrated by a quick comparison between the tone of one early Lady Macbeth passage, and
another from much later:

> Thy Letters have transported me beyond
> This ignorant present; and I feele now
> The future in the instant.
> > (TLN 408–10, 1.5.56–8)

> How now, my Lord, why doe you keepe alone?
> > (TLN 1161, 3.2.8)

Received in a part, the tonal change indicates to the actor of
Lady Macbeth a growing estrangement. Significantly, Macbeth
does not receive these same indications in his part. He continues
to call Lady Macbeth 'thee', 'love', 'deare Wife', and 'dearest
Chuck' throughout. So the Macbeth actor does not receive a part
that acknowledges or indicates that there is marital tension: he
continues to act familiarity while she becomes increasingly distant.

In short, Macbeth and Lady Macbeth do not share an understanding about the nature of their relationship – and the parts create the acting that reveals this.

Other theatrically telling information can be found in parts which sometimes contain information that may stand in for stage directions to other actors. The Duke in *Measure for Measure* asks a question which perhaps creates the appropriate action with his 'Doe you not smile at this, Lord *Angelo*?' (TLN 2535, 5.1.163). Alternatively the gulf between what the Duke says and the way Angelo actually looks is a hint to the audience. Similarly Iago constructs a certain kind of response in *Othello*:

Iago   I see this hath a little dash'd your Spirits:
Othello   Not a jot, not a jot.
Iago   Trust me, I feare it has.
                    (TLN 1835–7, 3.3.214–15)

Other kinds of detail actors would have been able to pick up from parts even before learning them would have been whether they were otiose or brief, curt or lyrical, full of questions or full of answers – and they would have spotted immediately the important moment at which any of their characteristics were changed or modified.

Even revision itself seems often to have happened along part lines, as is particularly apparent with the text of *Hamlet*. The alterations made to *Hamlet* between the quarto and folio text are mainly cuts, lines being taken, usually, from the middle of long speeches. Commentators have been left bemused, wondering why such minute passages were altered, and why cuts had not been made over, for instance, a whole scene. But, of course, cuts of this nature make absolute sense in playhouse terms: extracting the middle of a speech leaves the cues intact and so does not force more than one actor to relearn his part.

> O throwe away the worser part of it,
> And leave the purer with the other halfe,
> Good night, but goe not to my Uncles bed,
> Assume a virtue if you have it not,
> ~~That monster custome, who all sence doth eate~~
> ~~Of habits devil, is angel yet in this~~
> ~~That to the use of actions faire and good,~~

~~He likewise gives~~ a frock or Livery
~~That aptly is put on~~ refraine to night,
And that shall lend a kind of easines
To the next abstinence, ~~the next more easier:~~
~~For use almost can change the stamp of nature,~~
~~And either the devil, or throwe him out~~
~~With wonderous potency:~~ once more good night,
And when you are desirous to be blest,
Ile blessing beg of you, for this same Lord
I doe repent; but heaven hath pleasd it so
To punish me with this, and this with me,
That I must be their scourge and minster,
I will bestowe him and will answere well
The death I have him; so againe good night
I must be cruell only to be kinde,
This bad beginnes, and worse remaines behind.
On word more good Lady.
    (Q2, I4a-b; TLN 2540–55, 3.4.157–80)[23]

Indeed, in *Hamlet*, not all parts are revised, so many parts will never
have had to be returned to the prompter for rewriting. Only eight
parts are altered: Hamlet, Gertrude, Claudius, Horatio, Laertes,
Rosencrantz, Guildenstern, Osric (the five most important characters and the three clowns). This revision, then, happened not over
the whole text but along the length of some of the 'strands' in the
play.

So in many ways the internal structure of a play can be seen to
divide not so much into acts and scenes, plots and sub-plots, as into
stage orations, songs, 'parts': the plays are constructed from individual 'bits' that still keep some of their separate integrity. 'Parts'
explain a lot about acting technique at the time, but also about
writing technique. Shakespeare was an actor and, in writing plays
for other actors, seems to have included some of his instructions for
performance in the part-form itself.

7
From Stage to Printing House

The one written fragment that survives in what is thought to be Shakespeare's hand, passages from the play of *Sir Thomas Moore*, was discussed in Chapter 2. Here is another passage from the 'Shakespearean' part of that same document, repunctuated with stage directions added to show what the writer seems to want to be staged. 'Shrieve' is a variant of the word 'sheriff', 'a' is used for 'he':

Lincoln   Peace, I say! Peace! Are you men of wisdom, or what are you?
Surrey   [*aside*] What you will have them, but not men of wisdom.
[*some*]   We'll not hear my Lord of Surrey.
[*others*]   No, no, no, no, no! Shrewsbury, Shrewsbury!
Moore   [*to the nobles and officers*] Whiles they are o'er the bank of their obedience,
   Thus will they bear down all things.
Lincoln   [*to the prentices*] Shrieve Moore speaks. Shall we hear Shrieve Moore speak?
Doll   Let's hear him. A keeps a plentiful shrievaltry, and a made my brother, Arthur Watchins, Sergeant Safe's yeoman. Let's hear Shrieve Moore.
All   Shrieve Moore, Moore, Moore! Shrieve Moore!

The text as it is written, though, is much less clear. Shakespeare
– if this fragment is by him, and if it is representative of his usual
writing style – punctuated very lightly indeed and almost at
random.

Linc   Peace I say peace ar you men of Wisdome ~~ar~~ or what ar
          you
Surr   ~~But~~ what you will haue them but not men of Wisdome
all   weele not heare my L of Surrey, ~~all~~ no no no no no
          Shrewsbury shr
moor   whiles they ar ore the banck of their obedyenc
          thus will they bere downe all thing*es*
Linc   Shreiff moor speakes shall we heare shreef moor speake
Doll   Lett*es* heare him a keepes a plentyfull shrevaltry, and a
          made my Brother Arther watchin[s] Seriant Safes yeoman
          let*es* heare
          shreeve moore
all   Shreiue moor moor more Shreue moore[1]

In the passage above, the original text has two commas (after
'Surrey' and 'shrevaltry') and no full stops at all. There are also no
question-marks. The two commas, though positioned logically, are
absent from other places where they might be equally useful. The
capitalisation is slightly more explicable; it is used here for (some)
proper names and (some) nouns (at the time it was relatively normal
practice to capitalise nouns). Even then, however, the strategy that
determined which particular nouns should be singled out for capitalisation is obscure. So the first name 'Arthur' starts with a capital
letter, but not the surname 'watchin', the weighty term 'Wisdom' is
capitalised but not 'obedyenc', while 'Brother' and 'Serjant' are
selected for capitalisation when neither is particularly important. It
looks as though Shakespeare punctuated and capitalised more or
less according to whim.
    Much the same has to be said of Shakespeare's spelling prac-
tices. The last line in the passage above is spoken by 'all' (this
is what the massed crowd is meant to shout out) so its quirks
of spelling can hardly be supposed to suggest changes of accent
or pronunciation. Yet the spelling in that line is spectacularly vari-
able, for though it consists of only two words, 'shrieve' and 'Moore'
(the crowd is shouting out for sheriff Thomas Moore to come and
speak to them), each word is spelled in a variety of ways. 'Shrieve'

is rendered 'shreiue' or 'shreue', while the sentence before adds
another variant to the word, 'shreeve', and the sentence before
that presents two more: 'shreiff' and 'shreef'. As for what might
be taken to be a straightforward word, the name 'Moore', it has
three variant spellings simply within the one sentence spoken by
'all': 'moor', 'more' and 'moore'. Spelling had no fixed rules at
the time, but 'Shakespeare' is particularly wayward in his choices.

The punctuation and capitalisation to be found in early modern
printed texts, then, are unlikely to be authorial in origin. As will
be shown, it was normal for the scribe who might write a fair
copy of the author's rough draft to add punctuation of his own,
and for the compositors (typesetters) in the printing house to
impose their own punctuation on a text in the process of setting
the type. Some instances of textual uncertainty in the printed
plays of Shakespeare seem to relate to difficulties interpreting
punctuation in the underlying manuscripts. On occasion, two good
texts are printed in which the sense of the words is more or less
the same, but a choice of punctuation has altered the passage's
meaning.

Compare these two versions from 3.3 spoken by Iago in *Othello*,
one from the quarto (1622), one from the folio (1623). Both texts
are 'good', but both present their words in ways that alter the
meaning of the sentence:

> Good name in man and woman's deere my Lord;
> I[t]s the immediate Jewell of our soules:
> (Q G3b, 3.3.155–6)

That is to say, 'good name' is dear or 'precious' to man and
woman alike ('good name in man *and* woman's dear'), it is also
a jewel to our souls (Iago, who is speaking, probably means by
'our' himself and the addressee Cassio). Now follows the folio
(1623) version:

> Good name in Man, & woman (deere my Lord)
> Is the immediate Jewell of their Soules.
> (TLN 1768–9, 3.3.155–6)

Here 'dear' is attached to 'my lord': Iago reminds his dear lord
(Cassio) how important a jewel is 'good name' to men and women.
Both passages work, but each conveys a slightly different sense.

That word 'dear' is poised between the two: does it mean 'costly', as in passage one, or is it the chilling blandishment of passage two, where, as a phoney term of endearment for Cassio, it illustrates how Iago works his evil out of the language of love itself? Either way, the difference could be as much the result of variant punctuation as of variant text.

A similar problem besets the good quarto of *Hamlet* and the good folio version of that same play. The quarto (1604/5) has the following passage:

> What [a] peece of worke is a man, how noble in reason, how infinit in faculties, in forme and mooving, how expresse and admirable in action, how like an Angell in apprehension, how like a God.
>
> (Q2 F2a, 2.2.303–7)

The folio (1623) on the other hand, presents the passage like this:

> What a piece of worke is a man! how Noble in Reason? how infinit in faculty? in forme and moving how expresse and admirable? in Action, how like an Angel? in apprehension, how like a God?
>
> (TLN 1350–4, 2.2.303–7)

Passage two shows the commas towards the latter half of the text shifted a half-sentence along; the result is, again, a different meaning. Is man infinite in faculties *and* form *and* moving? Is he like an *angel* in apprehension? Or is he infinite in faculties, and express and admirable in form and moving? Is he like a *god* in apprehension? What is a modern editor to do faced with having to make a single text out of this? He or she has to choose one meaning, and, as a result, has to reject another – though the other might be the 'true' Shakespearean one. And, though textual notes to plays can easily point out editorial emendations to words, it is difficult to highlight altered commas, though the effect on meaning might be huge.

This chapter will explore what process plays went through from their inception to their first, 'foul paper', drafts, through scribal and actors' copies, to the printing house where they are turned into quartos and folios. The kinds of corrections, improvements and errors that result from the way texts were readied for 'production' as performance and printed text will be explored: even by the time of publication, Shakespeare's plays were considerably distanced from what he had written.

What a playwright first composed were his rough drafts or 'foul papers'. One or two of Shakespeare's foul-paper habits can be gleaned from looking at the *Thomas Moore* manuscript and at published texts of his thought to have been printed straight from draft. 'Shakespeare's' handwriting is not easy to read even by early modern standards, and his words are sometimes completely obscured by over-writing. There may, then, be errors in texts printed from Shakespeare's manuscripts that arise from misreadings of a difficult hand or from the fact that a worker in the printing house, unable to decipher a word, has substituted one of his own. After all, only concerned or invited playwrights might visit the printing house to proofread their texts, for plays belonged to the people who had paid for them in the Stationer's Register, not to their authors. In quartos 1 (1603) and 2 (1604/5) of *Hamlet*, the player's speech contains a reference to the 'mobled queen', a sentence that Polonius particularly likes (Q2 F4a, 2.2.504). But the word 'mobled' has no clear meaning. In the folio (1623) the word printed is 'inobled' (enobled) (TLN 1542), which at least makes some kind of sense (because the sentence remains obscure, some editors keep the word 'mobled' and attempt to provide meanings for it). Perhaps the letters 'i' and 'n' were written in a crabbed fashion in some of the manuscripts underlying *Hamlet*, a suggestion that becomes particularly important when considering the name 'Imogen', which exists only in Shakespeare's *Cymbeline*, and the name 'Innogen' which exists elsewhere. Is 'Imogen', as some editors believe, simply a misreading of Innogen?[2]

The *Thomas Moore* text, as discussed in Chapter 3, places the body of words to be spoken centre page, with the speech-prefixes roughly crammed into a space on the left hand side. Sometimes speech-prefixes do not quite match the start of the speaker's speech, indicating that, at any rate for a crowd scene, Shakespeare wrote the text first and put in the speech-prefixes later, creating a conversational babble, and then parcelling it out to different speakers. Possibly this is the reason why some characters are wrongly named in Shakespearean texts or are given floating names. For instance, Pistoll's wife in *Henry V* is called 'Nell' in Act 2, and 'Doll' in Act 5. In *Romeo and Juliet* there is some confusion between the Nurse's 'man', who is called Peter, and Romeo's 'man', who

is called at one stage 'boy', at another 'Balthazar', and at a third
also 'Peter'. Do Romeo and the Nurse share a man of uncertain
name? Does the same actor double as Romeo's man and the
Nurse's, the name being immaterial? Has Shakespeare written a
boy's part under the generic title of 'boy' and then later given
the character a couple of random names – leaving the tangled
problem for the prompter to sort out? Sometimes two different
'good' texts allot the same lines to different speakers – again,
maybe indicating a mind-change, or maybe indicating that
Shakespeare's wobbly designations were not obvious. In the first
'good' quarto of *Lear* (1608), Lear has this speech:

> Doth any here know me? Why, this is not *Lear*, doth *Lear*
> walke thus? speak thus? Where are his eyes, either his notion,
> weaknes [*sic*], or his discernings are lethargie, sleeping, or
> waking; ha? sure, tis no so, who is it that can tell me who I
> am? *Lears* shadow? I would learne that . . .
>
> (Q D1b, 1.4.226–32)

In the folio version Lear and the Fool have this dialogue:

Lear   Do's any heere know me?
    This is not *Lear*.
    Do's *Lear* walke thus? Speake thus? Where are his eies?
    Either his Notion weakens, his Discernings
    Are Lethargied. Ha! Waking? 'Tis not so?
    Who is it that can tell me who I am?
Fool   *Lears* shadow.
Lear   Your name, faire Gentlewoman?
                    (TLN 740–5, 1.4.226–32)

A mind-change? Quite possibly. But the continuous text of the
quarto might equally indicate that Shakespeare had not indicated
whether one or two people were speaking in the manuscript underlying the text. Either way makes a profound difference to the sense
of the passage. In the monologue Lear querulously asks whether he
is simply a shadow of the old Lear. In the dialogue he questions
who he is and is given as an external answer something he has not
dared to confront: that he is just the shadow of what he was.

    Completed foul papers seem often – but not always – to have
been written out again in 'fair' copy, either by the author himself

or by a playhouse scribe. This neat or 'fair copy' became the play-house 'book' (the version used by the prompter) unless the foul papers themselves were used for the 'book' instead. If a scribe were responsible for the rewriting, then he will have done more than simply copy the text: his job was to make sense out of a confusing script, and that will have included adding more punctuation, and, perhaps, supplying obviously missing stage directions, such as exits.

One of the scribes who worked for the King's Men was called Ralph Crane. His writing habits can be learned by looking at extant manuscripts that he penned (none, unfortunately, is Shakespearean), and by examining printed texts known to be set from his scripts. Crane-written plays are easy to identify, even through printed texts, because they supply what are known as 'massed entrances'. That is to say that, rather than include actors' entrances at the point in the scene at which they happened, he 'massed' or gathered all entrances at the top of the scene. This he seems to have learned while he was scribe to Ben Jonson, who liked to present his texts in 'literary' rather than playing form: 'massed entrances' work badly theatrically, but give a text the same physical appearance as a classical text published to be read rather than performed. It may be that Crane was especially commissioned by the printing house preparing the folio to rewrite messy or unreadable playbooks neatly, treating them as he had treated Ben Jonson's. It may be that the Crane manuscripts reached the printing house by other means (perhaps 'scribal copies', made for friends or patrons, were acquired for the publication of Shakespeare's folio). Folio texts with 'massed entrances' are *Two Gentlemen*, *Merry Wives* and *Winter's Tale*. So *Merry Wives* in folio (1623) begins

> *Enter Justice Shallow, Slender, Sir Hugh Evans, Master Page, Falstoffe, Bardolph, Nym, Pistoll, Anne Page, Mistresse Ford, Mistresse Page, Simple.*
>
> (TLN 1–3)

The quarto (1602) to that same play, on the other hand, begins with only the characters who are in fact to be on stage at the opening of the play – '*Enter Justice* Shallow, *Syr* Hugh, *Maister* Page, *and* Slender'. As 'massed entrance' texts are obviously difficult to act from, it is likely that Crane massed entrances only when he was writing a copy to be read rather than performed.

But if the text behind *Merry Wives* in folio is a gift or 'presentation copy' rather than a theatrical copy, might it contain other consciously 'literary' features? How should we think of such a text, with the hand of Crane lying so heavily upon it? What else might the scribe have altered?

The completed scribal manuscript, if one were made for the theatre, was then handed over to the prompter for further additions and alterations. The prompter would add to the text any missing entrances and exits and would often, additionally, indicate when actors were to be gathered in the tiring-house some lines in advance of their actual entrance. He did not expect anyone else to have dealings with his book however, so he wrote in a form he understood – he was under no obligation to have a system that an outsider could comprehend. Signs that a printed text may originate with the prompter include 'early' (reminder) entrances, and moments when a real actor's name is used instead of the name of the character he is playing (the prompter is more keen to know who is to be on stage at a certain point, than to know his character's stage-name). Examples include the second quarto *Romeo and Juliet's* 'enter Will Kempe' (Q2 K3b) for the Nurse's man Peter, that character of the questionable name. The prompter would also, if he could, be specific where the author is vague. Authors have a tendency to favour the fiction of the story over the practicalities of the playhouse; an author is likely to write 'enter gentleman on the walls of Rome', while a prompter is more likely to write 'enter above'. Indeed, clues of this nature help editors identify the lost text that lies behind a printed one. Where an author may give the vague 'enter . . . others as many as can be' (*Titus Andronicus*, Q A4a–b, 1.1 72, thought to have been set from foul papers), a prompter is likely to specify the number of spare people he can muster at this point in the acting. Specificity of numbers is said to be another sign of a prompter's book.[3]

Technically, the prompter was also supposed to remove dubious bits of text such as swear words and overtly political statements. And then he was supposed to hand this 'corrected' book (or another scribal copy of it) over to the authorities for 'approval'. At that time no play could be performed without being sanctioned first by the Master of the Revels, whose job was to ensure that nothing too seditious or blasphemous was played on the stage. So the Master of the Revels himself would also make his own amendments to the text, censoring bits he disapproved of, before returning the play to the theatre. The prompter would then either hand the 'improved' text back to the scribe to be written into actors' parts, or write the parts out himself – perhaps a bit of both. That, technically, was what was supposed to happen, though sometimes the order of events became a little muddled. One Master of the Revels, Henry Herbert (brother of the poet George Herbert), writes an angry note to the prompter for the King's Men in 1633, Edward Knight, whom he criticises for not having sufficiently 'purged' the submitted book. Herbert suggests extra amendments to be made to the text and to the parts that the prompter has rashly already distributed amongst the actors: 'Mr. Knight, In many things you have saved mee labour; yet wher your judgment or penn fayld you, I have made boulde to use mine. Purge ther parts, as I have the booke . . .'[4]

To summarise: the playwright's foul papers may have been written up in fair copy by a scribe who would then also have made 'scribal' alterations to the text; the neat text will have been given to the prompter who would have made prompter's alterations as well as censoring the play – and possibly both; that censored, scribal text will have been given to the Master of the Revels for final censoring and corrections before the play was returned to the playhouse and the actors' parts were created. In other words, even by the time actors received their parts, the text could be far removed from what the author had written. In the theatre, it was the authority of the practical men, the punctuators and the censurers, that mattered. Any Shakespeare text that can be traced to a prompter's book has already been repeatedly mediated by other hands.

A really successful play might survive longer than a year on stage. If that were the case, however, it would undergo a number of changes during that process. It might be cut down to be performed by the reduced, touring fragment of the company that did the rounds most summers when plague – *a* plague, if not *the* plague – caused London theatres to be closed. When actors were forced to go on 'peregrinations', temporary London players ('hired men') would be dropped, for strolling was a time of meagre salary for the actors; only the permanent sharers who had a financial stake in the company would perform regularly over the summer. Plays would therefore have to be reshaped. Minor characters might be abandoned or melded to form more major characters; extra doubling of parts would mean a change of entrances and exits; and, in general, travelling plays, which were shown to a less sophisticated audience, were kept shorter than non-travelling ones. One of the reasons why there are sometimes good texts in variant forms could be that one is for a travelling performance – this has been put forward as a possible explanation for the two versions of *King Lear*. Some 'bad' texts that are noticeably 'simpler' than their good counterparts, such as quarto 1 (1603) of *Hamlet*, may, amongst other forms of corruption, also preserve 'travelling' versions of plays.[5]

Even a play not adapted for strolling would be altered as topics of current interest changed: plays had a very short life in their first form. Often they have removable fragments of local gossip and in-jokes, as Chapter 2 showed. Themes of 'equivocation' which became modish at the time of the Gunpowder Plot (1605), as did the word itself, work their way into the porter's jokes in *Macbeth* ('Much Drinke may be said to be an Equivocator', TLN 773, 2.3.34). The first Gravedigger in *Hamlet* sends the second off to fetch 'a stoup of liquor' from a very un-Danish-sounding man of the name of 'Yaughan' – presumably the Welsh name 'Ewan' is intended (TLN 3250, 5.1.60). Yaughan is never mentioned again: the man was perhaps a tavern-keeper operating in or near the Globe, and this may be a local joke to the audience. Banks's celebrated dancing horse Marocco who could add numbers together and stamp out the product, is mentioned in *Love's Labour's Lost*: 'how easie it is to put yeres to the word three, and study three yeeres in two words, the dancing horse will tell you' (TLN 358–60, 1.2.51–4). Jokes, of course, stale quickly, and the subjects of jokes do not last. So a play would be regularly refreshed with the addition of new and topical references; were it to prove really popular, then it might also undergo a fuller revision between one season and another.

There is one practical reason why specific texts reflecting a particular point in time have survived. A discarded one-off text, or some foul-papers left over after the fair copy is made, would not necessarily be thrown away, for paper was expensive. They would, more likely, be kept as reserves in case something happened to the current theatrical book. Perhaps that is how some foul papers ended up at printers' shops for publication years after they were written. Similarly, when a book needed to be so thoroughly overhauled that it was written out again, the first copy too might end up at the printing house.

In other words, most 'good' quarto texts printed in Shakespeare's lifetime were good-but-outdated forms of plays – texts that someone had given up on in favour of a better, neater, or more modern version. So it is that quartos might have a lineage traceable either to foul papers or to the prompter's book, but relating either way to an earlier version of the play than that on stage at the time they were printed.

Once a text has been published, though, the playhouse might be tempted to use it even if it were slightly outdated: a printed text is neater and easier to read than a scribal copy, and also easier to replace. So what seems to have happened is that sometimes the playhouse would acquire the 'good' printed quarto for its prompter's book, but then supplement it in manuscript with all the additions that had subsequently been made to the play, plus prompt-markings. The printed text, with manuscript additions, becomes the playhouse's 'book'. This seems to be what has happened in the case of *Romeo and Juliet*, for which there is one 'bad' quarto, one 'good' quarto and a 'good' folio text. The 'good' quarto seems to have been used as a theatrical book on which manuscript additions were made, and the resultant text, though lost, appears to be behind what is printed in the folio. Folio *Romeo and Juliet* reproduces much of the spelling and lineation of the quarto – always revealing in a world in which there were no overall spelling rules – but contains some additional segments of text not present in the quarto.

Once a text, in whatever form, made it to the printing house, it was prepared for publication. This meant that it was marked out and the number of words that could be printed on each page was calculated – a process called casting off (or counting) copy. Copy had to be predetermined in this way, as books were generally not printed in the order in which they are bound and read ('seriatim') but were instead printed by 'formes'. This meant that the way the paper was to be folded would determine which pages were printed in which order on the sheet. To make a quarto, a sheet of paper would be folded twice after printing, which meant that pages 1, 4, 5, and 8 were all printed on the 'outer' forme (one side of the sheet), and pages 2, 3, 6, and 7 were printed on the inner forme (the other side of the sheet). To make a folio a sheet of paper had to be folded only once, but the way the 1623 folio was bound was that three sheets of paper were folded in half and interleaved, creating a 'quire' of six leaves (so twelve printed sides) – meaning that sheet one would have pages 1 and 12 on the outer forme and 2 and 11 on the inner forme; sheet two

would have 3 and 10 on the outer forme and 4 and 9 on the
inner forme; sheet three would have 5 and 8 on the outer forme,
and 6 and 7 on the inner forme. Instructions for the binder were
always printed on each sheet to indicate in what order the book
should be put together. A sign – generally a letter – was put at
the bottom of each quire, and the binder would set groups of
pages 'A' next to 'B' next to 'C'. Another binder's help was the
'catchword' at the bottom of each page which gave the first word
of the next page. This, too, helped the binder be sure that he was
placing pages in the right order.

Pages were set out of reading order – partly so that more than
one compositor could work on a play at once and partly so that (if
necessary because of shortage of type) one forme could be printed
and the type distributed before the pages to appear on the other
side of the sheet were set. But this affected the approach to the text.
A compositor setting, say, pages 1 and 12 for one sheet, while the
person next to him was composing, say, pages 3 and 10, could not
print either more or less of the manuscript text than had been designated for each page. Hence casting off copy (working out
how many pages it would fill) was a skilled business and any mis-
calculation simply had to be dealt with. The 1623 folio has pages
trying to compensate for too much or too little text in ways that
sometimes change the sense of the text itself. Peter Blayney explains
that if the compositor was still having difficulties with the layout of
his page after having added or removed space from around headings and stage directions, he would start to alter the text itself – as
happened in the case of *Much Ado About Nothing*. Comparison with
the quarto text (1600) shows that, on the overcrowded last folio
(1623) page of the play, the sentence 'heere comes the Prince and
Claudio', spoken just before a stage direction for the entrance of
those characters, has been removed. In straitened circumstances, it
would seem, the compositor thought bits of the play itself disposable. Similarly, where the quarto has 'They swore that you were
almost sick for me', 'they swore that you were wel-nye dead for me'
(Q I4a), the folio leaves out both instances of the word 'that' so that
the verse sentences will not spill over and use up the next line,
despite the fact that, as a result, the rhythm of the iambic
pentameter has been corrupted. Contractions are used throughout
the page, stage directions are crammed into the end of lines of
speech, even the 'finis' at the close of the play is in the line where
the catchword is supposed to be.[6]

Compositorial space problems may, too, have led to an awkward moment in the folio text (there is no other) of *Antony and Cleopatra*. A cramped page for 5.2 gives Proculeius two consecutive speech-prefixes (each is headed 'Pro'):

Cleo   Pray you tell him,
    I am his Fortunes Vassall, and I send him
    The Greatnesse he has got. I hourely learne
    A Doctrine of Obedience, and would gladly
    Looke him i'th'Face.
Pro   This ile report (deere Lady)
    Have comfort, for I know your plight is pittied
    Of him that caus'd it.
Pro   You see how easily she may be surpriz'd:
    Guard her till Caesar come.
                (TLN 3233–42, 5.2.27–36)

Proculeius addresses Cleopatra, the 'deere Lady', in the first speech, in the second his attention is on the guard; his manner of address between one speech and the other is also radically different. A bit of text appears to have been left out. Is a stage direction missing? Or – given that there is a half-line of verse before the capture and a complete one after it – could a half-line speech (possibly spoken by Cleopatra) have been edited away for space reasons?

In folio (1623) *King Lear*, the reverse appears to have happened and the compositor seems to have added some verbal padding to bulk out a section lacking sufficient words as Blayney points out. On the page in question which covers 4.7, various measures have been made to swell the text. Some complete lines of verse are printed as two half-lines so that they take up more room; gaps have been put above and below stage directions. But in addition there is a telling verbal difference on this page from the equivalent moment of play in the quarto (1608). In quarto Lear says that he is

    . . . a very foolish fond old man,
    Fourescore and upward, and to deale plainly
    I feare I am not in my perfect mind
                (Q K2b, 4.7.58–62)

A 'score' is 'twenty', so fourscore is eighty; fourscore and upward is therefore eighty-plus-a-little. In the folio (1623), however, Lear says he is (in broken verse)

> . . . a very foolish fond old man,
> Fourescore and upward,
> Not an houre more, nor lesse:
> And to deale plainely,
> I feare I am not in my perfect mind.
> (TLN 2824–18, 4.7.58–62)

How can Lear be neither an hour more nor less than an unde-fined number, eighty-something? The phrase 'not an hour more nor less' is senseless, and there is a strong suspicion that it originates in the printing house as a text-enhancing device.[7]

The people responsible for picking up the pieces of type and setting them were known as 'compositors'. They had in front of them two large trays or 'cases', the top one of which contained the pieces of type for capital letters, and the bottom one of which contained the type for small letters and for spaces. These days, capitals are still sometimes called 'upper-case letters' and small letters 'lower-case letters' because of the position they once occu-pied in the compositors' two type-cases. Holding a 'composing' stick that corresponded in width to the width of the line of type to be set, a compositor would pick up the requisite letters and spaces and fit them in, adding letters and spaces until he had made a tightly fitting line of type. On top of this he would set another line of type. When he had composed four or five lines of type, he would transfer them on to the 'galley', a wooden tray that would ultimately hold the full page of type. He would continue in this way until the galley was full and a whole page had been set. Naturally the very composing process affects what is printed.

The compositor was the Renaissance version of a touch-typist: he could have a manuscript at his side and, whilst keeping his eyes fixed on it, pick up the right pieces of type without looking at what he was doing. He set type every day, and had developed a 'feel' for the thickness of each letter and the position of each compartment in his type-case. But just as a good touch-typist still makes spelling errors, so a good compositor might still, on occasion, pick a letter out of the wrong section – usually the compartment next to the one he was aiming at. Equally, he might,

j			ae	oe	e		s						fl	fl
'	b	c	d		e		i	ſ	f	g	ſh		ſſ	ff
&													ſi	fi
ct	l	m	n	h			o	y	p	q	w			?
;													en	em
z	v	u	t	space			a	r	,	:		quad		
x									.	-				

Figure 7.1 Based, with grateful thanks, on the picture of Moxon's lower type case from Joseph Moxon, *Mechanick Exercises on the Whole Art of Printing* (1683), as supplied by David Bolton on his website http://members.aol.com/alembicprs/selcase.htm

when breaking up a printed page, 'distribute' a piece of type into the wrong compartment – usually, again, adjacent to the one intended. So there are common compositors' errors to look out for in Renaissance texts, though to spot them requires a sense of the layout of the compositors' boxes. Figure 7.1 shows a compositor's lower case of type (there were, of course, further cases that compositors used for italic type and for letters of different sizes). Two letters are shown when both occupy a single piece of type; 'ſ' represents a 'long s'; 'en' and 'em' are spaces the width of a letter 'n' and a letter 'm' respectively; 'k' is absent as it was placed amongst the capitals and numbers in the upper case box.

One compositors' error in the folio is in *Richard II*. Again, as there is also a quarto for that play, it is possible to see what the correct reading should be. The folio gives 'White Beares have arm'd their thin and hairelesse Scalps / Against thy Majestie' (TLN 1470–1, 3.2.112–13), as though a series of polar bears have joined the uprising against Richard II. The quarto provides the more reasonable 'White beards have armed their thin and hairless scalpes . . .' (Q F2a), where 'white beards' are 'old men'. Probably the folio compositor's hand has slipped into the 'e' box, which is next to the 'd' box. Similarly, Lear in quarto one is confronted by his daughters who ask the need why he should travel with so many men. He answers 'O reason not the deed'. The folio has what makes more sense at this point:

Gonoril   Heare me my Lord;
What need you five and twenty? Ten? Or five?

    To follow in a house, where twice so many
    Have a command to tend you?
Regan   What need one?
Lear   O reason not the need . . .
               (TLN 1559–64, 2.4.260–4)

Again, the 'n' box is next to the 'd' box, and, as both letters are
of a similar thickness, the compositor will not have 'felt' his mistake.
    Unlike a touch-typist, however, a compositor did not have
access to an infinite quantity of letters. Only when a full forme
had been printed could the type be 'broken up' and 'distributed'
back into the compositors' cases. In the meantime, the more type
a hard-working compositor set, the less he had to choose from.
As the compositor's stock of type dwindled, so his punctuation
and spelling habits would change. Extra 'e's on the ends of words
might go; punctuation might become lighter. For years people
wondered at the logic of the questions in this passage from the
quarto (1600) of *The Merchant of Venice*.

[Jewe]   if you deny it, let the danger light
      upon your charter and your Citties freedome?
      Youle aske me why I rather choose to have
      a weight of carrion flesh, then to receave
      three thousand ducats: Ile not aunswer that?
      But say it is my humour, is it aunswerd?
      What if my house be troubled with a Rat,
      and I be pleasd to give ten thousand ducats
      to have it baind? what, are you answered yet?
      Some men there are love not a gaping pigge?
      Some that are mad if they behold a Cat?
      . . .
Bass.   This is not aunswer thou unfeeling man,
      to excuse the currant of thy cruelty?
Jewe.   I am not bound to please thee with my answers?
Bass.   Doe all men kill the things they doe not love?
Jewe.   Hates any man the thing he would not kill?
Bass.   Every offence is not a hate at first?
Jewe.   What wouldst thou have a serpent sting thee twice?
               (Q G3b, 4.1.38–70)

Shylock and Bassanio have gone question-mad: all their questions are questioned back, all their statements are queried. What has sent two strong characters into such a flurry of uncertainty? Is the profusion of question marks here an acting note? No, for most of these 'questions' are obviously in fact statements. What has happened in this passage is that the compositor has run low on full stops (periods). His problem is that he has placed full-stops after speech-headings – but has not had the quantity of type for punctuation that such stop-heavy printing demands. Lacking the stops to sustain the passage of dialogue, the compositor has opted to use the next mark of punctuation along – the question mark. The punctuation here has little to do with the manuscript play or the punctuation desires of the printer, it simply reflects a printing house deficiency. The same may be behind the *King Lear* quarto's choice of the term 'Bastard' as opposed to 'Edmund' in the quarto speech-prefix and stage directions for that character. Often thought to be a weighted description of the nature of the man, his 'bastard' birth somehow shaping the person that Edmund is, the designation may equally reflect a printer's necessity. The capital italic 'E' is a letter much required in printed playtexts for the words 'Enter' and 'Exit'; in *Lear*, which also has a character called 'Edgar', italic 'E' will have been in great demand, and possibly the use of 'Bastard' was a way of preserving it.

The compositor was encouraged to improve the punctuation and spelling of the text in front of him. Compositors in William Jaggard's printing house (where Shakespeare's folio was set) specifically claimed, in 1622, that they would not be 'so madly disposed to tye themselves' to the spelling errors in Ralphe Brooke's manuscript book; had they 'given him leave to print his owne English . . . hee would (they say) have made his Reader, as good sport . . . as ever Tarleton did his Audience, in a Clownes part'.[8] Blindly following the manuscript in front of you without thinking was hazardous, though it did happen. In the quarto (and folio – set from quarto) text of *Love's Labour's Lost* there is a section where each of Berowne's speeches begins with an 'O'. Even at first glance these 'O's look extraordinary, and it is difficult to explain why Shakespeare has opted for rhetorical trickery of this kind. Is he giving the sophisticated Berowne a reserve that will contrast with the chattiness of the clown? The informality of the content of the dialogue strongly argues against that reading. Here is the passage exactly as it looks in the quarto, where Costard's speech-prefix varies between 'Cost' and 'Clow' ('Clown'), and Berowne's speech-prefix remains fixed at 'Ber'. The speech-prefixes are the clue to what seems to have happened in the printing house.

> *Enter Berowne.*
> *Ber.*   O my good knave *Costard,* exceedingly well met.
> *Clow.*   Pray you sir, How much Carnation Ribbon may
>   a man buy for a remuneration?
> *Ber.*   O what is a remuneration?
> *Cost.*   Marie sir, halfepennie farthing.
> *Ber.*   O, why then threefarthing worth of Silke.
> *Cost.*   I thanke your worship, God be wy you.
> *Ber.*   O stay slave, I must employ thee.
>   As thou wilt win my favour, good my knave,
>   Do one thing for me that I shall intreate.
> *Clow.*   When would you have it done sir?
> *Ber.*   O this after-noone.
> *Clow.*   Well, I will do it sir: Fare you well.
> *Ber.*   O thou knowest not what it is.
> *Clow.*   I shall know sir when I have done it.
> (Q D1a-b, 3.1.144–58)

It would seem that, in the manuscript behind this passage, Berowne's speech-prefix (here 'Ber.') has in fact been written 'Bero', but the compositor has misunderstood the 'o' as the start of Berowne's speeches. The compositor has been faithful to the manuscript but without bringing his own logic to bear on it.

Sometimes textual difficulties originate with the pieces of type – or even the inking. For years many thought that Ferdinand had a strange speech at the end of *The Tempest*. He has been granted what above all things he desired – Miranda's hand in marriage – but after Prospero has shown him a 'majestical vision', he appears to say

> Let me live here ever,
> So rare a wondred Father, and a wise
> Makes this place Paradise.
> (TLN 1785–7, 4.1.122–4)

How surprising, thought commentators, that Ferdinand wants to stay on the island because of the wonders and wisdom of his gruff father-in-law, rather than his lovely bride. But the word is not in fact 'wise' but 'wife' with the integument on the 'f' broken off leaving the letter resembling a long 's'. 'So rare a wondred Father, and a *wife* / Makes this place Paradise.' Another example occurs in *Antony and Cleopatra* where Cleopatra appears to say that death 'rids our dogs of languish' (TLN 3249, 5.2.41). 'Anguish' would undoubtedly make more obvious sense in this context, and what seems to have happened is that a space (which was also a piece of type) has been accidentally inked. Other instances do not seem to be resolvable. If long 's' and 'f' are confusable, how much more confusable are the letters that were used reversibly, such as 'u' and 'v' and 'i' and 'j'. So a word such as 'loud' in an uncertain context could conceivably represent 'loud' or 'lov'd'. Almost always, the context identifies the word intended, but there is a famous confusion resulting from i/j uncertainty in *Othello*. In 5.2 the folio has Othello, learning too late that the wife he killed was innocent, compare himself to

> . . . one, whose hand
> (Like the base Iudean) threw a Pearle away
> Richer then all his Tribe.
> (TLN 3657–9, 5.2.346–8)

In the quarto (1622) for that same passage he views himself as

> one whose hand,
> Like the base *Indian*, threw a pearle away,
> Richer then all his Tribe:
> (Q2 N2a, 5.2.346–8)

I or J for the first letter? And for the second letter, a 'u' or an 'n' (is one set upside-down by the compositor by mistake?) Or what? Indian or Judean? Or is the analogy a metaphorical one, in which case might the 'Judean' refer not so much to the Jews as to Judas, the cast-away pearl being Jesus? As no one yet has suggested an unambiguous source for the story of the man who threw a pearl away richer than all his tribe, there is no way to answer that question. Editors must simply make their own decision when preparing a text for this play.

When compositors did not copy blindly they imposed on the text their own individual habits of spelling and punctuation. This is very clear in the folio, which is set by up to eight different compositors, called by modern commentators A, B, C, D, E, F, G, H. Experts who study the folio's printing history can identify which page of which text was set by which compositor by recognising the compositors' spelling habits. For instance 'B' favours spelling the word 'do' 'doe', the word 'here' 'here', and the word 'dear' 'deare'. 'A' on the other hand, favours 'do', 'heere' and 'deere'.[9] Compositor 'E' working on the folio was probably apprentice to compositor 'B', as is suggested by the fact that 'E' has the same spelling quirks as 'B', but makes a lot more errors. 'E''s text has to be proofed and corrected (some of his proofed pages are bound into surviving folio texts – paper was too expensive to waste); no other compositor's texts seem to have been proofed in this way. Interestingly, the Jaggard printing house that was setting the folio at the time had a new apprentice compositor whose name was John Leason: was he 'E'?

So, the process of setting a play in the printing house puts the original text at one further remove. In addition, the printed texts themselves were prepared variously as quartos and folios and had differing concerns for accuracy (remember that as part of their sales pitch Heminges and Condell dismiss any previously published Shakespeare plays as not just stolen but 'maimed'). Quartos aimed at a readership of literate people prepared to pay a 'tester' (sixpence) to read a play – the price of an expensive seat at the Globe or a cheap seat at Blackfriars; the imposing folio was available only to those with fifteen shillings to a pound to spare.[10] The folio has been carefully designed so that it has coherence as a book. The first play, *The Tempest*, begins with 'a tempestuous noise of Thunder and Lightening', and the last play, *Cymbeline*, ends with 'such a Peace'. But in giving *Mr. William Shakespeares Comedies, histories & tragedies* its internal consistency and pleasing form, how greatly have the plays been altered?

The division of the folio into tragedies, histories and comedies, it was suggested in Chapter 3, placed plays in certain categories: that categorisation may also have necessitated the changing of play-titles to fit them into the system. During Shakespeare's lifetime, the play called in the folio *Henry VIII* and situated amongst the history plays was, in at least one of its manifestations, called *All Is True*, for that play was in performance when the first Globe theatre burnt down and its topic and title appear in letters and gossip of the time.[11]

Quarto titles to plays published while Shakespeare was alive presumably show the name of the play at that point in time. As against the folio designations, the quarto of *King Lear* is *M. William Shak-speare: His True Chronicle Historie of the life and death of King Lear and his three Daughters*, suggesting that Shakespeare called the play a 'history' rather than a 'tragedy', while *Richard III* is, in quarto, not just a 'tragedy', but *The Tragedy of King Richard the third. Containing, His treacherous Plots against his brother Clarence: the pittiefull murther of his innocent nephewes: his tyrannicall usurpation: with the whole course of his detested life, and most deserved death.* This title probably reflects the playbills that were hung up on posts around town to advertise the day's performance, while the folio displays the result of dividing plays into generic groups: *Richard III* is historical, and must therefore be a history play. But this is to muffle the tragic dimension of *Richard III*, overshadowing what may have been deeper underlying complications. 'History' is linear and goes on reaching forward through time to touch the head of the present monarch; 'tragedy' usually comes to an end with the death of the protagonist. By calling a play a 'tragedy' something permanent and irrevocable about its ending is implied that is lost in calling it a history. What else might folio logic have done to impose order on to a series of disparate texts? In fact, in the folio the designation for *Richard III* remains confused, for the play's actual title in the 'Catalogue' is 'the Life and Death of Richard the Third' which is also its 'running title' (the title that is placed along the top of each page). Calling the play 'the life and death' has the effect of making the death of Richard an important feature of what the play is about (imagine what a difference it would make if *Lear* were called 'the life and death of King Lear', the tragic close of the story already within the play as it opens). Does this title reflect what the play was called in one of its later manifestations? The heading for *Richard III* on its first page in the folio itself is, again, 'The Tragedy' (rather than history) 'of Richard the Third: with the Landing of Earle Richmond, and the Battell at Bosworth Field'. The final scene, the battle, is singled out, but the fact that Richard dies there is not the issue.

These variant titles – varied even within one text – provide examples of the unfixed and changeable nature of every aspect of a play from its name onwards. Early references show that many of Shakespeare's compositions swiftly became named after their protagonists even if their original titles had been more adventurous: *Twelfth Night* was commonly called *Malvolio*; indeed, Charles II's second folio Shakespeare survives, and in it the King has crossed out the heading *Twelfth Night* and substituted *Malvolio* as an alternative title. *All's Well that Ends Well* was known to Robert Burton as 'Benedicte and Betteris'.[12] And yet the choice of named character for a title will itself dictate, slightly, the way the audience sees a play – compare titles such as *Antony and Cleopatra* and *Romeo and Juliet*, both of which equally name two characters as protagonists, with titles such as *Othello* (rather than Othello and Desdemona) or *Macbeth* (rather than Macbeth and Lady Macbeth). If the play changes its title to reflect audience perception, as appears to be the case with *Malvolio*, then that too is illuminating, indicating that what stood out from the *Twelfth Night* comedy was its one tragic figure.

From content to title texts were fashioned by concerns brought about by the size and nature of the book in which they were published, and the context that book was conceived to have. The folio may have 'Mr William Shakespeare' as part of its title; quarto editions of Shakespeare's plays, published, some of them, before either Shakespeare or 'authorship' was particularly prized, are often printed without any authorial designation (Shakespeare is not named on any quarto title page until *Love's Labour's Lost* of 1598). The mediation that shapes the look and content of a book, however, does not stop in Shakespeare's time. A modern editor is generally concerned to produce an edition that will fit into a series – and each series has values of its own. Those values will determine the page size and quality, typeface and binding of the book. A series will also have certain demands – that spelling and punctuation should be modernised, that notes should be provided etc. Finally, modern editors have to deal with the printing house texts of Shakespeare's plays as we have them. Some texts are folio only; others exist both in folio and quarto. Not all quartos offer substantially different texts from the folio – but some do. When there are good-but-variant quartos and folios, it is still common policy for an editor to combine the two, which makes reading sense – most people do not want to read what is roughly the same play twice. It also ensures that the reader gets as much 'Shakespeare' as possible out of one reading. But it also produces a superimposition of all available texts one upon the other and is thus as far away as possible from what Shakespeare wrote at any one time.

8
Epilogue

The folio title of one of Shakespeare's later plays, *Cymbeline: King of Britain*, relates directly to recent historical events. 'Britain' was a new concept or, rather, an old concept revisited: the word had come into prominence after the Scottish King James came to the throne in 1603. Not only was it a weighted term, then; even the notion of a greater unified country was one that was open for exploration. Substituting 'Britain' where 'England' might more obviously be expected became a loaded joke, aired by Shakespeare also in his play *King Lear*, a story about a king who divides his united country into three distinct pieces. In *Lear*, the other half of the phrase 'fie, foh, and fumme', is completed not with 'I smell the blood of an English man', as the fairytale dictates, but 'I smell the blood of a Brittish man' (TLN 1967–8, 1.4.183–4). The fact of 'Britain' was a feature of Shakespeare's life from 1603 onwards, and Shakespeare's plays repeatedly harp on it. Yet the 'Britain' jokes are not exactly *about* the history of the time in which Shakespeare lived; rather, they are a product of it. Shakespeare responded to the events surrounding him; to understand his surroundings better is to understand better what he wrote.

Reading an old play in a modern edition, it is easy to lose more than just a sense of history or a sense of theatre. The reader can lose   or never gather – the oddly contingent facts about national and local life, circumstances of performance and personnel that defined the plays during their early productions and that fashioned the way they were written in the first place. Shakespeare was constantly affected by the conditions under which he wrote; if 'He was not of an age, but for all time!', yet he was *from* an age, and the timelessness of some of his utterances must be balanced by the contemporary rootedness of others.[1]

Given that any surviving play is at a remove from what Shakespeare was creating – a text to be spoken on the stage, not to be printed – the 'Shakespeare' that is bought in a modern bookshop is very different from anything the playwright might have anticipated. But as *Making Shakespeare* has argued, it is not different simply because 'performance' would have supplied a visual dimension absent on the printed page. The very layout and building of the stage itself provided, for an audience trained to look at playhouses in a particular way, a manner of 'reading' the performance, in which place of entrance and exit were part of what a play was saying, and props and music had symbolic ramifications that cannot be instantly interpreted now as they could in Shakespeare's day. Early modern London too has been shown to be part of the plays written to be performed there, as have the particular actors for whom roles were specifically composed. Players worked their habits, their body-types and their performances in other plays into every production they mounted. This book has attempted to highlight and elucidate the extent to which place, people and props – the physical and material context in which plays were performed – were elements of the way a play was interpreted and of the statements it made.

The textual as well as physical production of plays has also been considered, and they have been presented as assemblages of different parts – prologues, epilogues, songs, letters, actors' speeches – rather than as consistent, tightly unified 'whole' texts. Factors which Shakespeare embraced and which in turn moulded his writing are shown to be not additional to the plays but deeply embedded within them.

For these reasons, Shakespeare the man has not been particularly addressed, not because he is not important but because he is not all-important. 'Decentring' textual authority, both by pointing out that it is not there, and by redistributing it more broadly around the various people who put together a published playtext, reopens, excitingly, questions about what 'Shakespeare' really can be said to be. For too long his plays have been treated as sacrosanct and fixed in ways that patronise the fluidity of his working pattern, and exclude the excitingly collaborative nature of his writing. Seeing Shakespeare's plays in production in playhouse and printing house, raises new questions about the construction – the making – of 'Shakespeare'. Most important of all, it forces us to ask what the study of that phenomenon ought to involve.

Notes

Chapter 1

1 David Scott Kastan, *Shakespeare After Theory*, London and New York: Routledge, 1999, 16.

2 Other important contributors to the revision movement include Steven Urkowitz, John Kerrigan and Randall McLeod (who, as an illustration of textual indeterminacy, sometimes writes under the name 'Random Cloud'). E. A. J. Honigmann's *The Stability of Shakespeare's Text*, London: Edward Arnold, 1965, considered Shakespeare as a reviser in ways that came to be of concern in the 1980s – its title 'stability' rather than 'instability' had probably prevented its coming to prominence previously. In the wake of these accounts other important books were written: Grace Ioppolo wrote *Revising Shakespeare*, Cambridge, MA: Harvard University Press, 1991; Thomas Clayton edited *The Hamlet First Published (Q1, 1603): Origins, Form, Intertextualities*, Newark: University of Delaware Press, 1992; and John Jones produced *Shakespeare at Work*, Oxford: Clarendon Press, 1995.

3 Brian Vickers shows to what extent co-authorship was usual in his *Shakespeare Co-author*, Oxford: Oxford University Press, 2003, combining a variety of methodologies to determine the co-authorship of five Shakespeare plays. Other recent and important contributions to the field include Jonathan Hope's *The Authorship of Shakespeare's Plays*, Cambridge: Cambridge University Press, 1994; Gordon McMullan's *The Politics of Unease in the Plays of John Fletcher*, Amherst, MA: Studies in Early Modern Culture, 1994; and Jeffrey Masten's *Textual Intercourse*, Cambridge: Cambridge University Press, 1997.

4 'What Is a Text?' was written by Stephen Orgel in *Research Opportunities in Renaissance Drama*, 24, 1981, 3–6. The whole division of Shakespeare texts into 'good' and 'bad' was questioned and redefined by Paul Werstine in 'Narratives about Printed Shakespeare Texts: "Foul Papers" and "Bad" Quartos', *Shakespeare Quarterly*, 41, 1990, 65–86, and by Laurie Maguire in *Shakespearean Suspect Texts: The 'Bad' Quartos and their Contexts*, Cambridge: Cambridge University Press, 1996.

5 Andrew Gurr has written the most accessible and inspiring accounts of the early modern theatre in general: *The Shakespearean Stage, 1574–1642*, 3rd edn, Cambridge: Cambridge University Press, 1992, and *Playgoing in Shakespeare's London*, 2nd edn, Cambridge: Cambridge University Press, 1996; other thought-provoking accounts are provided by Peter Thomson, *Shakespeare's Theatre*, 2nd edn, London: Routledge, 1992, and Arthur Kinney, *Shakespeare by Stages*, Oxford: Blackwell, 2003. Tremendous research added to the field of theatre history and helped redefine it – in particular, the work on contemporary staging pictures by R. A. Foakes, *Illustrations of the English Stage, 1580–1642*, London: Scolar Press, 1985; on playhouses by Herbert Berry, *Shakespeare's Playhouses*, New York: AMS, 1987; on censorship by Richard Dutton, *Mastering the Revels: The Regulation and Censorship of English Renaissance Drama*, Iowa City: University of Iowa Press, 1991; on repertory by Roslyn Knutson, *The Repertory of Shakespeare's Company, 1594–1613*, Fayetteville: University of Arkansas Press, 1991; on the developments that led to the playhouses by William Ingram, *The Business of Playing*, Ithaca: Cornell University Press, 1992; on stage directions by Alan Dessen, *Recovering Shakespeare's Theatrical Vocabulary*, Cambridge: Cambridge University Press, 1995; and on companies by Scott McMillin and Sally-Beth MacLean, *The Queen's Men and Their Plays*, Cambridge: Cambridge University Press, 1998.

6 Chadwyck-Healey's Literature on Line, 'LION', contains (virtually) all plays and poems and many works of prose from the early modern period; Early English Books Online, 'EEBO', contains (virtually) all early modern rare books. The internet sites, for which a substantial subscription is required, are at http://lion.chadwyck.co.uk and http://wwwlib.umi.com/eebo.

7 Other recent and important stage-to-page books are Robert Weimann's *Author's Pen and Actor's Voice*, Cambridge: Cambridge University Press, 2000, which explores the duality between playing and writing; David Scott Kastan's *Shakespeare After Theory*, which contextualises Shakespeare's plays in the rich densities of the world in which they were created, and Douglas Brooks's *From Playhouse to Printing House*, Cambridge: Cambridge University Press, 2000, which examines the shifting relationship between theatre and publisher. My own *Rehearsal from Shakespeare to Sheridan*, Oxford: Clarendon Press, 2000, investigates early modern theatrical rehearsal as a way of exploring the revision of texts. Peter Holland and Stephen Orgel are preparing two collections of essays on *Redefining Theatre History* in the early modern period, London: Palgrave, forthcoming; one will examine actors and companies, theatre buildings and staging; the other considers evidence of playtexts and concepts of authorship.

Chapter 2

1 'Petition from the Watermen of the bankside to Lord Howard 1592', in W. W. Greg, *Henslowe Papers*, London: A. H. Bullen, 1907, 43.

2 Steven Mullaney, *The Place of the Stage*, Chicago: University of Chicago Press, 1988, 22.

3 William Shakespeare, *Mr. William Shakespeares Comedies, Histories, & Tragedies* – hereafter, *The First Folio* (1623). *First Folio* quotations are taken throughout from the Norton Facsimile, prepared by Charlton Hinman, New York: Norton, 1968, using the through-line-numbers (TLN) of that edition. For more information, see the textual note, p. xiv.

4 G. B. Besant, *London Bridge*, London: Selwyn and Blount, 1927, 120.

5 For ways of blacking the face see Andrew Gurr, *The Shakespearean Stage, 1574–1642*, 3rd edn, Cambridge: Cambridge University Press, 1992, 199–200, and W. J. Lawrence, 'The Black-a-vised Stage Villain', in *Old Theatre Days and Ways*, London: G. G. Harrap & Co. Ltd, 1935, 124–9.

6 John Stow, *Survey of London*, 1598, 33.

7 Henry Vaughan, 'A Rhapsodie: Occasionally written upon a meeting with some of his friends at the Globe Taverne, in a Chamber painted over head with a Cloudy Skie, and some few dispersed Starres . . .', in *The Works of Henry Vaughan*, ed. L. C. Martin, Oxford: Clarendon Press, 1957, 10–11.

8 William Harrison, *Chronologie*, 1588, I.liv, quoted in E. K. Chambers, *The Elizabethan Stage*, 4 vols, Oxford: Clarendon Press, 1923, 2: 396.

9 Chambers, *Elizabethan Stage*, 2: 392.

10 John Northbrooke, *A Treastise wherein Dicing, Dauncing, Vaine plaies . . . are Reproved . . .*, 1579, 29b.

11 Quoted in Chambers, *Elizabethan Stage*, 2: 415.

12 For the dating of *Henry V* see William Shakespeare, *Henry V*, ed. Gary Taylor, Oxford: Oxford University Press, 1982, 4.

13 William Parkes, *The Curtaine-Drawer of the World*, 1612, 47.

14 See Christine Eccles, *The Rose Theatre*, London: Nick Hern Books, 1990, 72.

15 Thomas Heywood, *The English Traveller*, 1633, I6a.

16 'A Funerall Elegye on ye Death of the famous Actor Richard Burbedg who dyed on Saturday in Lent the 13 of March 1618', quoted in Edwin Nungezer, *A Dictionary of Actors*, New Haven: Yale University Press, 1929, 75–6.

17 Tiffany Stern, 'Was *Totus Mundus Agit Histrionem* Ever the Motto of the Globe Theatre?', *Theatre Notebook*, 51, 1997, 122–7.

18 Passages in the manuscript behind this folio, 1623, text of *Hamlet* are dated in *William Shakespeare, a Textual Companion*, ed. Stanley Wells and Gary Taylor, Oxford: Clarendon Press, 1987, 400.

19 Chambers, *Elizabethan Stage*, 2: 508.

20 William Lambarde, *Perambulation of Kent*, 1596, 233.

21 For an exploration of Shakespeare's spectacular use of stage violence for its entertainment value see R. A. Foakes, *Shakespeare and Violence*, Cambridge: Cambridge University Press, 2003.

22 Samuel Rowlands, *The Letting of Humours Blood in the Head-Vaine*, 1600, A7a.

23 Barnaby Rich, *Faultes Faults, and nothing else but Faultes*, 1606, 4b.

24 John Stephens, *Satyrical Essayes Characters and Others*, 1615, 276.

25 John Marston, *Scourge of Villanie*, 1598, H4a.

26 See Jonathan Hope, 'Shakespeare's "Natiue English"', in *A Companion to Shakespeare*, ed. David Scott Kastan, London: Blackwell, 1999, 248.

27 Sir John Harington, *A New Discourse of a Stale Subject, called the Metamorphosis of Ajax*, 1596, C2b.

28 Sir John Harington, *Ulysses upon Ajax*, 1596, D1a.

29 *The Actors Remonstrance, or Complaint*, 1643, 5.

30 Richard Flecknoe, *Miscellania*, 1653, 103–4.

31 The Swan drawing's inaccuracy is discussed in R. A. Foakes, *Illustrations of the English Stage*, London: Scolar Press, 1985, 52–5.

32 Peter Razzell, ed., *The Journals of Two Travellers in Elizabethan and Early Stuart England: Thomas Platter and Horatio Busino*, London: Caliban Books, 1995, 26.

33 Ben Jonson, *The Works*, ed. C. H. Herford and P. and E. Simpson, 11 vols, Oxford: Clarendon Press, 1947, 8: 439.

34 Thomas Middleton, *The Blacke Booke*, 1604, B1a.

35 Philip Henslowe, *Henslowe's Diaries* ed. R. A. Foakes, Cambridge: Cambridge University Press, 2002, 319; *The Second Report of Doctor John Faustus . . . Written by an English Gentleman student in Wittenberg . . .*, 1594, E2b.

36 Jonathan Bate in his Arden edition of William Shakespeare, *Titus Andronicus*, London and New York: Routledge, 1995, writes powerfully about the use of the trap in his introduction to that play, 4–21.

37 John Tatham, *The Fancies Theater*, 1640, H3; Richard Tarlton, *Tarltons Jeasts*, 1638, B2a–b.

38 John Davies, *Wits Bedlam*, 1617, F7a.

39 For an account of the Midland Uprising of 1607/8 see William Shakespeare, *Coriolanus*, ed. R. B. Parker, Oxford: Clarendon Press, 1994, 34–7; for William Shakespeare's corn hoarding see Katherine Duncan Jones, *Ungentle Shakespeare*, London: Arden, 2001, 121–2.

40 Joseph Hall, *Virgidemiarum* 2, Liber 1, satire 3, 1598, in *Poems of Joseph Hall*, ed. A. Davenport, Liverpool: Liverpool University Press, 1949, 14–15.

41 Francis Lenton, *The Young Gallants Whirligigg*, 1629, 14.

42 The dimensions of the stage are discussed in Gurr, *Shakespearean Stage*, 157; and Andrew Gurr and Mariko Ichikawa, *Staging in Shakespeare's Theatres*, Oxford: Oxford University Press, 2000, 29–32.

43 Richard Brathwait, *Whimzies*, 1631, 51–2.

Chapter 3

1 See E. A. J. Honigmann, 'The Unblotted Papers', in *The Stability of Shakespeare's Text*, London: Edward Arnold, 1965, 22–35.

2 Richard West, 'To the pious Memory of my deare Brother in Law, Mr Thomas Randolph' in Thomas Randolph, *Poems*, 1640, B4b.

3 Jonson, *Works*, 8: 583.

4 'To the Memory of Ben Johnson' in Jasper Mayne, *Jonsonus Virbius*, 1638, 30.

5 First identified as Shakespeare's hand in a *Notes and Queries* article by Richard Simpson in 1871, and now commonly accepted to be so. But see Paul Ramsey, 'The Literary Evidence for Shakespeare as Hand D in the Manuscript Play Sir Thomas More: A Re-re-consideration', *The Upstart Crow*, 11, 1991, 131–55, for a disputation of this designation.

6 Transcription is provided in Wells and Taylor, *Textual Companion*, 463–7; modernised version is my own.

7 More on revision in *Love's Labour's Lost* can be found in John Kerrigan, 'Shakespeare at Work: the Katharine–Rosaline Tangle in *Love's Labour's Lost*', *Review of English Studies*, NS 33, 1982, 134–6; '*Love's Labour's Lost* and Shakespearean Revision', *Shakespeare Quarterly*, 33, 1982, 337–9.

8 For more on this topic see Randall McLeod (Random Cloud), 'The Marriage of Good and Bad Quartos,' *Shakespeare Quarterly*, 33, 1982, 421–31.

9 Cassius also changes his character between these two sections, a point made by Grace Ioppolo, *Revising Shakespeare*, Cambridge, MA: Harvard University Press, 1991, 115.

10 See Thomas Dekker, *Newes from Hell*, 1606, in *The Non Dramatic Works of Thomas Dekker*, 5 vols, ed. Alexander B. Grosart, 1884, New York: Russell and Russell, 1963, 2:146, who writes about 'a Cobler of Poetrie called a play-patcher'. More on the playwright as playpatcher can be found in Tiffany Stern, 'Repatching the Play', in Peter Holland and Stephen Orgel, eds, *Redefining the Theatre*, London: Palgrave, 2004, forthcoming.

11 Reproduced in William Shakespeare, *Antony and Cleopatra*, ed. Michael Neill, Oxford: Clarendon Press, 1994, appendix A, 327–62.

12 See Ben Jonson, *Sejanus*, in Jonson, *Works*, 4: 351.

13 See Ben Jonson's *Sejanus*, 1605. More on this subject can be found in Mark Bland, 'The Appearance of the Text in Early Modern England', in *TEXT*, 11, 1998, 91–127.

14 The distinction is importantly redefined by Laurie Maguire in *Shakespearean Suspect Texts: The 'Bad' Quartos and Their Contexts*, Cambridge: Cambridge University Press, 1996. For an argument against using 'foul papers' and 'bad/good' quartos as technical terms see Werstine, 'Narratives about Printed Shakespeare Texts'.

15 Thomas Heywood, *Pleasant dialogues and dramma's*, 1637, 249.

16 Peter Blayney, 'The Publication of Playbooks', in John D. Cox and David Scott Kastan, eds, *A New History of Early English Drama*, New York: Columbia University Press, 1997, 383–422.

17 These terms of opprobrium come from Thomas Bodley's instructions to the keeper of the Bodleian Library, reproduced in Sir Thomas Bodley, *Letters of Sir Thomas Bodley to Thomas James, First Keeper of the Bodleian Library*, ed. G. W. Wheeler, Oxford: Clarendon Press, 1926,

219. He adds, 'Happely some plaies may be worthy the keeping: but hardly one in fortie', 222.

18 Sir John Mennes, *Wits Recreations*, 1641, F4a.

19 William Prynne, *Histriomastix*, 1633, **6b.

20 Jonson, *Works*, 8: 584.

21 Jonson, *Works*, 6: 280.

22 Thomas Fuller, *Worthies of England*, 1662, 253.

23 For the suggestion that the line in question is not actually supposed to be verse see Thomas A. Pendleton, '"This is not the man": On calling Falstaff Falstaff', *Analytical and Enumerative Bibliography*, NS 4, 1990, 59–71.

24 'The Glutton's Speech' in Ahasuerus, *The Wandering Jew*, 1640, F3b.

25 See Andrew Gurr's introduction to his edition of Shakespeare's *Henry V*, Cambridge: Cambridge University Press, 1992, 7.

26 Quoted in Chambers, *Elizabethan Stage*, 4:338–9.

27 For the argument that the names were changed for Oxford performance see William Shakespeare, *Hamlet*, ed. G. R. Hibbard, Oxford: Clarendon Press, 1987, 74–5. The bad quarto names are used in a German play from the eighteenth century, *Der Bestrafte Brudermord*, which seems to be descended from an early modern version of *Hamlet* that made its way to Germany.

28 Robert Armin, *A Nest of Ninnies*, 1608, G3b.

29 'A Funerall Elegye on ye Death of . . . Richard Burbedg', reproduced in Nungezer, *Dictionary*, 74. The phrase featured, as early accounts make clear, in the Ur-*Hamlet*: perhaps Burbage borrowed it from there.

30 Robert Chamberlain, *A New Booke of mistakes. Or, Bulls with tales, and buls without tales* (1640), 50.

31 For more on the way changes between the two good texts of *Hamlet* alter the hero see John Jones, 'Hamlet', *Shakespeare at Work*, Oxford: Clarendon Press, 1995.

32 Jerome McGann, *A Critique of Modern Textual Criticism*, Chicago and London: University of Chicago Press, 1983, 4–5.

33 For the history of the *Lear* texts see Wells and Taylor, *Textual Companion*, 509.

34 All in Gary Taylor and Michael Warren, eds, *The Division of the Kingdoms*, Oxford: Clarendon Press, 1983.

35 Ioppolo in *Revising Shakespeare*, 167.

36 Ioppolo in *Revising Shakespeare*, 50, includes a list of quartos by a variety of playwrights which state on their title pages that they have been 'corrected', 'amended', 'augmented' without mention of the author's name.

Chapter 4

1 See *Henslowe's Diary*, ed. R. A. Foakes, 2nd edn, Cambridge: Cambridge University Press, 2002.

2 *A Banquet of Jeasts*, 1630, 57.

3 For more on the life of William Kempe and the characters he played see David Wiles, *Shakespeare's Clown: Actor and Text in the Elizabethan Playhouse*, Cambridge: Cambridge University Press, 1987.

4 Armin, *Nest of Ninnies*, B2b.

5 John Davies, *The Complete Works* collected by Alexander B Grosart, 2 vols, repr. New York: AMS Press, 1967, 2: 60.

6 Robert Armin, *The Italian Taylor and his Boy*, 1609, A3a.

7 Henry Glapthorne, *Poems*, 1639, 28.

8 F. W. Sternfeld, *Music in Shakespearean Tragedy*, London: Routledge and Kegan Paul, 1967, 79.

9 John Manningham, *Diary of John Manningham, of the Middle Temple*, ed. J. Bruce, 1868, 39.

10 Rowlands, *The Letting of Humours Blood in the Head-Vaine*, A2a; *Mercurius Bellicus* no. 5, 1648, 4.

11 Richard Corbet, *Certain Elegant Poems*, 1647, 12.

12 'A Funerall Elegye on ye Death of . . . Richard Burbedg', reproduced in Nungezer, *Dictionary*, 74.

13 Henry Glapthorne, *Ladies Priviledge*, 1640, A3b.

14 V. C. Clinton-Baddeley, *It'll be Alright on the Night*, London: Putnam, 1954, 43.

15 For more on the playwright's 'reading' and the entire rehearsal process see Tiffany Stern, *Rehearsal from Shakespeare to Sheridan*, Oxford: Clarendon Press, 2000, 59–61.

16 Samuel Pepys, *The Diary*, ed. Robert Latham and William Matthews, 11 vols, London: G. Bell and Sons Ltd, 1970–83, 3: 243–4.

17 Dulwich College MS I, Item 138. Reproduced as facsimile with transcript in W. W. Greg, ed., *Dramatic Documents from the Elizabethan Playhouses; Stage Plots, Actors' Parts, Prompt Books*, 2 vols, Oxford: Clarendon Press, 1931, 2, and against the text of the 1594 quarto to *Orlando Furioso* in W. W. Greg's *Two Elizabethan Stage Abridgements*, Oxford: Malone Society, 1922.

18 Edmund Gayton, *Pleasant Notes upon Don Quixote*, 1654, 94–5.

19 John Marston, *The Plays*, ed. H. Harvey Wood, 3 vols, London: Oliver and Boyd, 1934, 1: 5.

20 For more on instruction see Stern, *Rehearsal*, chapters 2 and 3 passim.

21 This proposition is put forward by Scott McMillin in his fascinating 'The Sharer and His Boy', in Peter Holland and Stephen Orgel, eds, *Redefining Theatre History*, London: Palgrave, 2004, forthcoming.

22 More on the early modern concept of passions can be found in Joseph R. Roach's *The Player's Passion*, Newark: University of Delaware Press, 1985.

23 Thomas Wright, *The Passions of the mind in Generall*, 1604, 174.

24 BL Ms Sloane 3709, fol. 8r quoted in Gurr, *The Shakespearean Stage 1574–1642*, 3rd, 1992, 100.

25 Thomas Heywood, *Apology for Actors*, 1612, C4b.

26 'A Funerall Elegye on ye Death of . . . Richard Burbedg', reproduced in Nungezer, *Dictionary*, 74.

27 *The Three Parnassus Plays*, ed. J. B. Leishman, London: Ivor Nicholson and Watson Ltd, 1949, 341.
28 See John Downes, *Roscius Anglicanus*, ed. J. Milhous and R. D. Hume, London: Society for Theatre Research, 1987, 51, 55.
29 Thomas Davies, *Dramatic Miscellanies*, 3 vols, Dublin, 1784, 1: 138.
30 For the position of the prompter in the early modern theatre see Tiffany Stern, 'Behind the Arras: the Prompter's Place in the Shakespearean Theatre', *Theatre Notebook*, 55, 2001, 110–18.
31 Richard Flecknoe, *Love's Kingdom . . . with a short Treatise of the English Stage*, 1664, G7a.
32 Stephens, *Satyrical Essayes*, 297.
33 This is an idea put forward by Harold Jenkins in his edition of *Hamlet*, London and New York: Methuen, 1982, 62.

Chapter 5

1 See Alan C. Dessen, 'Elizabethan Darkness and Modern Lighting', in *Elizabethan Stage Conventions and Modern Interpretations*, Cambridge: Cambridge University Press, 1984.
2 Thomas Kyd, *The Spanish Tragedy* ed. Philip Edwards, Manchester: Manchester University Press, 1977, 4th edn, l.63, 127.
3 Inventory reproduced from Greg, *Henslowe Papers*, 116.
4 John Taylor, *The Water-Cormorant his complaint: Against a brood of Land-Cormorants*, 1622, A4a; James Shirley, *Poems*, 1646, 147.
5 *A Warning for Faire Women*, 1599, A3a; 'A Funerall Elegye on ye Death of . . . Richard Burbedg', reproduced in Nungezer, *Dictionary*, 74.
6 Discussed in more detail in Dessen's *Elizabethan Stage Conventions*, 36.
7 Alan C. Dessen, *Recovering Shakespeare's 'Theatrical' Vocabulary*, Cambridge: Cambridge University Press, 1995, 151.
8 William Rowley, *A Search for Money*, 1609, C2b.
9 W. W. Greg, *A Bibliography of the English Printed Drama to the Restoration*, 4 vols, 1939–59, 172.
10 John Marston, *Antonio and Mellida* in *The Plays*, 1:5–7.
11 Sternfeld, *Music*, 223–4.
12 Sternfeld, *Music*, 205.
13 Sternfield, *Music*, 86. The resemblance is questioned by Peter J. Seng, *The Vocal Songs in the Plays of Shakespeare: A Critical History*, Cambridge, MA: Harvard University Press, 1967, 212, but his translation of the full 'Veni Creator' lyric seems, in fact, to draw attention to the similarities he is trying to disprove.
14 For more on the 'late play' qualities revised out of *Lear* see John Jones, 'King Lear: Romance into Tragedy', in *Shakespeare at Work*, Oxford: Clarendon Press, 1995.
15 See 'Tradition of Vocal and Instrumental Music in Tragedy' in Sternfield, *Music*.
16 For other verbal themes that relate to the upside-down world, particularly for the play's use of hendiadys, see George T. Wright, 'Hendiadys and Hamlet', *PMLA*, 96, 1981, 168–93, and Frank Kermode, *Shakespeare's Language*, London: Penguin Books, 2000, 100–2.

Chapter 6

1 James Shirley, *The Duke's Mistress*, 1638, C1b.
2 Other examples of 'lost songs' can be found in William Bowden, *The English Dramatic Lyric*, New Haven: Yale University Press, 1951, 87–94.
3 Edward Cape Everard, *Memoirs of an Unfortunate Son of Thespis*, Edinburgh, 1818, 49.
4 Quoted from Rowley, *All's Lost by Lust*, A3b.
5 'to ye Q. by ye players 1598', reproduced in *The Riverside Shakespeare*, ed. G. Blakemore Evans *et al.*, 2nd edn, Boston and New York: Houghton Mifflin, 1997.
6 'A young witty Lad playing the part of Richard the third: at the Red bull: the Author because hee was interested [*sic*] in the Play to incourage him, wrote him this Prologue and Epilogue', in Thomas Heywood, *Pleasant dialogues and dramma's*, 247.
7 For inflated first performance entrance charges see Chambers, *Elizabethan Stage*, 2: 532.
8 Jonson, *Works*, 6: 397. Beaumont and Fletcher, *The Dramatic Works in the Beaumont and Fletcher Canon*, ed. Fredson Bowers *et al.*, 10 vols, Cambridge: Cambridge University Press, 1966, 3: 491; Peter Hausted's *The Rivall Friends*, 1632, title page.
9 This argument, with reference to early modern plays in general, is given with much more detail in Tiffany Stern, 'A Small-beer Health to his Second Day': Playwrights, Prologues, and First Performances in the Early Modern Theatre', *Studies in Philology*, 2004, forthcoming.
10 *Dramatic Works* collected by Richard Herne Shepherd, 6 vols, London, 1874, 2: 165; Edward Phillips, *The Mysteries of Love and Eloquence*, 1658, A3a.
11 Beaumont and Fletcher, *The Woman Hater*, 1607, in *Dramatic Works*, 1: 157.
12 Andrew Gurr, 'Maximal and Minimal Texts: Shakespeare v. The Globe', *Shakespeare Survey*, 52, 1999, 68–87.
13 Discussed in Peter W. M. Blayney, 'The Publication of Playbooks' in John D. Cox and David Scott Kastan, eds., *A New History of Early English Drama*, New York: Columbia University Press, 1997, 383–422 and Lukas Erne, *Shakespeare as Literary Dramatist*, Cambridge: Cambridge University Press, 2003, 87.
14 This is an argument put forward by G. I. Duthie, 'The Quarto of Shakespeare's *Henry V*' in *Papers, Mainly Shakespearian*, Edinburgh: Oliver & Boyd, 1964, 106–30.
15 The fullest history of early modern parts to date is provided by Tiffany Stern, *Rehearsal*, chapters 1 and 2. But see Simon Palfrey and Tiffany Stern, *Shakespeare in Parts*, Oxford: Oxford University Press, 2004, forthcoming. The parts of Poore (from a lost play), Polypragmaticus (from Robert Burton's Latin *Philosophaster*), Amurath (from Thomas Goffe's *The Tragedy of Amurath*), Antoninus (from the anonymous *Antoninus Bassianus Caracalla*), four non-professional university parts

from the 1620s in the Houghton Library, Harvard, give longer cues and name the cue-speaker. They are typical of parts for university production which offer more information than parts for professional players.

16 Thomas Heywood, *The Royall King, and the Loyall Subject*, 1637, C1a.

17 See James Boswell, *Life of Johnson*, ed. R. W. Chapman, Oxford: Oxford University Press, 1979, 616; Thomas Davies, *Memoirs of the Life of David Garrick*, 2 vols, 2nd edn, 1780, 1: 177n.

18 Thomas Killigrew's *The Princess*, 1664, 21; Marston, *The Plays*, 3: 22.

19 John Davies, *Wits Bedlam*, 1617, F7a: 'of all Glory, purchas'd by the small, / A *Play-wright*, for his *Praise*, payes most of all!'

20 For the date of *Hamlet* see *The Riverside Shakespeare*, 1184.

21 BBC interview, quoted in Peter Hay, *Theatrical Anecdotes*, Oxford: Oxford University Press, 1987, 60–1.

22 Distinctions between 'you' and 'thou' are discussed in Hope, 'Shakespeare's "Natiue English"', 246–7. For the performance ramifications of 'you' and 'thou' and for clues to look for when performing from actors' parts see Patrick Tucker, *Secrets of Acting Shakespeare*, London and New York: Routledge, 2002, 207.

23 Other within-speech cuts occur at 1.2.60; 2.2.210; 2.2.393; 2.2.320; 3.2.205; 3.4.72; 3.4.73; 3.4.190; 4.1.39; 4.7.88; 4.7.99; 5.1.100. For more on the subject of parts and revision in *Hamlet* see Stern, *Rehearsal*, 106–10.

Chapter 7

1 This text is reproduced from Wells and Taylor, *Textual Companion*, 463–67, the modernised transcript is my own.

2 This belief led Stanley Wells and Gary Taylor to substitute the name 'Innogen' for 'Imogen' in their William Shakespeare, *Complete Works*, Oxford: Oxford University Press, 1986. The change is problematic, however, because the manuscript speech-heading must have been at least 'Im' (or 'In') to differentiate it from the name 'Iachimo'. Moreover, the folio text of *Cymbeline* is set by at least two compositors. How likely is it that both would continually misread the speech-heading and the full name?

3 William Long, however, provides a useful caveat against concluding too much from such textual characteristics. See his 'Precious Few: the Surviving English Manuscript Playbooks', in David Scott Kastan, ed., *A Companion to Shakespeare*, Oxford: Blackwell, 1999, 414–33.

4 N. W. Bawcutt, *The Control and Censorship of Caroline Drama*, Oxford: Clarendon Press, 1996, 183.

5 See William Shakespeare, *King Lear*, ed. George Ian Duthie and John Dover Wilson, Cambridge: Cambridge University Press, 1961, 131; and Kathleen O. Irace, '"Origins and Agents of Q1 *Hamlet*", in Thomas Clayton, ed., *The Hamlet First Published*, Newark: University of Delaware Press, 1992, 90–122 (100).

6 Peter W. M. Blayney, *The First Folio of Shakespeare*, Washington: Folger Shakespeare Library, 1991, 14.

7 These examples, and some others, are provided with more detail in Blayney, *The First Folio*, 13–14.

8 Augustine Vincent, *A Discoverie of Errours*, 1622, π6b.

9 Blayney reproduces two pages of folio illustrating 'A' and 'B''s spelling habits in *First Folio*, 10–11.

10 For entrance charges see Chambers, *Elizabethan Stage*, 2: 531–4, 556. For the price of a quarto see Blayney, 'Publication of Playbooks', 383–422; for the price of a folio see Kastan, *Shakespeare After Theory*, 82.

11 See, for instance, Sir Henry Wotton, Letter to Sir Edmund Bacon, 2 July 1613, in *The Life and Letters*, ed. Logan Pearsall Smith, 2 vols, Oxford: Clarendon Press, 1907, 2: 32–3. For a discussion of this letter as a critical reading of the play *Henry VIII* see Gordon McMullan's edition of William Shakespeare, *Henry VIII*, London: Thomson, 2000, 59–62.

12 See John Munro, *The Shakspere Allusion-Book*, 2 vols, Oxford: Oxford University Press, 1932, 324–5.

Chapter 8

1 Ben Jonson, 'To the memory of my beloved, the author Mr. William Shakespeare: and what he hath left us' in the preliminary matter to *The First Folio* (1623), A4b.

Bibliography and Further Reading

Primary Sources

Actors Remonstrance, or Complaint, The, 1643.
'Ahasuerus', *The Wandering Jew*, 1640.
Armin, Robert, *The Italian Taylor and his Boy*, 1609.
Armin, Robert, *A Nest of Ninnies*, 1608.
Banquet of Jeasts, A, 1630.
Beaumont, Francis and John Fletcher, *The Dramatic Works in the Beaumont and Fletcher Canon*, ed. Fredson Bowers *et al.*, 10 vols, Cambridge: Cambridge University Press, 1966.
Bodley, Thomas, *Letters of Sir Thomas Bodley to Thomas James, First Keeper of the Bodleian Library*, ed. G. W. Wheeler, Oxford: Clarendon Press, 1926.
Boswell, James, *Life of Johnson*, ed. R. W. Chapman, Oxford: Oxford University Press, 1979.
Brathwait, Richard, *Whimzies*, 1631.
Chamberlain, Robert, *A New Book of mistakes. Or, Bulls with tales, and buls without tales*, 1640.
Corbet, Richard, *Certain Elegant Poems*, 1647.
Davies, John, *The Complete Works*, collected by Alexander B. Grosart, 2 vols, repr. New York: AMS Press, 1967.
Davies, John, *Wits Bedlam*, 1617.
Davies, Thomas, *Dramatic Miscellanies*, 3 vols, Dublin, 1784.
Davies, Thomas, *Memoirs of the Life of David Garrick*, 2 vols, 2nd edn, 1780.
Dekker, Thomas, *The Non Dramatic Works of Thomas Dekker*, 5 vols, ed. Alexander B. Grosart, 1884, New York: Russell and Russell, 1963.
Downes, John, *Roscius Anglicanus*, ed. J. Milhous and R. D. Hume, London: Society for Theatre Research, 1987.
Everard, Edward Cape, *Memoirs of an Unfortunate Son of Thespis*, Edinburgh, 1818.
Flecknoe, Richard, *Love's Kingdom ... with a short Treatise of the English Stage*, 1664.
Flecknoe, Richard, *Miscellania*, 1653.
Fuller, Thomas, *Worthies of England*, 1662.
'A Funerall Elegye on ye Death of the famous Actor Richard Burbedg who dyed on Saturday in Lent the 13 of March 1618', in Edwin

Nungezer, *A Dictionary of Actors*, New Haven: Yale University Press, 1929.

Gayton, Edmund, *Pleasant Notes upon Don Quixote*, 1654.

Glapthorne, Henry, *Ladies Priviledge*, 1640.

Glapthorne, Henry, *Poems*, 1639.

Hall, Joseph, *Poems of Joseph Hall*, ed. A. Davenport, Liverpool: Liverpool University Press, 1949.

Harington, John, *A New Discourse of a Stale Subject, called the Metamorphosis of Ajax*, 1596.

Harington, John, *Ulysses upon Ajax*, 1596.

Hausted, Peter, *The Rivall Friends*, 1632.

Henslowe, Philip, *Henslowe's Diary*, ed. R. A. Foakes, 2nd edn, Cambridge: Cambridge University Press, 2002.

Heywood, Thomas, *Apology for Actors*, 1612.

Heywood, Thomas, *Dramatic Works* collected by Richard Herne Shepherd, 6 vols, London, 1874.

Heywood, Thomas, *The English Traveller*, 1633.

Heywood, Thomas, *Pleasant dialogues and dramma's*, 1637.

Heywood, Thomas, *The Royall King, and the Loyall Subject*, 1637.

Hill, Aaron, *The Prompter*, ed. William A. Appleton and Kalman A. Burnim, New York: B. Blom, 1966.

Jonson, Ben, *The Works*, ed. C. H. Herford and P. and E. Simpson, 11 vols, Oxford: Clarendon Press, 1947.

Killigrew, Thomas, *The Princess*, 1664.

Kyd, Thomas, *The Spanish Tragedy*, ed. Philip Edwards, Manchester: Manchester University Press, 1977.

Lambarde, William, *Perambulation of Kent*, 1596.

Lenton, Francis, *The Young Gallants Whirligigg*, 1629.

Manningham, John, *Diary of John Manningham, of the Middle Temple*, ed. J. Bruce, 1868.

Marston, John, *The Plays*, ed. H. Harvey Wood, 3 vols, London: Oliver and Boyd, 1934.

Marston, John, *Scourge of Villanie*, 1598.

Mayne, Jasper, *Jonsonus Viribus*, 1638.

Mennes, John, *Wits Recreations*, 1641.

Mercurius *Bellicus* no. 5, 1648.

Middleton, Thomas, *The Blacke Booke*, 1604.

Northbrooke, John, *A Treatise wherein Dicing, Dauncing, Vaine plaies . . . are Reproved*, 1579.

Parkes, William, *The Curtaine-Drawer of the World*, 1612.

Pepys, Samuel, *The Diary*, ed. Robert Latham and William Matthews, 11 vols, London: G. Bell and Sons Ltd, 1970–83.

Phillips, Edward, *The Mysteries of Love and Eloquence*, 1658.

Prynne, William, *Histriomastix*, 1633.

Northbrooke, John, *A Treastise wherein Dicing, Dauncing, Vaine plaies . . . are Reproved . . .*, 1579.

Randolph, Thomas, *Poems*, 1640.

Razzell, Peter, ed., *The Journals of Two Travellers in Elizabethan and Early Stuart England: Thomas Platter and Horatio Busino*, London: Caliban Books, 1995.

Rich, Barnaby, *Faultes Faults, and nothing else but Faultes*, 1606.
Rowlands, Samuel, *The Letting of Humours Blood in the Head-Vaine*, 1600.
Rowley, William, *All's Lost by Lust*, 1633.
Rowley, William, *A Search for Money*, 1609.
The Second Report of Doctor John Faustus . . . Written by an English Gentleman student in Wittenberg . . ., 1594.
Shakespeare, William, *Antony and Cleopatra*, ed. Michael Neill, Oxford: Clarendon Press, 1994.
Shakespeare, William, *Complete Works*, ed. Stanley Wells and Gary Taylor, Oxford: Oxford University Press, 1986.
Shakespeare, William, *Coriolanus*, ed. R. B. Parker, Oxford: Clarendon Press, 1994.
Shakespeare, William, *Hamlet*, ed. G. R. Hibbard, Oxford: Clarendon Press, 1987.
Shakespeare, William, *Hamlet*, ed. Harold Jenkins, London and New York: Methuen, 1982.
Shakespeare, William, *Henry V*, ed. Andrew Gurr, Cambridge: Cambridge University Press, 1992.
Shakespeare, William, *Henry V*, ed. Gary Taylor, Oxford: Oxford University Press, 1982.
Shakespeare, William, *Henry VIII*, ed. Gordon McMullan, London: Thomson, 2000.
Shakespeare, William, *King Lear*, ed. George Ian Duthie and John Dover Wilson, Cambridge: Cambridge University Press, 1961.
Shakespeare, William, *Mr. William Shakespeares Comedies, Histories, & Tragedies (The First Folio)*, facsimile prepared by Charlton Hinman, New York: Norton, 1968.
Shakespeare, William, *The Riverside Shakespeare*, ed. G. Blakemore Evans *et al.*, 2nd edn, Boston and New York: Houghton Mifflin, 1997.
Shakespeare, William, *Titus Andronicus*, ed. Jonathan Bate, London and New York: Routledge, 1995.
Shirley, James, *The Duke's Mistress*, 1638.
Shirley, James, *Poems*, 1646.
Stephens, John, *Satyrical Essayes Characters and Others*, 1615.
Stow, John, *Survey of London*, 1598.
Tarlton, Richard, *Tarltons Jeasts*, 1638.
Tatham, John, *The Fancies Theater*, 1640.
Taylor, John, *The Water-Cormorant his complaint: Against a brood of Land-Cormorants*, 1622.
Three Parnassus Plays, The, ed. J. B. Leishman, London: Ivor Nicholson and Watson Ltd, 1949.
Vaughan, Henry, *The Works of Henry Vaughan*, ed. L. C. Martin, Oxford: Clarendon Press, 1957.
Vincent, Augustine, *A Discoverie of Errours*, 1622.
Warning for Faire Women, A, 1599.
Wotton, Henry, *The Life and Letters*, ed. Logan Pearsall Smith, 2 vols, Oxford: Clarendon Press, 1907.
Wright, Thomas, *The Passions of the mind in Generall*, 1604.

Secondary Sources

Astington, John H., *English Court Theatre, 1558–1642*, Cambridge: Cambridge University Press, 1999.

Barroll, J. Leeds, *Politics, Plague, and Shakespeare's Theater*, Ithaca: Cornell University Press, 1991.

Bate, Jonathan and Russell Jackson, *Shakespeare: An Illustrated Stage History*, Oxford: Oxford University Press, 1996.

Bawcutt, N. W., *The Control and Censorship of Caroline Drama*, Oxford: Clarendon Press, 1996.

Beckerman, Bernard, *Shakespeare at the Globe, 1599–1609*, New York: Macmillan, 1962.

Bentley, G. E., *The Jacobean and Caroline Stage*, 7 vols, Oxford: Clarendon Press, 1941–68.

Bentley, G. E., *The Profession of Dramatist in Shakespeare's Time, 1590–1642*, Princeton: Princeton University Press, 1971.

Bentley, G. E., *The Profession of Player in Shakespeare's Time, 1590–1642*, Princeton: Princeton University Press, 1971.

Berry, Herbert, *Shakespeare's Playhouses*, New York: AMS, 1987.

Besant, G. B., *London Bridge*, London: Selwyn and Blount, 1927.

Bevington, David, *Action Is Eloquence: Shakespeare's Language of Gesture*, Cambridge, MA: Harvard University Press, 1984.

Bland, Mark, 'The Appearance of the Text in Early Modern England', *TEXT*, 11, 1998, 91–127.

Blayney, Peter W. M., *The First Folio of Shakespeare*, Washington: Folger Shakespeare Library, 1991.

Blayney, Peter W. M., 'The Publication of Playbooks', in *A New History of Early English Drama*, ed. John D. Cox and David Scott Kastan, New York: Columbia University Press, 1997, 383–422.

Blayney, Peter W. M., *The Texts of 'King Lear' and their Origins, I: Nicholas Okes and the First Quarto*, Cambridge: Cambridge University Press, 1982.

Bowden, William, *The English Dramatic Lyric*, New Haven: Yale University Press, 1951.

Bowers, Fredson T., *Bibliography and Textual Criticism*, Oxford: Clarendon Press, 1964.

Bowers, Fredson T., *On Editing Shakespeare and the Elizabethan Dramatists*, Philadelphia: University of Pennsylvania Press, 1955.

Bowers, Fredson T., *Textual Study and Literature Criticism*, Cambridge: Cambridge University Press, 1959.

Bradbrook, M. C., *The Rise of the Common Player*, London: Chatto & Windus 1962.

Bradley, David, *From Text to Performance in the Elizabethan Theatre: Preparing the Play for the Stage*, Cambridge: Cambridge University Press, 1992.

Braunmuller, A. R. and M. Hattaway, eds, *The Cambridge Companion to English Renaissance Drama*, Cambridge: Cambridge University Press, 1990.

Brooks, Douglas A., *From Playhouse to Printing House: Drama and Authorship in Early Modern England*, Cambridge: Cambridge University Press, 2000.

Chambers, E. K., *The Elizabethan Stage*, 4 vols, Oxford: Clarendon Press, 1923.

Chambers, E. K., *William Shakespeare: A Study of Facts and Problems*, 2 vols, Oxford: Clarendon Press, 1930.

Clayton, Thomas, ed., *The Hamlet First Published (Q1, 1603): Origins, Form, Intertextualities*, Newark: University of Delaware Press, 1992.

Clinton-Baddeley, V. C., *It'll be Alright on the Night*, London: Putnam, 1954.

Coghill, Nevill, *Shakespeare's Professional Skills*, Cambridge: Cambridge University Press, 1964.

Cook, Ann Jennalie, *The Privileged Playgoers of Shakespeare's London, 1576–1642*, Princeton: Princeton University Press, 1981.

Cox, John D. and David Scott Kastan, eds, *A New History of Early English Drama*, New York: Columbia University Press, 1997.

Dawson, Anthony B. and Paul Yachnin, *The Culture of Playgoing in Shakespeare's England: A Collaborative Debate*, Cambridge: Cambridge University Press, 1995.

Dessen, Alan C., *Elizabethan Drama and the Viewer's Eye*, Chapel Hill: University of North Carolina Press, 1977.

Dessen, Alan C., *Elizabethan Stage Conventions and Modern Interpretations*, Cambridge: Cambridge University Press, 1984.

Dessen, Alan C., *Recovering Shakespeare's 'Theatrical' Vocabulary*, Cambridge: Cambridge University Press, 1995.

Dillon, Janete, 'Is There a Performance in this Text?', *Shakespeare Quarterly*, 45, 1994, 74–86.

Duncan Jones, Katherine, *Ungentle Shakespeare*, London: Arden, 2001.

Duthie, G. I., *Papers, Mainly Shakespearian*, Edinburgh: Oliver & Boyd, 1964.

Dutton, Richard, *Licensing, Censorship and Authorship in Early Modern England*, Basingstoke: Palgrave, 2000.

Dutton, Richard, *Mastering the Revels: The Regulation and Censorship of English Renaissance Drama*, Iowa City: University of Iowa Press, 1991.

Eccles, Christine, *The Rose Theatre*, London: Nick Hern Books, 1990.

Erne, Lukas, *Shakespeare as Literary Dramatist*, Cambridge: Cambridge University Press, 2003.

Foakes, R. A., *Illustrations of the English Stage, 1580–1642*, London: Scolar Press, 1985.

Foakes, R. A., 'The Player's Passion: Some Notes of Elizabethan Psychology and Acting', *Essays and Studies*, NS 7, 1954, 62–77.

Foakes, R. A., *Shakespeare and Violence*, Cambridge: Cambridge University Press, 2003.

Gaskell, Philip, *A New Introduction to Bibliography*, Oxford: Clarendon Press, 1972.

Greg, W. W., *A Bibliography of the English Printed Drama to the Restoration*, 4 vols, London: Bibliographical Society, 1939–59.

Greg, W. W., ed., *Dramatic Documents from the Elizabethan Playhouses; Stage Plots, Actors' Parts, Prompt Books*, 2 vols, Oxford: Clarendon Press, 1931.

Greg, W. W., *Henslowe Papers*, London: A. H. Bullen, 1907.

Greg, W. W., *Some Aspects and Problems of London Publishing between 1550 and 1650*, Oxford: The Clarendon Press, 1956.

Greg, W. W., ed., *Two Elizabethan Stage Abridgements*, Oxford: Malone Society, 1922.

Gurr, Andrew, 'Maximal and Minimal Texts: Shakespeare v. The Globe', *Shakespeare Survey*, 52, 1999, 68–87.

Gurr, Andrew, *Playgoing in Shakespeare's London*, 2nd edn, Cambridge: Cambridge University Press, 1996.

Gurr, Andrew, *The Shakespearean Stage, 1574–1642*, 3rd edn, Cambridge: Cambridge University Press, 1992.

Gurr, Andrew and Mariko Ichikawa, *Staging in Shakespeare's Theatres*, Oxford: Oxford University Press, 2000.

Harbage, Alfred, *Shakespeare's Audience*, New York: Columbia University Press, 1941.

Harbage, Alfred and S. Schoenbaum, *Annals of English Drama, 975–1700*, London: Methuen, 1964.

Harris, Jonathan Gil and Natasha Korda, eds, *Staged Properties in Early Modern English Drama*, Cambridge: Cambridge University Press, 2002.

Harris, Michael and Robin Myers, *The Stationers' Company and the Book Trade, 1550–1990*, Winchester: St Paul's Bibliographies, 1997.

Hartnoll, Phyllis, ed., *Shakespeare and Music*, London: Macmillan, 1964.

Hattaway, Michael, *Elizabethan Popular Theatre*, London: Routledge and Kegan Paul, 1982.

Hay, Peter, *Theatrical Anecdotes*, Oxford: Oxford University Press, 1987.

Honigmann, E. A J., *The Stability of Shakespeare's Text*, London: Edward Arnold, 1965.

Honigmann, E. A. J., *The Texts of Othello and Shakespearian Revision*, London: Routledge, 1996.

Hope, Jonathan, *The Authorship of Shakespeare's Plays*, Cambridge: Cambridge University Press, 1994.

Hope, Jonathan, 'Shakespeare's "Natiue English"', in *A Companion to Shakespeare*, ed. David Scott Kastan, London: Blackwell, 1999.

Howard-Hill, T. H., *Ralph Crane and Some Shakespeare First Folio Comedies*, Charlottesville: University Press of Virginia, 1972.

Howard-Hill, T. H., *Shakespeare and 'Sir Thomas More' – Essays on the Play and its Shakesperian Interest*, Cambridge: Cambridge University Press, 1989.

Hunter, G. K., '"Flatcaps and Bluecoats": Visual Signals on the Elizabethan Stage', *Essays and Studies*, 30, 1980, 16–47.

Ingram, William, *The Business of Playing: The Beginnings of the Adult Professional Theater in Elizabethan London*, Ithaca: Cornell University Press, 1992.

Ioppolo, Grace, *Revising Shakespeare*, Cambridge, MA: Harvard University Press, 1991.

Ioppolo, Grace, ed., *Shakespeare Performed: Essays in Honour of R. A. Foakes*, Newark: University of Delaware Press, 2000.

Irace, Kathleen O., 'Origins and Agents of Q1 *Hamlet*', in *The Hamlet First Published*, ed. Thomas Clayton, Newark: University of Delaware Press, 1992.

Irace, Kathleen O., *Reforming the 'Bad' Quartos; Performance and Provenance of Six Shakespearian First Editions*, Newark: University of Delaware Press, 1994.

Jones, Ann Rosalind and Peter Stallybrass, *Renaissance Clothing and the Materials of Memory*, Cambridge: Cambridge University Press, 2001.

Jones, John, *Shakespeare at Work*, Oxford: Clarendon Press, 1995.
Joseph, Bertram, *Elizabethan Acting*, London: Oxford University Press, 1951.
Joseph, Bertram, *Elizabethan Acting* rev. edn, London: Oxford University Press, 1964.
Kastan, David Scott, ed., *A Companion to Shakespeare*, Blackwell Companions to Literature and Culture, Oxford: Blackwell, 1999.
Kastan, David Scott, *Shakespeare After Theory*, London and New York: Routledge, 1999.
Kastan, David Scott, *Shakespeare and the Book*, Cambridge: Cambridge University Press, 2001.
Kermode, Frank, *Shakespeare's Language*, London: Penguin Books, 2000.
Kerrigan, John, '*Love's Labour's Lost* and Shakespearean Revision', *Shakespeare Quarterly*, 33, 1982, 337–9.
Kerrigan, John, 'Shakespeare at Work: the Katharine–Rosaline Tangle in *Love's Labour's Lost*', *Review of English Studies*, NS 33, 1982, 134–6.
Kinney, Arthur F., *Shakespeare by Stages: An Historical Introduction*, Oxford: Blackwell, 2003.
Knapp, Robert S., *Shakespeare: The Theater and the Book*, Princeton: Princeton University Press, 1989.
Knutson, Roslyn Lander, *The Repertory of Shakespeare's Company, 1594–1613*, Fayetteville: University of Arkansas Press, 1991.
Lawrence, W. J., *Old Theatre Days and Ways*, London: G. G. Harrap & Co., Ltd, 1935.
Lawrence, W. J., *Those Nut-cracking Elizabethans*, London: Argonaut Press, 1935.
Leech, Clifford and T. W. Clark, eds, *The Revels History of Drama in English*, vol. 3, *1576–1613*, by J. Leeds Barroll *et al.*, London: Methuen, 1975.
Linthicum, Marie Channing, *Costume in the Drama of Shakespeare and His Contemporaries*, Oxford: Clarendon Press, 1936.
Long, John H., *Shakespeare's Use of Music: A Study of the Music and its Performance in the Original Production of Seven Comedies*, Gainesville: University of Florida Press, 1955.
Long, John H., *Shakespeare's Use of Music: The Final Comedies*, Gainesville: University of Florida Press, 1961.
Long, John H., *Shakespeare's Use of Music: The Histories and Tragedies*, Gainesville: University of Florida Press, 1971.
Long, William B. '"A Bed for Woodstock": a Warning for the Unwary', *Medieval and Renaissance Drama in England*, 2, 1985, 91–118.
Long, William B., '"Precious Few": the Surviving English Manuscript Playbooks', in *A Companion to Shakespeare*, ed. David Scott Kastan, Blackwell Companions to Literature and Culture, Oxford: Blackwell, 1999, 414–33.
Long, William B., 'Stage directions: a Misinterpreted Factor in Determining Textual Provenance', *TEXT: Transactions of the Society for Textual Scholarship*, 2, 1985, 121–37.
McDonald, Russ, *The Bedford Companion to Shakespeare: An Introduction with Documents*, London: Palgrave, 1996.

McDonald, Russ, *Shakespeare and the Arts of Language*, Oxford: Oxford University Press, 2001.

McGann, Jerome, *A Critique of Modern Textual Criticism*, Chicago: University of Chicago Press, 1983.

McGann, Jerome, ed., *Textual Criticism and Literary Interpretation*, Chicago and London: University of Chicago Press, 1985.

MacIntyre, Jean, *Costumes and Scripts in the Elizabethan Theatre*, Edmonton: University of Alberta Press, 1992.

McKenzie, D. F., 'Printers of the Mind: Some Notes on Bibliographical Theories and Printing-house Practices', *Studies in Bibliography*, 22, 1969, 1–75.

McKerrow, R. B., *An Introduction to Bibliography for Literature Students*, Oxford: Clarendon Press, 1928.

McLaverty, James, 'The Concept of Authorial Intention in Textual Criticism', *The Library*, 6th ser., 1984, 121–38.

McLeod, Randall (Random Cloud), 'Fiat flux', in *Crisis in Editing: Texts of the English Renaissance*, ed. Randall McLeod, New York: AMS Press, 1988.

McLeod, Randall (Random Cloud), 'The Marriage of Good and Bad Quartos', *Shakespeare Quarterly*, 33, 1982, 421–31.

McMillin, Scott, *The Elizabethan Theatre and 'The Book of Sir Thomas More'*, Ithaca: Cornell University Press, 1987.

McMillin, Scott, 'The Sharer and His Boy', in *Redefining Theatre History*, ed. Peter Holland and Stephen Orgel, London: Palgrave, 2004, forthcoming.

McMillin, Scott and Sally-Beth MacLean, *The Queen's Men and Their Plays*, Cambridge: Cambridge University Press, 1998.

McMullan, Gordon, *The Politics of Unease in the Plays of John Fletcher*, Amherst: Studies in Early Modern Culture, 1994.

Maguire, Laurie, *Shakespearean Suspect Texts: The 'Bad' Quartos and their Contexts*, Cambridge: Cambridge University Press, 1996.

Marotti, Arthur F., *Manuscript, Print, and the English Renaissance Lyric*, Ithaca: Cornell University Press, 1995.

Masten, Jeffrey, *Textual Intercourse*, Cambridge: Cambridge University Press, 1997.

Melchiori, Giorgio, 'The Continuing Importance of New Bibliography', in Ann Thompson and Gordon McMullan, *In Arden: Editing Shakespeare*, London: Thomson, 2003.

Mullaney, Steven, *The Place of the Stage: License, Play, and Power in Renaissance England*, Chicago: Chicago University Press, 1988.

Munro, John, *The Shakspere Allusion-Book*, 2 vols, Oxford: Oxford University Press, 1932.

Naylor, Edward, *Shakespere and Music*, 2nd edn, 1896, London: J. M. Dent and Sons, Ltd, 1931.

Nungezer, Edwin, *A Dictionary of Actors*, New Haven: Yale University Press, 1929.

Orgel, Stephen, 'The Authentic Shakespeare', *Representations*, 21, 1988, 1–25.

Orgel, Stephen, *Impersonations: The Performance of Gender in Shakespeare's England*, Cambridge: Cambridge University Press, 1996.

Orgel, Stephen, 'What Is a Text?', *Research Opportunities in Renaissance Drama*, 24, 1981, 3–6.

Palfrey, Simon and Tiffany Stern, *Shakespeare in Parts*, Oxford: Oxford University Press, 2005, forthcoming.

Pendleton, Thomas A., '"This is not the man": on Calling Falstaff Falstaff', *Analytical and Enumerative Bibliography*, NS 4, 1990, 59–71.

Potter, Lois and Arthur F. Kinney, eds, *Shakespeare, Text and Theater*, Newark: University of Delaware Press, 1999.

Ramsey, Paul, 'The Literary Evidence for Shakespeare as Hand D in the Manuscript Play Sir Thomas More', *The Upstart Crow*, 11, 1991, 131–55.

Rasmussen, Eric, 'The Revision of Scripts', in *A New History of Early English Drama*, ed. John D. Cox and David Scott Kastan, New York: Columbia University Press, 1997, 441–60.

Roach, Joseph R., *The Player's Passion*, Newark: University of Delaware Press, 1985.

Rutter, Carol Chillington, ed., *Documents of the Rose Playhouse*, rev. edn, Manchester: Manchester University Press, 1999.

Seng, Peter J., *The Vocal Songs in the Plays of Shakespeare: A Critical History*, Cambridge, MA: Harvard University Press, 1967.

Shand, G. B. and Raymond Shady, *Play-texts in Old Spelling*, New York: AMS Press, 1984.

Shapiro, Michael, *Gender in Play on the Shakespearian Stage: Boy Heroines and Female Pages*, Ann Arbor: University of Michigan Press, 1994

Sheavyn, Phoebe Anne, *The Literary Profession in the Elizabethan Age*, 2nd edn, Manchester: Manchester University Press, 1967.

Stern, Tiffany, 'Behind the Arras: the Prompter's Place in the Shakespearean Theatre', *Theatre Notebook*, 55, 2001, 110–18.

Stern, Tiffany, *Rehearsal from Shakespeare to Sheridan*, Oxford: Clarendon Press, 2000.

Stern, Tiffany, 'Repatching the Play', in *Redefining the Theatre*, ed. Peter Holland and Stephen Orgel, London: Palgrave, 2004, forthcoming.

Stern, Tiffany, '"A Small-beer Health to his Second Day": Playwrights, Prologues, and First Performances in the Early Modern Theatre', *Studies in Philology*, 2004, forthcoming.

Stern, Tiffany, 'Was *Totus Mundus Agit Histrionem* Ever the Motto of the Globe Theatre?', *Theatre Notebook*, 51, 1997, 122–7.

Sternfeld, F. W., *Music in Shakespearean Tragedy*, London: Routledge and Kegan Paul, 1963.

Taylor, Gary, *Reinventing Shakespeare: A Cultural History from the Restoration to the Present*, New York: Oxford University Press, 1989.

Taylor, Gary and John Jowett, *Shakespeare Reshaped 1606–1623*, Oxford: Clarendon Press, 1993.

Taylor, Gary and Michael Warren, eds, *The Division of the Kingdoms: Shakespeare's Two Versions of 'King Lear'*, Oxford: Clarendon Press, 1983.

Thompson, Ann and Gordon McMullan, *In Arden: Editing Shakespeare*, London: Thomson, 2003.

Thomson, Peter, *On Actors and Acting*, Exeter: University of Exeter Press, 2000.

Thomson, Peter, *Shakespeare's Theatre*, 2nd edn, London: Routledge, 1992.

Tucker, Patrick, *Secrets of Acting Shakespeare: The Original Approach*, London and New York: Routledge, 2002.

Urkowitz, Steven, *Shakespeare's Revision of King Lear*, Princeton: Princeton University Press, 1980.

Urkowitz, Steven, ' "Well-Sayd Olde Mole": Burying Three Hamlets in Modern Editions', in *Shakespeare Study Today*, ed. Georgianna Ziegler, New York, 1986.

Vickers, Brian, *Shakespeare, Co-author: A Historical Study of Five Collaborative Plays*, Oxford: Oxford University Press, 2003.

Weimann, Robert, *Author's Pen and Actor's Voice*, Cambridge: Cambridge University Press, 2000.

Wells, Stanley W., *Re-editing Shakespeare for the Modern Reader: Based on Lectures Given at the Folger Shakespeare Library, Washington DC*, Oxford: Clarendon Press, 1984.

Wells, Stanley and Lena Cowen Orlin, eds, *Shakespeare: An Oxford Guide*, Oxford: Oxford University Press, 2003.

Wells, Stanley W. and Gary Taylor, *Modernizing Shakespeare's Spelling with Three Studies in the Text of Henry V*, Oxford: Clarendon Press, 1979.

Wells, Stanley and Gary Taylor, eds, *William Shakespeare, a Textual Companion*, Oxford: Clarendon Press, 1987.

Werstine, Paul, 'Narratives about Printed Shakespeare Texts: "Foul Papers" and "Bad" Quartos', *Shakespeare Quarterly*, 41, 1990, 65–86.

Werstine, Paul, 'Plays in Manuscript', in *A New History of Early English Drama*, ed. John D. Cox and David Scott Kastan, New York: Columbia University Press, 1997, 481–97.

West, Anthony James, *The Shakespeare First Folio: The History of the Book*, Oxford and New York: Oxford University Press, 2001–.

Wickham, Glynne, *Early English Stages, 1300 to 1660*, 3 vols in 4, London: Routledge and Kegan Paul, 1959–81.

Wickham, Glynne, Herbert Berry and William Ingram, *English Professional Theatre, 1530–1660*, Cambridge: Cambridge University Press, 2001.

Wiggins, Martin, *Shakespeare and the Drama of His Time*, Oxford: Oxford University Press, 2000.

Wiles, David, *Shakespeare's Clown: Actor and Text in the Elizabethan Playhouse*, Cambridge: Cambridge University Press, 1987.

Williams, George Walton, *The Craft of Printing and the Publication of Shakespeare's Works*, Washington: Folger Shakespeare Library, 1985.

Worthen, W. B., *Shakespeare and the Authority of Performance*, Cambridge: Cambridge University Press, 1997.

Wright, George T., 'Hendiadys and Hamlet', *PMLA*, 96, 1981, 168–93.

Wright, George T., *Shakespeare's Metrical Art*, Berkeley and Los Angeles: University of California Press, 1988.

Index